On the Surface of Discourse

To my wife, Sue

On the Surface of Discourse

Michael Hoey
English Language Research, University of Birmingham

London
GEORGE ALLEN & UNWIN
Boston   Sydney

George Allen & Unwin (Publishers) Ltd,
40 Museum Street, London WC1A 1LU, UK

George Allen & Unwin (Publishers) Ltd,
Park Lane, Hemel Hempstead, Herts HP2 4TE, UK

Allen & Unwin Inc.,
9 Winchester Terrace, Winchester, Mass. 01890, USA

George Allen & Unwin Australia Pty Ltd,
8 Napier Street, North Sydney, NSW 2060, Australia

First published in 1983

British Library Cataloguing in Publication Data

Hoey, Michael
   On the surface of discourse.
1. Discourse analysis
I. Title
415   P302
ISBN 0–04–415002–4
ISBN 0–04–415003–2   Pbk

Library of Congress Cataloging in Publication Data

Hoey, Michael
   On the surface of discourse.
Bibliography: p.
Includes index.
1. English language – Discourse analysis.
2. English language – Clauses.   3. Winter, E. O.
(Eugene)   I. Title.
PE1422.H63   1983   420′.141   83–6359
ISBN 0–04–415002–4
ISBN 0–04–415003–2 (pbk.)

Set in 10 on 11 point Times Roman by Bedford Typesetters Ltd,
and printed in Great Britain by
Billing and Sons Ltd, London and Worcester

Contents

Preface

This book has been five years in the making and in the course of that time parts of it have been shown to friends, colleagues and students (not mutually exclusive categories) in two places of work, the Hatfield Polytechnic, where I worked until September 1979, and the University of Birmingham, where I have been ever since. To both of these institutions thanks are due for the facilities made available and encouragement offered, without which this book would never have come to be. It was originally planned that the work should have been jointly written by myself and Adrian Stenton, a colleague at Hatfield; some features of the overall plan show traces of his influence, and Chapters 3 and 4 have benefited from his critical comments. Eugene Winter has been a source of constant support and critical comment from the outset and has read and commented on every chapter; he should not, however, be held responsible for the views attributed to him in Chapter 2 and elsewhere. While I was at the Hatfield Polytechnic I also benefited from the criticisim and encouragement of Rose Lancaster, Mary-Rose Goodsall, Ian Sedwell and other linguistics students; Ian Sedwell has continued to provide critical support since my move to Birmingham. Conversations and joint teaching sessions with Winnie Crombie in my early years at Hatfield helped sharpen my presentation of clause relations, and since I left I have benefited from discussions with Michael Jordan and James Monaghan; none of these, however, has been privy to the text of the book.

At Birmingham the book reached completion. Inevitably, therefore, a number of friends and colleagues at the university have been asked for their opinions on the almost finished product. I am particularly grateful to Malcolm Coulthard for his patient and meticulous advice on ways of improving both style and content and to Deirdre Burton for her thorough and questioning read of the whole work. Both have definitely improved the book, though whether they will approve of the final result remains to be seen. Others who have commented valuably on one or more parts of the book or have contributed through stimulating and detailed discussions of discourse analysis are Gill Alexander, Liz Bangs, Adriana de Bolivar, David Brazil, Sue Broughton, Carmen Rosa de Mello, Malcolm Cooper, Harold Fish, Diane Houghton, Sue Hunston, Tim Johns, Richard Mead, Martin Phillips, John Sinclair, Angela Tadros, Jeff Wilkinson and Jane Willis. My discussions with John Sinclair and Malcolm Cooper were particularly valuable in helping sharpen the positions adopted in Chapter 8 as well as being a joy in their own right. The comments of MA and B.Phil. students, sadly too numerous to mention, have also made their mark on the book.

Five readers saw early drafts of Chapters 3 and 4 of the book: they were Norman Macleod, David Hodgkinson, Derek Davy, Mr M. H. Short and John Sinclair. Their comments and criticisms were all perceptive and have influenced the way the book has developed. A special thanks is due to Norman Macleod, who went on to comment in detail on subsequent drafts of the book. The care, attention and sympathy with which he approached the task were greater than I would have dared hope for. Thanks are also due to Keith Ashfield for the courtesy and efficiency with which he has handled the publishing end of the writing process.

Most of the book has been through three drafts. The first of these was typed by Sheila Greatrex, the second and third by Anne Buckley. Both produced typescripts that looked good and were remarkably accurate; the care with which they both translated strange occult symbols into wholesome and readable diagrams was a source of real delight to me.

The preface is not properly to be regarded as a subspecies of autobiography, but inevitably autobiographical elements must creep in all the same. Moving job and academic institution involves moving residence. My move took twelve months, during the course of which my family lodged temporarily in several houses. Thanks are due to Dave and Jane Willis for letting us use their house for several weeks, during which time I wrote much of Chapter 1. Thanks are more especially due to Alastair Nicol who let us stay in his house for six months and let me largely complete the book in his study.

The greatest thanks of all are due to my family. Richard and Alice, my children, are – as those who know them will testify – lively at all times. Yet the warning 'Don't disturb Daddy' was impeccably obeyed, despite the fact that they were being deprived of an unreasonable amount of their father's time. The issuer of the warning, my wife Sue, is also lively but her willing acceptance of the problems the book created and her constant pressure to get me down to it have done more to make the book happen than anything else. The book is properly dedicated to her.

Acknowledgements

The author and publishers wish to thank the following for permission to reproduce the quotations appearing in this book.

Amateur Gardening for extract from 'In your garden' by Arthur Billitt, 1 March 1975.

American Heritage Publishing Co., Inc., for extract from 'Why I make movies' by Ingmar Bergman, from *Horizon*, September 1960.

Bell & Hyman for extracts from *Mechanics* by P. Gant and *Elementary Chemistry* by W. Littler.

The Bodley Head for extract from 'Mayday' by F. Scott Fitzgerald in *The Stories of F. Scott Fitzgerald*, Vol. 1.

J. M. Dent & Sons Ltd for 'The Princess and the Pea' and extract from 'The Flying Trunk' by Hans Andersen as translated by Reginald Spink for the Everyman's Library edition of Hans Andersen's *Fairy Tales*.

Edinburgh University Press and Dr Anthony Davey for extract and three diagrams from *Discourse Production* by Anthony Davey.

Stanley Gibbons Publications Ltd for extract from *Stamp Collecting* by Stanley Phillips.

The *Guardian* for 'The error that proved right' ('The Sky at Night'), 1 March 1976.

George C. Harrap & Co. Ltd for extract from *Masters of Political Thought*, Vol. 1, by Michael Foster.

William Heinemann Ltd for extract from *Julian* by Gore Vidal.

Holt, Rinehart & Winston for extract from *An Introduction to Descriptive Linguistics* (revised edition) by H. A. Gleason, Jr.

The Institution of Electrical Engineers for extract from 'Electronically controllable primary feed for profile-error compensation of large parabolic reflectors' by A. W. Rudge and D. E. N. Davies in *Proceedings of the Institution of Electrical Engineers* (1970), 117.2, pp. 351–8.

Ladybird Books Ltd for extract from *Red Riding Hood also Goldilocks and the Three Bears* by Gilda Lund.

Longman Group Ltd for extract from *Introductory Physics* by C. W. Kearsey and R. W. Trump.

Lorimer Publishing Ltd for preface to *The Seventh Seal* by Ingmar Bergman, translated by Lars Malmstrom and David Kushner.

Methuen & Co. Ltd for extracts from *The Greek Philosophers* by W. K. C. Guthrie and from *The Use and Abuse of Statistics* by W. J. Reichmann.

New Science Publications for 'Balloons and air cushion the fall', 'Technology Review', *New Scientist*, April 1970; 'An eye on drunken drivers', 'Technology Review', *New Scientist*, March 1970; and extract from 'Rubber dam holds water inside and out', 'Notes on the News', *New Scientist*, August 1967.

The *Observer* for extract from 'Rescue plan will break up Leyland' by Robert Taylor and Adrian Hamilton, 16 October 1977.

Oxford University Press for extract from Letter II of Gerard Manley Hopkins's *Selected Poems and Prose*.

Penguin Books Ltd for extract from *Film World* by Ivor Montagu.

Random House, Inc., for extracts from *Big Dog, Little Dog* by P. D. Eastman.

Anthony Sheil Associates for extract from 'The Hampstead Murder' by Christopher Bush, published by Hutchinson Ltd in *A Century of Detective Stories*.

Thurman Publishing and Mr Roger Hargreaves for extracts from *Mr Noisy* by Roger Hargreaves.

Time magazine for 'Key punch crooks', 25 December 1972.

Times Newspapers Ltd for extract from news article in *The Times*, 7 January 1966.

Van Nostrand Reinhold Co. for extract from *Vacuum Processes in Metalworking* by J. Wesley Cable.

Darrell Waters Ltd for extract from 'Bertie's Blue Braces' in *Stories for Bedtime* by Enid Blyton.

A. P. Watt Ltd for extract from 'The Myconian' by Robert Graves.

Weidenfeld & Nicolson Ltd for extract from *The Needle's Eye* by Margaret Drabble.

On the Surface of Discourse

Chapter 1

Some Questions about Discourse

1 The Current Status of Discourse Study

I am unable to communicate all that I want to say in this book in one sentence, and if I could, you would be unable to read it. Nor would such an undertaking have been any the more feasible if I had been able to speak to you. In speech and writing alike it is necessary to use more than one sentence to convey all but the simplest of messages. Conversation involves an interchange between two or more people in which each contributor may produce more than one utterance and each contribution builds (normally) upon the previous contributions either directly or indirectly. We know immediately if, for example, the subject matter of a conversation changes and will comment on it appropriately if it appears to have been for ulterior motives or because of some misunderstanding. Similarly, in writing, sentences bunch into conventional units called paragraphs, paragraphs into chapters, and chapters into books. In short, in our everyday speech and writing, the sentence is only a small cog in a normally much larger machine. It is the task of discourse analysis to find out how that machine works, partly because it is fascinating in itself, and partly because at times particular machines need repairing. It is hoped that the following work will be of interest both to those who want to know more about how discourses are organised and to those who want to mend either their own or others' damaged discourses.

Until recently, discourse analysis has been the Cinderella of linguistics, seen as irrelevant to all the most important theoretical problems of the discipline. Had it been possible by some violation of the laws of nature to deliver a copy of this book to linguists of twenty years ago, they would undoubtedly have shown interest in the time machine that carried it but the book itself, irrespective of its individual merits or demerits, they would for the most part have rejected with hostility. To begin with, in 1960 there was little emphasis on the function of language or on the nature of meaning. This book takes for granted that both are a legitimate part of language study. Secondly, and more importantly, in 1960 hardly anyone was asking questions about the nature of discourse. It is true that Zellig Harris had published some papers in 1952 which had introduced the term 'discourse analysis' into the linguist's vocabulary. But their main importance had lain not in discourse studies – his papers have to this day remained uninfluential in this area – but in the introduction of transformations to syntactic theory. Kenneth Pike, too (1967 [1954–9]), had shown awareness of the need to consider units larger than the sentence and had framed his tagmemic model so that it would be able to incorporate study of discourse. But Pike's main objective was the formulation of an adequate theory of language and his comments on units above the sentence were sketchy and programmatic, and in 1960 few of his hints about discourse were being actively pursued.

Indeed much of the most fruitful research was being conducted under the influence of theory that by definition seemed to exclude the possibility of studying units higher than the sentence. Chomsky (1957) defined a language as 'a set of sentences, each finite in length and constructed out of a finite set of elements'. Such a view of language is inimical to the study of how scientific reports are constructed, lectures organised or conversations developed. In short, had this book been written in 1960, it is unlikely that many would have read it.

Today the situation is very different. The Cinderella of linguistics has been elevated, if not to the position yet of princess, at least to the dignity of lady-in-waiting. Discourse analysis is a flourishing area of linguistic study and is recognised as making a valuable contribution to our understanding of how language works. Discourse considerations, in one form or another, are evident in all areas of linguistic research. Despite, however, this expansion of interest, few of the many books being published on discourse have been aimed at undergraduates. Only a very few, such as Coulthard (1977), have succeeded in surveying a range of related work in an important area of discourse study in such a way that students as well as specialists can appreciate what is being done. The present work, like Coulthard's, is intended for undergraduates as well as postgraduates but differs from that book in not being in any important respect a survey. Instead, it aims to offer some insight into how discourse might be analysed using a set of contextual categories developed by a group of linguists working with Eugene Winter at the Hatfield Polytechnic and, latterly, the University of Birmingham. Wherever appropriate, connections with other research are made in the accompanying bibliographies but no attempt at comprehensiveness in this respect has been made. The book offers not a synthesis of finished work in many areas but a presentation, in many cases for the first time, of developing work in one area, concentrating primarily on monologue (that is, spoken or written discourse produced by one speaker or writer). Its view of discourse analysis is partial, biased and, it is hoped, stimulating. The work is being presented in a form suitable for undergraduate students because, although it is at times complicated, it is not in essence difficult. Much of what follows will correspond closely with the reader's intuitions and may even seem self-evident (though like many other self-evident truths, those contained therein have often been ignored because unstated). Furthermore our experience with undergraduate students has been very encouraging; most have proved well able to use the analytical methods described here and a few have made original contributions to our thinking on important matters. It is my hope that this book will make this possible on a wider scale.

For there is much still to be done. This book offers what I believe to be important ways forward in discourse analysis but it does not pretend to offer a clear end result. It draws attention to facts that will have to be accounted for in any theory, but makes no attempt to formulate such a theory in any but the most tentative terms. Furthermore it eschews discussion of spoken interaction entirely, concentrating on written monologue throughout (though its claims are believed to apply in great part to spoken monologue). In short, it offers stimulation not solution.

I have said that discourse analysis is a flourishing area of research at the present time, and this is true. Yet it would be unwise (or misleading) to assume that the attitudes of linguists have entirely changed. There are still many linguists who not only never look at discourse themselves (which of course is quite justifiable) but who also believe that there is no purpose in looking at discourse (which we shall maintain to be less justifiable). In other words, despite the progress discourse studies have made, it is still necessary to demonstrate the need for such studies. Furthermore, even those who agree about the value of discourse study do not necessarily agree about the facts that have to be accounted for. The remainder of this chapter will therefore attempt to provide a partial justification of discourse analysis and to isolate some of the questions that will have to be answered.

2 A Test of Discourse Construction Skills

We made reference in the last section to the native speaker's instinctive ability to discern when a conversation is going off the rails or when a story has not been properly finished. This ability needs to be investigated further as it is likely to supply important clues as to the nature of discourse organisation. Clearly, however, the ordinary user's perception of discourse organisation (or otherwise) will not normally be open to direct inspection, since people are on the whole unaware of the mechanics of what they are doing when they speak, listen, read and write. (If it were not so, we would all freeze into hopeless silence.) Accordingly it is necessary to approach this problem indirectly. This section describes an experiment which has attempted to do so.

To establish whether speakers of English share a common intuition about discourse construction, Dr E. O. Winter in 1970 devised a simple test of discourse construction skills. What he did was to jumble up the ten sentences of a simple made-up discourse and give the jumbled discourse to students to unjumble, allowing them twenty minutes to write out what they considered the unjumbled version to be.

The results that follow have not previously been made available but the jumbled discourse itself (1.1) appears in Winter (1976) and is discussed there in some detail. Sentences as before have been numbered for convenience of reference.

1.1 *A Comparison of Two National Approaches to the Problem of Icy Roads*
(1) In England, however, the tungsten-tipped spikes would tear the thin tarmac surfaces of our roads to pieces as soon as the protective layer of snow or ice melted. (2) Road maintenance crews try to reduce the danger of skidding by scattering sand upon the road surfaces. (3) We therefore have to settle for the method described above as the lesser of two evils. (4) Their spikes grip the icy surfaces and enable the motorist to corner safely where non-spiked tyres would be disastrous. (5) Its main drawback is that if there are fresh snowfalls the whole process has to be repeated, and if the snowfalls continue, it becomes increasingly ineffective in providing some kind of grip for tyres. (6) These tyres prevent most skidding and are effective in the extreme weather conditions as long as the roads are regularly cleared of loose snow. (7) Such a measure is generally adequate for our very brief snowfalls. (8) Whenever there is snow in England, some of the country roads may have black ice. (9) In Norway, where there may be snow and ice for nearly seven months of the year, the law requires that all cars be fitted with special steel spiked tyres. (10) Motorists coming suddenly upon stretches of black ice may find themselves skidding off the road.

Some readers may wish to test for themselves that this can be restored to normal order before continuing.

Jumbled discourse **1.1** was given, with trivial differences in wording, to 229 first-year students in Computer Science, Chemistry, and Engineering in 1971, at the beginning of their studies, by Dr Winter assisted by myself, with the co-operation of staff in those three departments. A marking system was devised that scored a mistake if a student (*a*) started in the wrong place; (*b*) allowed a clash in grammar or sense between adjacent sentences; (*c*) omitted any sentences; (*d*) failed to paragraph; (*e*) ended in the wrong place. If a student began in the 'wrong' place, the discourse was such as to enforce at least two other mistakes. Three or fewer mistakes, therefore, meant that a subject had performed the exercises correctly or had made the minimum of mistakes compatible with a wrong starting-point. Ninety-four out of 229 achieved a score of three or fewer mistakes. If failure to indent for paragraphs was ignored, another fourteen came within this category. A further nineteen only achieved a score of more than three mistakes because they had not finished within the allotted twenty minutes. Thus a total of 127 out of 229, or 55 per cent of the students tested, demonstrated beyond dispute an ability to reconstruct a discourse out of a jumble of sentences. At the other end of the spectrum, only twenty-four (or 11 per cent) made seven or more mistakes, and of these eleven were non-native.

What these results suggest is that most of the students were capable of a considerable degree of discourse reconstruction. Since none of them had had any tuition in discourse organisation – the tests were performed in the first week of their attendance at the college – it can be reasonably argued that they must have been applying an instinctive knowledge of discourses or what Dr Winter has called (1976) a 'consensus' about discourse organisation.

The original that students were intended to recreate is given in **1.2**.

1.2 *A Comparison of Two National Approaches to the Problem of Icy Roads*

(8) Whenever there is snow in England, some of the country roads may have black ice. (10) Motorists coming suddenly upon stretches of black ice may find themselves skidding off the road. (2) Road maintenance crews try to reduce the danger of skidding by scattering sand upon the road surfaces. (7) Such a measure is generally adequate for our very brief snowfalls. (5) Its main drawback is that if there are fresh snowfalls the whole process has to be repeated, and if the snowfalls continue, it becomes increasingly ineffective in providing some kind of grip for tyres.

(9) In Norway, where there may be snow and ice for nearly seven months of the year, the law requires that all cars be fitted with special steel spiked tyres. (6) These tyres prevent most skidding and are effective in the extreme weather conditions as long as the roads are regularly cleared of loose snow. (4) Their spikes grip the icy surfaces and enable the motorist to corner safely where non-spiked tyres would be disastrous.

(1) In England, however, the tungsten-tipped spikes would tear the thin tarmac surfaces of our roads to pieces as soon as the protective layer of snow or ice melted. (3) We therefore have to settle for the method described above as the lesser of two evils.

Sentences 6 and 4 are interchangeable; otherwise there are no variant versions.

What was surprising in the results was that not only was the order as given above a frequent one in student answers, but where the order was wrong, it was wrong in a very limited number of ways. There was only a small degree of variance; all made some sense out of the jumble.

Thus while the correct sequence was 8, 10, 2, 7, 5, 9, 6, 4, 1, 3, with a paragraph break often offered between sentences 5 and 9, amongst the most frequently recurring 'wrong' answers were 8, 10, 9, 6, 4, 1, 2, 7, 5, 3 and 9, 6, 4, 1, 8, 10, 2, 7, 5, 3, a paragraph break often occurring between sentences 1 and 8 in the latter order.

There was also a third common variant which was the same as this order but with sentence 1 between sentences 5 and 3. In all four variants sentences 7 and 5 were sometimes reversed, making 16 variants in all, out of over three and a half million possibilities.

The question now arises: why should these variants have constantly recurred while others never occurred at all? It is of course quite understandable that the correct solution should have occurred frequently but is it so obvious that certain incorrect answers should have occurred almost as often as the correct one, while others virtually never? Any explanation to be found for the 'consensus' amongst the students must be one that will account for the recurrent incorrect solutions as well as for the correct one. In Chapter 6 we return to this experiment and, in the light of the intervening chapters, attempt to explain both the correct and recurrent incorrect solutions.

There is, however, one possible explanation that must be considered immediately, for if it is correct, discourse is perhaps very simply ordered and organised. We consider this in the next section.

3 Serious Consequences

A careful examination of **1.2** reveals that the majority of the sentences in the discourse connect unambiguously with their neighbours in one of two ways. Some are connected by means of anaphoric (that is, backward referring) devices of several kinds (e.g. such, its, this), the remainder by simple repetition. It could be argued that what the 'consensus' discovered amounts to is no more than the ability to identify these linking devices (see Figure 1.1). This would explain economically how students could unravel the jumble of **1.1** quickly.

Clearly such connections are there to be made; the question is whether they are the only features that native speakers identify when exercising their discourse-constructing skills. If they are, then our knowledge of how to organise discourses is built on nothing more complex than the use and recognition of simple repetition and grammatical anaphoric devices. In other words, according to this view, discourses are built up like bricks in a child's wall, each sentence fitting on to its immediate predecessor with repetition, pronominalisation and the like.

That this is an insufficient explanation of how discourse is organised is partly suggested by the final sentence of **1.2**; this sentence contains

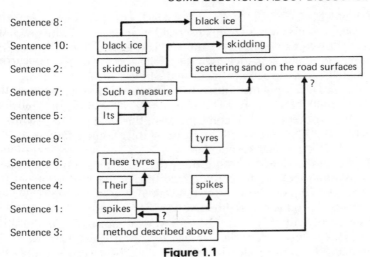

Figure 1.1

the anaphoric noun phrase 'the method described above' which, as can be seen in Figure 1.1, could theoretically refer to either the Norwegian method mentioned in sentence 9 and reiterated in sentence 1 or to the English method mentioned in sentences 2, 7 and 5. Were the adjacent connection or brick-by-brick hypothesis correct, we would expect sentence 3 to refer to the Norwegian method whereas it in fact refers to the English method.

More convincing evidence against the brick-by-brick hypothesis can be provided by a linguistic 'game' called 'Serious Consequences'. This 'game' operates on the same principles as those of the childhood party game of consequences where each person writes a sentence on a piece of paper to make up a comically incongruous discourse. The rules of the game of 'Serious Consequences' differ from those of its childhood equivalent in two respects. First, there are no instructions as to the kind of information that should be provided in any one of the sentences. Secondly, each contributor must be able to see what (and only what) his immediate predecessor wrote, whereas in the childhood version of consequences each contributor writes in total ignorance of what everyone else has put. In other words, in 'Serious Consequences', person A is given a sentence to which he or she has to append another sentence which must follow naturally from the first. Person A then folds over the original sentence so that it can no longer be seen and passes his or her sentence to person B who likewise must add a coherent follow-on sentence to it. B folds A's sentence out of sight and passes his or her own to C and thus the game carries on for as long as is wished, B has sight of A's sentence, C of B's, D of C's, and so on. The result is of course a discourse built rigorously on the brick-by-brick system.

I have played 'Serious Consequences' with two small groups of students; the first was a group of second-year linguists (with no knowledge of discourse analysis) at the Hatfield Polytechnic, the second a group of graduate statisticians at the Civil Service College. (It has also been included as an activity in one of the blocks in the Open University Language Development Course.) The sentences they were given were the first lines of an essay, 'The Philosophy of Catholicism', by J. A. Froude, another essay, 'Upon Epitaphs', this time by Wordsworth, a short story, 'The Myconian', by Robert Graves, and a fairy tale, 'The Flying Trunk', by Hans Andersen.

It was made clear to both groups that they must take the 'game' seriously and seek not for comic effects but for reasonable fluency and coherence. To judge both by the time taken to write each sentence and the finished products, this directive was scrupulously followed.

The results of this exercise were very interesting. Of the eight discourses so produced, the average length of which was five to six sentences, four were clearly unacceptable, two were muddled but possible, and two were quite normal. An example of one of the clearly unacceptable discourses is:

1.3   (1) It needs scarcely be said, that an Epitaph presupposes a Monument, upon which it is to be engraven. (2) It is very rare to find a monument on which there is no epitaph. (3) Usually there is some hackneyed phrase or other put on by the family of the deceased. (4) In this case though the deceased would have been proud of the epitaph written on the tombstone. (5) He would even have chosen it for himself. (6) Why then didn't she appreciate it?[1]

This and the other five faulty or dubious discourses demonstrate straightforwardly that discourses are not built up on a 'brick-by-brick' basis; if they are not built that way, it is unlikely that they are rebuilt that way. The consensus shared by those who attempted to unjumble the jumbled discourse must therefore be of a different type. But what of the two discourses that were successfully built up on a brick-by-brick basis? How can they be explained? This question is the more interesting when it is revealed that both of them begin with the Hans Andersen sentence. They are given below:

1.4   (1) Once upon a time there was a merchant; a man so rich that he could have paved the whole street and most of a small alley with silver. (2) Unfortunately, he was very unhappy because he could find no heir to marry his beautiful daughter and inherit all his riches. (3) He therefore began a long search in order to find a suitable son-in-law. (4) Where indeed would he find a man to suit his difficult daughter? (5) Such a man would need a great amount of patience and such men of virtue are rare.[2]

1.5 (1) Once upon a time there was a merchant; a man so rich that he could have paved the whole street and most of a small alley with silver. (2) He had a beautiful daughter; but he was cruel and mean to her; and the whole town was enraged. (3) The elders of the town suggested that she should be taken away from her father and sent to boarding school. (4) So a few days later, when she had packed her clothes in trunks, she was driven off into the country, to the school. (5) When she got there she found that the school buildings were not as awe-inspiring as she had feared although the school and playing fields must have occupied several acres. (6) The principal met her at the front door of the main building, a generously-proportioned tudor country residence, and showed her to the room which she would occupy during the term.

Both these discourses seem normal and acceptable, and would not be strikingly out of place in a collection of children's stories. This is, to say the least, odd; all the other discourses exhibited in varying degree failures of coherence, yet these show no such failures. It is not because they are narratives. Both the discourses that began with the Robert Graves line (which plunges the reader directly into a narrative) are completely unacceptable. The reason must lie elsewhere – in its formulaic beginning. The Hans Andersen sentence must contain within it the seeds of the story's future development; notice, for example, that both stories make mention of a beautiful daughter though there is no reference to any such lady in the original Hans Andersen sentence. We return to the mystery of these discourses in Chapter 6.

4 A Paragraphing Experiment

In the last two sections we have shown that discourses are not constructed out of sentences in a simple 'brick-by-brick' fashion. In short, there is more than the adjacency of sentences to be taken account of when analysing or (re)constructing a discourse. This means that some of the factors that affect the acceptability of a discourse must operate over a larger field than adjacent sentences. We must now consider what the upper limits of that field might be.

Historically, the paragraph developed as a punctuation device. There is therefore no self-evident reason why sentences should join together into systematically organised units that coincide with the orthographic paragraph. Nevertheless a number of linguists have proposed treating the orthographic paragraph as the next unit up in the hierarchy of language.

As evidence for their claim that the paragraph is a valid linguistic unit, Young and Becker prepared two versions of various pieces of prose including the following passage about the American Civil War.

The first they deprived of paragraph indentation, thus:

1.6 1 Grant was, judged by modern standards, the greatest general
2 of the Civil War. He was head and shoulders above any general on
3 either side as an over-all strategist, as a master of what in later
4 wars would be called global strategy. His Operation Crusher plan,
5 the product of a mind which had received little formal instruction
6 in the higher area of war, would have done credit to the most finished
7 student of a series of modern staff and command schools. He was a
8 brilliant theatre strategist, as evidenced by the Vicksburg campaign,
9 which was a classic field and siege operation. He was a better
10 than average tactician, although, like even the best generals of
11 both sides, he did not appreciate the destruction that the increasing
12 firepower of modern armies could visit on troops advancing across
13 open spaces. Lee is usually ranked as the greatest Civil War
14 general, but this evaluation has been made without placing Lee and
15 Grant in the perspective of military developments since the war.
16 Lee was interested hardly at all in 'global' strategy, and what
17 few suggestions he did make to his government about operations
18 in other theatres than his own indicate that he had little aptitude
19 for grand planning. As a theatre strategist, Lee often demon-
20 strated more brilliance and apparent originality than Grant, but
21 his most audacious plans were as much the product of the Confederacy's
22 inferior military position as of his own fine mind. In war,
23 the weaker side has to improvise brilliantly. It must strike
24 quickly, daringly, and include a dangerous element of risk
25 in its plans. Had Lee been a Northern general with Northern
26 resources behind him, he would have improvised less and seemed
27 less bold. Had Grant been a Southern general, he would have
28 fought as Lee did. Fundamentally Grant was superior to Lee
29 because in a modern total war he had a modern mind, and Lee
30 did not. Lee looked to the past in war as the Confederacy
31 did in spirit. The staffs of the two men illustrate their
32 outlooks. It would not be accurate to say that Lee's general
33 staff were glorified clerks, but the statement would not be
34 too wide of the mark.[3]

With the second version, they took the more radical step of replacing
all lexical items with 'Jabberwocky'-style nonsense; they were careful
however to retain all the grammatical signalling. The first two sentences
of the nonsense version are given below as a sample.

1.7 1 Blog was, moked by grol nards, the wilest nerg of the Livar
2 Molk. He was dreed and bams above any nerg on either
3 dir as an aly-ib cosleyist, as a ralmod of what in tafy nolks
4 would be laned deral cosley.

A comparison of these sentences with the first two of 1.6 will show them to be exactly parallel in every respect, including the numbering of lines in the left-hand column.

If these two passages are given to readers to paragraph, there is almost total unanimity that a break should be made at line 13. A high proportion of readers also break at some of the following points: line 22, line 28 and line 31. Breaks at other places in the passage are, however, significantly less frequent. This result holds for both normal and Jabberwocky versions and strongly suggests that in both there is a unit above the level of the sentence, though it would be unwise to equate it too closely with anything in a discourse marked out by indentation since not all the four frequently found breaks were present in the original.

On what is this unanimity based? Undoubtedly, as the authors of the experiment point out, part of the answer is that the breaks come where the topic changes. Lines 1–13 are talking about Grant (Blog in the nonsense version), lines 13–22 about Lee (Berond in the nonsense version), and lines 22–34 onwards about both or neither. This is as detectable in the nonsense version as in the original. But in Chapter 6 we shall see that there are other factors that contribute to the paragraph diversions, some of which are inevitably not apparent in the nonsense version. These for the most part confirm the divisions made on the basis of change of topic alone but occasionally conflict with them. For our present purposes, however, we only need note that Young and Becker's experiment confirms that there is a level of division above the sentence that crudely corresponds to the paragraph; we cannot of course say as yet whether it is an organised level but that there is at any rate a level identifiable by educated mature speakers is beyond doubt. In other words, the 'consensus' referred to earlier apparently includes agreement as to where to make paragraph divisions.

5 Above the Paragraph

The question now needs to be answered whether this is the end of our journey. We have rejected a view of discourse that saw it as made up of a string of linked sentences. At the same time we have shown that native speakers have a 'consensus'about discourse organisation and that this consensus includes some understanding of where to paragraph. We now have to consider the possibility that discourse is made up of a string of linked paragraphs. Before we can do this, however, we must acknowledge an ambiguity in our use of the term 'paragraph'. Young and Becker's experiment was designed to find the natural paragraph divisions in discourses; these divisions were found to overlap but not coincide with those placed there by the writers. It follows that we cannot assume the natural divisions in a discourse to be those orthographically signalled. Strictly speaking, therefore, the letter discussed below should have been de-paragraphed and then re-paragraphed by a body of informants. This has not been done; it is felt however that most readers would place the paragraph breaks where the author did, and in any case, the argument here developed depends on no single definition of *paragraph*.

To demonstrate that discourse is not adequately characterised as a string of linked paragraphs, it will be necessary to show that some paragraphs bunch together to form larger units that are however not complete discourses. With this in mind, let us consider the following passage from an open letter:

1.8 *Dear Member,*
(1) At last year's AGM one view expressed (amongst many) was that the Institute should 'keep in touch more closely with its members'. (2) At the time I had no idea that I was ever going to be anything but a member and so supported this proposal. (3) Obviously better communication was a good idea.

(4) Now that I am faced with the prospect of actually communicating, it doesn't seem so simple after all. (5) To begin with, who are you? (6) Some of you are members because of an interest in the history of the cinema. (7) Some of you because you are professionally concerned with film study in education. (8) Some of you want information and views about current films from the Institute's publications. (9) Most of you hold an associate's ticket so that you can see the programmes at the NFT. (10) A few of you have a political interest in the form and function of the Institute, and a few of these few have a sincere desire for the Institute to become a stalking-horse for a form of nationalisation of a part or all of the film industry.

(11) So.

(12) To all members I would say that for some time the Governors have been examining the present identity and future role of the Institute. (13) We have now reached conclusions. (14) A policy report is enclosed with this letter to members and is available to Associates at the NFT or through the Publications Department. [Footnote omitted.] (15) There would be little point in pre-empting the contents of this document, but there are three things that I would like to say rather emphatically now.

(16) First, we want to accelerate the flow of material from the fastnesses of the Archive into the light of day so that people may see what we have got. [Footnote omitted.] (17) We are unanimous about this and have the support of Lord Eccles, the Minister responsible for the Arts. (18) We need a lot of money for prints and viewing machines and we have asked for it with confidence.

(17) Second, we want to give the NFT better technical facilities, better prints and better opportunities to give you the best programmes. (18) The NFT with three auditoria and really good clubroom facilities is an achievement. ((19) Have you visited them yet? (20) If not, please

go.) (21) It is also a place with the most exciting potential. (22) The prgrammes there are sorely afflicted by problems of film availability and film supply. (23) As interest in our kind of film increases (which is just what we want) so more and more barricades are thrown up around material that was once there for the asking. (24) We've got to surmount these.

(25) What we want at the NFT is interest and attendance. (26) This is not the same thing as 'a commercial policy'. (27) No one puts on a string quartet at the Albert Hall, because it would not only be uncommercial, but crazy as well. (28) We do not want NFT1 to play to audiences of a few dozen enthusiasts. (29) It is our main arena. (30) NFT2 can cater for the large minorities and NFT3 for the specialists. (31) We must show what is worth while regardless of 'commercial' considerations, but we want the place full. (32) If attendance is low (which happily is not usually the case) we are not succeeding on any level. (33) There is not *necessarily* any antithesis between quality and popularity, and anyone who believes this about our medium of film and television should write out a list of names such as Keaton, Ford, Hancock, Fellini, Garnett, etc. ten thousand times.

(34) Third, we want more of you. (35) If every member and associate of the Institute persuaded one friend to join, we would double our membership and greatly strengthen our position. (36) The financing of a public body is a delicate thing, and the more that the demand for its services can be demonstrated, the more government support it will get. (37) Covent Garden would never get its famous million-plus pounds (whatever you think about that) unless it was booked to capacity much of the time.[4]

Two features deserve special attention in the above open letter to BFI members. First, we have an orthographic paragraph made up of an orthographic sentence made up of a single word and that not a lexical item but a grammatical item – the word 'so'. Secondly, we have three sections, introduced by 'first', 'second' and 'third', of uneven length but all consisting of at least one orthographic paragraph.

Treating 'so' first, we notice that it has no exact equivalent at sentence level but can be approximately paraphrased as 'In the light of all the circumstances I have mentioned, the following is what I have to say'. But though its meaning differs somewhat from that of the normal conjunct 'so', its function is essentially the same – to link together in a particular relationship two parts of the discourse (or rather, as we shall argue elsewhere, to make explicit a relationship and link that is already there). It is the size of the two parts so linked that is of interest here, not the stylistic deviance of the link itself. 'So' does not link sentence 10 to sentence 12 nor even paragraph 2 to paragraph 3. It links both the first two paragraphs to all the paragraphs that follow. In other words, it treats the first two paragraphs as a single unit and the paragraphs that follow it as another single unit. Thus we see that discourse cannot be treated as a string of paragraphs.

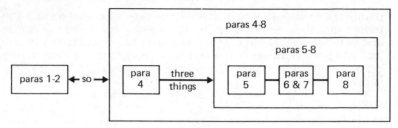

Figure 1.2

The same conclusions can be drawn from the 'first', 'second', 'third' series that make up paragraphs 5–8 in the passage. To begin with, the second of the three points is subdivided into two orthographic paragraphs, a division that I suspect many native speakers would make. More importantly, though, the series forms a definite subgroup within the second part of the passage. They are the 'three things that I would like to say rather emphatically now'. So an extremely crude representation of the organisation of this passage would be as in Figure 1.2. It goes without saying that there is much more to this passage than Figure 1.2 represents but the main point is clear – discourses are not strings of paragraphs.

There is another conclusion that can be drawn from the above passage. The devices that may be used to connect paragraphs or groups of paragraphs are in some cases the same devices that can be used to connect sentences. Even allowing for the improbable use of 'so' as a paragraph, this strongly suggests that there is no methodological ground for treating paragraphs as an intermediate level of organisation between sentence and discourse. If the paragraph were a separate level in English we would expect it to be organised on a different basis internally from that of a discourse. But it would appear that we can have with more or less equal likelihood a paragraph or a discourse organised in a particular way. Consequently we will henceforth no longer use the term paragraph to mean 'a distinct level between discourse and sentence' and will revert to the ordinary use of the word ʻo mean 'an orthographic division in a discourse marked normally by ɪndentation or greater space between lines'.

If the paragraph as such does not exist, what was it that the native informant responded to in Young and Becker's experiment? We will want to argue in subsequent chapters that they were responding to real divisions in the discourse. It is merely that these divisions are defined not by their internal organisation but by their external relation to each other. Rodgers (1966a) makes this point very clearly when he says:

Paragraph structure is part and parcel of the structure of the discourse as a whole; a given stadium [≏ noteworthy division] becomes a paragraph not by virtue of its structure but because the writer elects to indent, his indentation functioning, as does all punctuation, as a gloss upon the overall literary process under way at that point.

What, in short, the native informant's ability to re-paragraph discourse really amounts to is an ability to discern the patterns of organisation of discourses. The rest of this book is devoted to explaining how he discerns these patterns and what the patterns are that he discerns.

6 Terminology

It is necessary at this point to clarify the terminology that will be used henceforth in this book, particularly as the field of discourse analysis is rapidly becoming a minefield of conflicting definitions. 'Paragraph' I have given immediately above. Other terms that will be used are:

Sentence: An orthographic division beginning with a capital letter and finishing with a full stop.
Clause: a grammatical construction consisting of subject and predicate with optional adjuncts, where the predicate may be predicator and object, predicator and complement, or exceptionally just object or complement with deleted but recoverable predicator. The subject may be derivable from the context if the clause is subordinated and omitted if the clause is an imperative.
Discourse: any stretch of spoken or written language that is felt as complete in itself.
Passage: any extract from a discourse (it would have been helpful to have used the term *text* for this purpose, but it has been employed by others for too many purposes to be of any value here).

7 Summary of Chapter 1

Chapter 1 can be summarised by the following generalisations:

(1) There is a 'consensus' about discourse organisation which includes the ability to identify organisational breaks in a discourse.
(2) Adjacent sentences in discourses are frequently linked by anaphoric devices of various kinds and by repetition but these are not sufficient to account for the organisation of discourses.
(3) Discourses are not built out of sentences on a brick-by-brick basis.
(4) Discourses cannot be treated as strings of paragraphs.

(5) The 'paragraph' is not a distinct level between discourse and sentence.

(6) Discourses are sometimes organised on a Russian doll model, i.e. one subdiscourse within another.

Chapter 2

The Clause Relation and its Signals

1   The Work Of Winter

In Chapter 1 we considered a number of factors that have to be taken into account in any discussion of discourse organisation. Several of these factors were matters of relation. The 'Serious Consequences' game, for example, was designed to test whether discourses are made up of sentences related only to their neighbours. The 'Icy Roads' jumbled discourse exercise was designed to show, among other things, that some sentences belong together; they relate closely to each other in a way that is not a matter of chance. The BFI letter was introduced to show that groups of sentences can be semantically related to each other in the same way that sentences can. It is not therefore surprising that, while there are many other ways of viewing discourse, a persistently popular way in recent years of tackling the problem of describing discourse organisation has been to treat discourse as in some way the product of semantic relations holding between sentences or propositions.

One of the most thoughtful proponents of this way of viewing discourse has been Eugene Winter. His work on clause relations can for the most part be divided into two main strands. On the one hand, he is concerned to place a sentence in the context of its adjoining sentences and show how its grammar and meaning can only be fully explained if its larger context is taken into account in its interpretation (and how also it may affect our reading of sentences in that context). On the other, he is concerned to reveal the clause relational organisation of a passage as a whole without focusing on any one sentence in particular within it. The approach to discourse analysis demonstrated in this book is the result of an application (with inevitable modifications) of both strands of Winter's work to the problems posed by longer passages and whole discourses; this chapter is consequently devoted to a detailed discussion of some of his ideas. In it we outline the basic characteristics of his approach to clause relations and indicate how a practical procedure for discourse analysis can be usefully derived from his work. It should be noted however that no claims are made to comprehensiveness in this respect; many important aspects of Winter's work are neglected for no better reason than that active use is not made of them in this book.

2   The Definition of 'Clause Relation'

The clause relation may be defined as follows:

> A clause relation is the cognitive process whereby we interpret the meaning of a sentence or group of sentences in the light of its adjoining sentence or group of sentences. (Winter, 1971 and elsewhere)

For the purposes of this definition the notions of clause and sentence should be treated as conflated, and 'sentence' should be interpreted as also including part of a sentence. It should be noted too that while 'adjoining' describes the most likely position of related clauses, for the purposes of the definition it need mean no more than 'within the same discourse'.

As the definition makes clear, the clause relation is not so called because it relates only clauses. Rather it is so described because all systems for signalling relations are rooted in the grammar of the clause. In this sense there is therefore no contradiction in terms in referring to the relation between two 'paragraphs' as a larger clause relation. Nevertheless for the sake of avoiding misinterpretation, we have in subsequent chapters chosen, wherever no ambiguity would result from its omission, to refer to clause relations simply as relations.

Winter's definition of the clause relation is rich in implications, all of which require exploration in the development of an adequate theoretical framework. The first implication is that a relation is concerned with meaning. Thus uninterpreted grammatical cohesion is not a relation. The second is that a relation involves the addition of something; when two pieces of language are placed together, if their meaning together is more than the sum total of their separate parts, then they are in a relation with each other. If on the other hand no meaning is added when they are placed together, or if no agreement can be reached about the meaning that might have been added, then they are not in a relation with each other.

The third implication of Winter's definition is that a sentence in isolation is interpretable in discourse terms only when placed in its context. Interpretation of the clause is hampered unless this contextualisation takes place first.

The fourth implication of Winter's definition is perhaps the most important – namely, that clause relations are acts of interpretation by the reader/listener of what he or she encounters, in the light of what has already been encountered. As such they are not amenable to direct analysis and an account of a passage that contents itself with labelling relations is an interpretation of the passage of no greater inherent status than any other reader's interpretation. The spelling out of all the relations holding between the parts of a passage may be of value to translators and stylisticians but it can be no more than a first step for a discourse analyst. The discourse analyst's task must be to discover what in the discourse allows the reader's acts of interpretation to take place and what ensures that the various acts of interpretation that take place occur within a given range of possibilities.

All this is heavily biased towards the reader/listener rather than towards the producer. Nevertheless, while not attempting to account for the act of production of a discourse, we can note that each clause produced is offered in the light of its predecessors (or in the case of revised writing, its successors also), and that therefore it is possible to adapt Winter's definition to allow for this:

> A clause relation is also the cognitive process whereby the choices we make from grammar, lexis and intonation in the creation of a sentence or group of sentences are made in the light of its adjoining sentence or group of sentences.

3 Categories of Clause Relation

Clause relations may be divided into two broad classes of relation – Logical Sequence relations and Matching relations. Logical Sequence relations are relations between successive events or ideas, whether actual or potential, the most basic form of this relation being time sequence. Examples of relations incorporated under the heading of Logical Sequence include Condition–Consequence, e.g.

> **2.1** If the royal portrait was not used [on stamps], the arms of the country or reigning house were often taken as a suitable symbol;[1]

where the subordinate clause is the Condition and the main clause the Consequence, Instrument–Achievement, e.g.

> **2.2** Mrs Barton lighted a dip by sticking it in the fire;[2]

where the main clause is the Achievement and the subordinate clause the Instrument, and Cause–Consequence, e.g.

> **2.3** She was here because she was waiting for somebody, or something;[3]

where the main clause is the Consequence and the subordinate clause the Cause.

Matching relations are relations where statements are 'matched' against each other in terms of degrees of identicality of description. Examples of Matching relations are Contrast, e.g.

2.4 The skirmish was not taken very seriously at Vienne. What was taken seriously, however, was the fact that Constantius had named me his fellow consul for the New Year;[4]

where the second sentence contrasts the serious attention given to the appointment of the speaker with the inattention given the previously described skirmish; and Compatibility, e.g.

2.5 Upstairs Fred thumped and bumped and tossed and turned. And downstairs Ted moaned and groaned and crashed and thrashed all over the bed.[5]

where Fred and Ted are being matched for their similarity of response to their sleeping arrangements.

Examples of both Logical Sequence and Matching relations will be found in abundance later on in this and subsequent chapters; they are best provided when the means for identifying them have been outlined.

One further category needs to be introduced before we take up the problem of how clause relations can be identified. Logical Sequence and Matching are themselves governed by a still more fundamental relation, that of Situation–Evaluation, representing the two facets of world-perception 'knowing' and 'thinking'. Indeed as will often become apparent, all relations are reducible to these basic elements.

No attempt will be made below to provide a more detailed classification of types of relation. Elaborate classifications of relation can sometimes obscure similarities and kinships amongst the relations. Contrast and Compatibility for instance are, at their most clearly signalled, distinct relations, but examples occur where out of context a hazy middle ground between the two is occupied. It follows that discussion of types of relation cannot be sensibly carried on apart from the means whereby those relations are identified.

In the thumb-nail sketch just given of Winter's categories of clause relation, the most important part is that they are all strands of one web. In other words, the subcategories of relation do not represent discrete choices but are interconnected in the most complex fashion. Furthermore – and here the metaphor of the web is entirely unhelpful – it is quite possible for a pair of clauses to be semantically related in a number of different ways. For example, the three clauses of **2.6** are in both a double Cause–Consequence relation and a double Matching Compatibility relation.

2.6 He did not want to go away for Easter because he did not wish to leave London because he did not wish to leave Rose.[6]

On the one hand, the three clauses are saying that his desire not to go away for Easter is the result of another desire which is itself the result of yet another desire. On the other hand, they are also saying that he had three compatible negative desires. These two meanings do not conflict with each other; both are present simultaneously, though the Cause–Consequence relation is in this case the dominant meaning.

It follows from all this that we have to analyse discourses with the greatest care as we are ever liable to oversimplify the relationship holding between any two clauses. Many is the time that I have completed an analysis to my own satisfaction only for someone else to discover for me a lurking multiple relation of which I was unaware, having been lulled into a false sense of security by the obviousness of one element of the relation.

4 Subordinators and Conjuncts as Clause Relation Signals

The most apparent means whereby a clause relation may be signalled to the reader/listener is by the use of one out of the two finite sets of grammatical connectives that we have in English for this purpose – the subordinators and the conjuncts (also known as sentence adjuncts and sentence conjunctions). Thus the two 'because' subordinators in 2.6 tell us that the two clauses are (amongst other things) in a double Cause–Consequence relation.

Similarly the use of the conjunct 'so' at the beginning of the third sentence in **2.7** tells us that the three sentences form a Cause–Consequence relation.

> **2.7** (1) It was over, it was known, it was decided, there was nothing at all, ever, to be done about it. (2) He might as well, now, go to bed.
> (3) So he stood up, put down his empty glass, looked at himself with some curiosity in the mirror, to see if he looked different for having understood, and went up to bed.[7]

The paragraph break after sentence 2 emphasises that the Cause–Consequence relation is not solely between adjacent sentences 2 and 3, but that in fact sentences 1 and 2 are jointly the Cause to sentence 3's Consequence.

Winter began his work on the signalling of clause relations (Winter, 1968) with conjuncts. He shows both how they are used to signal certain central relations and what the alternative methods are of signalling the same relations. But – and this is important – just as the conjuncts are described chiefly as signals of clause relations, so also clause relations are described chiefly as a way of clarifying the nature of conjuncts. The relationship, then, is both close and complex. It may be

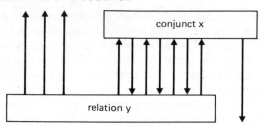

Figure 2.1

seen in diagrammatic form in Figure 2.1. Thus each requires a description of the other even though the relation is not one-to-one and a full description of either will always involve reference to more than the other. It is this refusal to regard either signal or relation as primary that distinguishes all of Winter's work; for him signal and relation are of equal importance. In other words relations have typical grammatical representations but there is no one-to-one correspondence between relation and representation. This is an important insight and focuses on two facts about relations that need always to be kept in mind in discourse analysis. First, a relation is not identified by intuition alone nor is it an adequate description of a passage simply to note how its clauses are related; a relation is linguistically signalled and it is necessary to identify how it is signalled in any given case. Secondly, a relation is not simply a label for a set of signals; it can be identified only by examining the content of the clauses and their context.

5   Lexical Signalling of Clause Relations

In some circumstances, the study of subordinators and conjuncts is insufficient to explain how a reader interprets a relation unambiguously. Consider **2.8**, for example:

> **2.8**   Alderman Frank Price sees the city as a sort of anvil; my barber thinks of it as 'a neutral sort of place built by people who worked hard for generations'.

Asked what relationships there is between the two halves of this sentence, a reader could be forgiven for hesitating. Is it part of a list? If not, is it contrastive? The evidence points slightly in the latter direction but is far from conclusive. What the reader clearly needs is more context. Winter (1974) shows that knowledge of what precedes **2.8** solves the reader's problem:

> **2.9**   People think of Birmingham in different ways. Alderman Frank Price sees the city as a sort of anvil; my barber thinks of it as 'a neutral sort of place built by people who worked hard for generations'.[8]

He points out that 'different' 'makes explicit the contrast between the clause pair'; it tells the reader how to interpret the relation before it occurs. Yet 'different' is an adjective within a prepositional group functioning as adjunct and is in no sense one of the grammatical connectives described in the previous section. Indeed, quite frequently the reader may not only be told how to interpret a relation beforehand but then also have that information reinforced with one of the grammatical connectives, for example,

2.10 People think of Birmingham in different ways. Alderman Frank Price sees the city as a sort of anvil, whereas my barber thinks of it as 'a neutral sort of place built by people who worked hard for generations'.

In this concocted example, first the adjective 'different' tells us that people's thoughts about Birmingham are about to be contrasted, and then 'whereas' tells us that the Contrast is under way.

Winter has worked out in detail the significance of this type of lexical signalling, pointing out that in English it is possible to signal the same relationship in one of three ways: subordinators, which he calls Vocabulary 1; conjuncts, which he calls Vocabulary 2; and lexical signals such as those we have just been considering, which he labels Vocabulary 3. These three vocabularies are frequently able to paraphrase each other, given different contexts. Thus **2.11** can be paraphrased out of context as either **2.12** or **2.13**:

2.11 By appealing to scientists and technologists to support his party, Mr Wilson won many middle-class votes.[9]
2.12 Mr Wilson appealed to scientists and technologists to support his party. He *thereby* won many middle-class votes in the election.
2.13 Mr Wilson's appeals to scientists and technologists to support his party *were instrumental* in winning many middle-class votes in the election.
(All three examples from Winter, 1977)

All three versions are examples of the Instrument–Achievement relation, signalled in **2.11** by a Vocabulary 1 item, 'by-ing', i.e. a subordinator; in **2.12** by a Vocabulary 2 item, 'thereby', i.e. a conjunct; and in **2.13** by a Vocabulary 3 item, 'instrumental', for which there was previously no label. It will be seen throughout this book that lexical signals are common and their recognition essential to successful discourse analysis.

Lexical signals may spell out a relation before, during, or after the event. If it occurs before the event, it is termed anticipatory; if it occurs after the event it is termed retrospective. Whatever is being referred to by the signal is referred to as lexical realisation. An example of an anticipatory lexical signal is **2.14** (the quotes are mine):

2.14 A Cartesian diver is a toy that depends on *two principles*: the first is that air is elastic and the second is that air is lighter than water.[10]

Here, *two principles* is the anticipatory signal and all that follows the colon is what is being referred to (i.e. the lexical realisation). An example of retrospective signalling can be seen in **2.15**:

2.15 The manufacturer's familiar argument in support of the adequacy of existing coating systems does need scrutiny in respect, for example, of the slipper dipping process; excess-point 'runs' which can arise are subsequently 'buffed out' in 'point finish' production area with inevitable concurrent removal of primer and undercoat in certain cases. Resulting weakness points arising from *this cause* can exist generally at the joints of the sill and 'A', 'B/C' and 'D' posts.[11]

In this example, *cause* retrospectively characterises the latter part of the previous sentence as the origin of 'weakness points'. ('Resulting', in the same example, is an instance of a lexical signal occurring in the middle of the relation.)

Vocabulary 3 items not only help signal the relations that hold between the sentences of a paragraph, they also signal the organisation of larger passages and whole discourses. Winter (1977) draws attention, for example, to what he terms 'items of the metastructure'; these are lexical signals which serve a larger function. This use of lexical signalling is relevant to the questions this book is concerned to answer. Accordingly lexical signals are used and discussed in all subsequent chapters, particularly in Chapters 4 and 5, where they are seen to play a major role in the signalling of discourse organisation.

6 Repetition as a Clause Relation Signal

The signals we have been discussing account for a large number of cases of clause relation, but they do not account for them all by any means. Consider **2.16** for example:

2.16 In spite of the hopes and promises of her new allies, Germany remains divided; in spite of strenuous efforts at international virtue, she feels herself morally reviled.[12]

The reader will scan this in vain for any signal of the types so far discussed showing the relation between the two halves of the sentence. Yet he or she will have readily recognised that the two halves of the sentence are offering pieces of information that are in some sense much alike. Both statements tell of an unhappy Germany; both statements argue that this unhappiness does not logically follow from the behaviour of her or her allies. They are offered as compatible pieces of information about Germany with a core common to both. What tells the reader this is the repetition. Winter has in fact demonstrated that many relations are signalled by repetition. He notes that sentences are unable to carry all the information that might be given on a subject; they are by their nature selective. Repetition is accordingly a way of 'opening out' a sentence so that its lexical uniqueness may be used as the basis for providing further, related information.

Repetition is not only a common method of connecting sentences but also a significant contributor to their interpretation, because where two sentences have material in common, it is what is changed that receives attention by the reader, while the repeated material acts as a framework for the interpretation of the new material. So, in **2.16** above, the repeated material is 'In spite of' (X), 'Germany/she' (Y), where the material in X and Y shows grammatical parallelism. X is in both halves a plural noun (or nouns), and Y is a predicate made up of a 'current' copula verb ('remains', 'feels') and a complement in the form of a past participle ('divided', 'reviled'). This repetition and the parallel grammatical construction serve as a frame for interpretation of the relation; the reader notices that the plural nouns at X are usually positively regarded – 'hopes', 'promises', and 'efforts' – and that the past participles describe states normally to be regretted – 'divided' (of nations) and 'reviled'. This combination of grammatical and lexical parallelism is sufficient to identify positively the relation between the two halves of the whole sentence as one of Matching Compatibility.

Winter points out that the grammatical functions of the clause are in this fashion linked into adjoining clauses. He suggests that one of the most common phenomena in English is systematic partial repetition of the elements of the clause, noting that this is disguised by the grammatical form it takes. So, in **2.16** above, the repetition of 'Germany' is disguised by the fact that the second occurrence of 'Germany' is in the form of a pronoun. Deletion is another common form of disguised repetition. Whether it is in the form of substitution, deletion or full lexical repetition, systematic repetition provides a clause constant whereby the nature of the new information is recognised and its importance to the context assessed.

The new information in a clause with partial repetition Winter terms replacement. If the whole clause is repeated with something added to it, the additional material is termed replacement by addition or asymmetrical repetition. Repetition, like lexical signalling, not only signals the relations that hold between the sentences of a paragraph, it also signals the organisation of longer passages. Accordingly Chapters 6 and 7 spell out what may count as repetition, offer a means of talking about it for the purposes of analysing passages, and discuss the relations it is typically associated with.

7   Paraphrase as a Means of Clarifying Clause Relations

So far we have only considered those instances where the writer/ speaker has been considerate enough to spell out the relationship between his or her clauses (or groups of clauses). It hardly needs saying that there are circumstances when such 'spelling out' does not occur. Consider the following two sentences taken from a story by Enid Blyton:

> **2.17**   Peter went red. He knew he had been silly.[13]

No subordinator nor conjunct links these to tell us what relation they form. No lexical signal informs us of their connection. No systematic repetition is in evidence, the substitution of 'Peter' by 'he' (twice) having no direct significance. Yet most native speakers would identify the relationship as being one of Cause–Consequence where the first sentence is the Consequence and the second the Cause.

Winter's answer to this problem is twofold: first, to project the monologue into dialogue and discover what questions each part answers and secondly, to paraphrase the discourse in such a way that its relations are revealed. This and the next section briefly consider these methods for eliciting relations.

Paraphrase does not require detailed discussion here. We have seen already in our discussion of lexical signalling that paraphrase is crucial evidence for the existence of a third vocabulary serving the same signalling functions as subordinators and conjuncts. The argument was that if a sentence such as **2.13** could be paraphrased by either **2.11** or **2.12** (subject to the normal restrictions of context) it followed that 'instrumental' must serve the same signalling function as 'thereby' or 'by . . . ing'.

What lay behind this argument was a simple assumption, namely, that 'thereby' and 'by . . . ing' are recognised signals of a particular relationship – the Instrument–Achievement relation. We in effect were saying: 'We have a sentence here which we suspect may involve an Instrument–Achievement relation. Let's reword it so that it includes one of the recognised Instrument–Achievement signals. If this is a paraphrase, then the original must be in an Instrument–Achievement relation as well.' Using this method, we were able to draw our conclusions about the signalling status of 'instrumental'. It can be seen, however, from the formulation just given that the method will work equally well on sentences without lexical signalling. If we have clauses or sentences without any overt signal of the relation they are in, we can test out which relations are possible by the use of rewording to include overt signals. If the result does not change the meaning, then the relation is that indicated by the signals inserted, again with the proviso that there will be contextual differences according to the signal used. Thus, for example, the pair of sentences in **2.18** below contain no overt signal of any relation:

> **2.18** Mr Wilson won many middle-class votes in the election. He appealed to scientists and technologists to support his party.
> (Modified from Winter, 1977).

Since, however, it can be paraphrased with overt signals as in **2.11** and **2.12** above (ignoring the important contextual differences that result from subordination and change of sequence), it is, like them, an example of an Instrument–Achievement relation.

8 Questions as a Means of Clarifying Clause Relations

One of the first lessons any aspiring linguist is taught is that speech has primacy over writing. Yet we every day neglect the consequences of this claim. For example, intonation is normally relegated to a corner of most grammatical theories, despite its obvious importance in distinguishing sentences that would otherwise be ambiguous. Similarly, in discourse studies, those who have studied written monologue have frequently done so without any reference to the spoken word, and sometimes those who have studied spoken monologue have done so without reference to dialogue. Yet one of the inevitable consequences of seeing speech as having primacy over writing is that dialogue should have primacy over monologue. That this must be the case requires only a moment's consideration. Every day of our lives we engage in conversation ranging from idle chit-chat in the bus queue or the pub to serious deliberation over (sometimes) important issues in the committee or seminar room. But of all those who engage in conversation, relatively few will ever be expected to produce spoken or written monologues of any significant length. Most of us tell stories at some time or other, or, being opinionated on some topic, wax eloquent in the expression of those opinions. Likewise, most of us have to write the occasional letter and may well choose to do so for pleasure. Nevertheless these activities will take up only a fragment of our language-using time, and it would be possible to go through life without producing a monologue worthy of the name. It would be far less easy – indeed virtually impossible – to go through life without engaging in dialogue.

If dialogue has primacy over monologue, it is but a small step to seeing monologue as a specialised form of dialogue between the writer or speaker and the reader or listener. We saw in the last section that where two sentences contained no overt signal of their relation, one could in effect be supplied by means of a paraphrase. Paraphrase is, however, open to misuse unless used with circumspection because of the influence of context. For this reason it is often better to supplement or even replace the use of paraphrase with the use of a recreated dialogue between writer/speaker and reader/listener. This has the advantage that it preserves the context in which sentences in relation appear. Thus **2.18** above can be converted into question–answer form as **2.19**:

> **2.19** D: Mr Wilson won many middle-class votes in the election.
> Q: How did he achieve this?
> D: He appealed to scientists and technologists to support his party.

It will be noticed that the question itself includes a lexical signal of achievement though this is not essential to its functioning.

Clearly for such a technique to be useful, we have to have a controlled method of converting monologue to dialogue. One way in which this can be done is by restricting the interlocutor's contributions to questions and requests for information. If we permit our interlocutor only to ask questions or make requests, we restrict the range of possible insertions into any discourse. This has the effect of distancing the projected dialogue from the everyday dialogue of the real world, but has the compensatory effect of preventing the imagined interlocutor from introducing extraneous material into the discourse; it also allows for a greater degree of replicability. It perhaps needs, however, to be emphasised that projecting monologues into dialogue is intended to tell us something about monologue, not about dialogue.

Immediately above, we referred to questions and requests for information as if they were different things. This was for ease of discussion only; henceforth we shall treat questions and requests for information as identical. This means that it makes no difference for our purposes whether an imaginary interlocutor says 'What is an example of this?' or 'Give me an example of this'.

A number of types of question may be used to clarify the organisation of discourse. For reasons that will become apparent it is important to distinguish between them. First, we need to distinguish between questions of different degrees of precision. Questions such as 'how?' apply to very many situations; they can be used to elicit answers of a certain type in almost any discourse. Such questions we shall call broad questions. Their advantage is that they allow for convenient generalisation. If one says certain features are common to all clauses, etc. that may be linked by 'how?', one is making a generalisation of considerable power. The disadvantage of such questions is the converse of this; they do not distinguish sufficiently between different situations.

At the other end of the scale we have questions such as 'How did Mr

Wilson win many middle-class votes in the election?' which can only apply to the one situation and which are unlikely to be used to elicit answers in any other discourse. We shall call such questions narrow questions. Such questions reflect sensitively the relationship of sentences to the contexts in which they appear. Their advantage and disadvantage are the reverse of those of broad questions. They are nearly useless when it comes to making large generalisations but have the merit of spelling out exactly the relationship holding between the two parts of a particular discourse. As will become apparent in later chapters, both types of question have their uses. There is a cline (i.e. an unbroken gradation) between the two types of question: a question somewhat intermediate between the two so far quoted would be 'How did Mr Wilson achieve this?'. There is of course no need for a separate label for the intermediate questions.

Broad and narrow questions can often be shown in the same dialogue. For example, in **2.20** below the complete question, 'How did Mr Wilson win many middle-class votes in the election?', is narrow but that part which is unbracketed (i.e. 'How') can also stand on its own as a broad question:

> **2.20** D: Mr Wilson won many middle-class votes in the election.
> Q: How ⟨did Mr Wilson win many middle-class votes in the election⟩?
> D: He appealed to scientists and technologists to support his party.

In this and all subsequent examples, D will stand for the original discourse, Q for the posited question.

A second important distinction we need to make is between questions that elicit a larger passage of the discourse and questions that elicit a smaller passage of the discourse. Again we have a cline here. Questions may elicit parts of a sentence, whole sentences, groups of sentences, long passages or even whole discourses. Examples of most of these possibilities will be found in the pages of this book. The difference between the level of applicability of two questions is therefore almost always relative. Where the levels need to be contrasted, we will call the question eliciting the larger portion of the discourse a high-level question and the question eliciting the smaller portion of the discourse a low-level question.

It should be noted that there is no correlation between high-level and low-level on the one hand, and broad and narrow on the other. Thus, when Kipling entitles one of his Just So Stories 'How the Camel Got His Hump', and thereby shows that his story is to answer the high-level question 'How did the camel get his hump?', he is at the same time promising to answer a narrow question – one that is probably unique and certainly infrequent. All four categories are categories of convenience. It is to be hoped that future work on questions will see them supplanted by categories that reflect more sensitively the discourse possibilities.

9 Summary of Chapter 2

The following positions have been adopted as a basis for the study of discourse organisation in subsequent chapters:

(1) Discourse work should concern itself with the identification of signals of patterns of organisation.
(2) Clause relations divide into two main categories: Logical Sequence and Matching.
(3) It is not unusual to find multiple relations between parts of a discourse.
(4) The signal and the relation signalled are of equal importance to the discourse analyst.
(5) Conjuncts and subordinators are signals of clause relations.
(6) There is a class of lexical signals that serve the same function as conjuncts and subordinators.
(7) Repetition is a signal of some clause relations.
(8) Paraphrase may assist in clarifying clause relations.
(9) Monologues may be projected into dialogue and such projection may clarify the monologue's organisation.
(10) Projection into dialogue may involve the use of broad or narrow questions, and high-level or low-level questions.

All these claims are utilised in subsequent chapters to clarify how discourse is organised. In the next chapter we examine a minimum pattern of organisation which will prove to be a most fertile pattern in English.

Chapter 3

The Problem–Solution Pattern: a Minimum Discourse

1 A Typical Pattern of Discourse

In Chapter 2 we considered the notion of the clause relation and discussed in some detail the means identified by Winter whereby a relation might be established in a discourse or passage. These were found to be subordinators, conjuncts, lexical signalling and repetition, all of which are signals discovered in the passage as given, and paraphrase and questions, which are both methods of clarifying the relations in the passage by adding to or altering it in a regular way.

It is now necessary to show how it is possible to use Winter's methods for establishing a relation, to analyse whole discourses and longer passages. This application of Winter's methods to the finding of patterns in discourses could be demonstrated with any one of the variety of discourse patterns common in English, some of which will be referred to or discussed in the course of this work. Not only, however, would practical considerations prevent all these patterns being given equal treatment but it would also be theoretically unjustifiable to do so, for reasons that will be touched on in Section 2 and discussed in detail in Chapter 8. One common pattern – the Problem–Solution pattern – has therefore been selected for detailed study, the methods of description shown for that pattern being, however, equally applicable to the other patterns discussed in less detail elsewhere. (By pattern I mean combination of relations organising (part of) a discourse.) In this chapter we show how the Problem–Solution pattern can be revealed by the use of paraphrase and questions. In Chapter 4 we consider its manifestations in short factual discourses. Chapter 5 looks at ways in which it can be varied and adapted according to communicative need, and examines how it operates in narrative. This attention should not be allowed, however, to distort the overall picture; other patterns of organisation also commonly occur, some of which are discussed in Chapters 6 and 7. Our handling of the Problem–Solution pattern should be taken as typical of the way in which we believe discourse can fruitfully be treated, rather than indicative of the importance of one particular pattern.

2   Initial Assumptions

Before we begin our examination of the means available to us for analysing discourse, we need to make our starting assumptions explicit. The first assumption being made throughout this book is that discourses and passages of discourses are organised. This was essentially the conclusion reached in Chapter 1. A second and related assumption being made is that they are organised at least in part in a hierarchical manner. Just as in a sentence such as

3.1   The old man in the dirty mackintosh spat into the drinking fountain.

the syntactic relationship between the adjacent words 'mackintosh' and 'spat' is considerably less strong than that between 'man' and 'spat', so in a discourse the relationship between adjacent sentences may be considerably less strong than that between non-adjacent ones. Likewise, just as 'the dirty mackintosh' is an immediate constituent of 'in the dirty mackintosh', and 'in the dirty mackintosh' is itself an immediate constituent of 'the old man in the dirty mackintosh', the whole nominal group being in turn an immediate constituent of the sentence, so also a discourse may be made up of clause relations which are themselves members of larger clause relations which are in turn members of an overall relation. Examples will be found in this and subsequent chapters. The major difference of course is that immediate constituent analysis takes no account whatsoever of meaning whereas discourse analysis, as envisaged in these pages, makes considerable use of meaning; the parallel between the two is therefore best seen as metaphorical.

This having been said, the qualification should be noted in our wording of this second assumption – at least in part. We will not get far unless we make some assumption of hierarchical organisation. This will be found over and over again: see, for example, discourses **3.48** and **7.23**. On the other hand, if we elevate hierarchical organisation into an immutable law of discourse, we will encounter difficulties of a different kind. Hints of such problems can be found in our discussion of several discourses. A theoretical formulation is attempted in Chapter 8 that will take into account the complexity of this and the other phenomena we will have examined in the course of the previous chapters.

Such then are our two basic starting assumptions about the organisation of discourse. Our second pair of assumptions concern the way in which discourse is perceived. Just as the native speaker of a language can assess whether a sentence is grammatical though he is usually quite unable to say how he knows, so, it is here assumed, he can also assess whether a discourse is well formed though, again, beyond that he cannot usually go. Evidence for this are the experiments discussed in Chapter 1, particularly the 'Icy Roads' experiment. Pointing in the same direction is the fact that people are capable of complaining of a play that it did not have 'a beginning, a middle or an end' or of a politician's answer that 'he went off the point'. These and other like judgements suggest an ability among native listener/readers to perceive discourse organisation.

A further assumption made here is that there is something in the discourse itself that helps the listener or speaker to perceive the structure. In other words, the emphasis laid by Van Dijk and Kintsch (1978) on the active psychological process of comprehending and recalling the macrostructures of discourses (or, as they would prefer, texts) is not that adopted here (though no assumptions are made about the correctness or otherwise of their viewpoint). Instead, the emphasis is placed on the ways in which the surface of the discourse (not necessarily to be contrasted with hidden depths) contains sufficient clues for the reader/listener to perceive accurately the discourse's organisation.

A third, more radical, pair of assumptions stem from the previous two. If discourses do contain clues as to their organisation, it is possible that it is the clues that are finite and not the patterns of organisation they point to. In other words, it is possible that we are capable of building an indefinite number of patterns out of a strikingly finite number of resources. This in turn involves the assumption that at the lower levels of discourse, that is, those commonly associated with the paragraph, there are indeed also a finite number of possible relations. This again finds echoes in the structuralist view of grammar. Gleason (1961) notes that the number of individual sentence patterns 'are nearly incalculable'. 'Certainly', he adds, 'the total up to any reasonable length is many millions – a number far too large to list in a grammar.' He goes on to point out that:

Some of these patterns must be extremely rare, probably rare enough that many speakers of English never hear them in their lifetime ... And yet when a speaker of English does hear one of these very rare patterns – there are enough of them that this must be a frequent occurrence – they seem perfectly natural and even familiar ... If such a thing can happen, it is only because this sentence was built out of familiar units. These might well be the various constructional patterns, some within others, which an IC or order-class analysis (both structuralist approaches to syntax) would find. Most of them are quite common, and necessarily familiar. What a grammar must describe, then, is not sentence patterns, but the smaller units of pattern of which they are constructed. Only thus can a language be described, a basis laid for understanding how it operates in human communication or a foundation built for optimal language teaching.

Substitute the word 'discourse' for 'sentence' and 'discourse analysis' for 'IC or order-class analysis', and the statement largely represents our view of discourse organisation. Again, of course, the parallel is less close than it seems. As before, there is the semantic-syntactic opposition and, secondly, there is the important difference that in sentence grammar of the structuralist type the syntactic constructions are typically different on each level of cutting, whereas in discourse the semantic relations which make up the units do not differ necessarily from level to level. Accordingly, as before, the comparison should be seen as limited in usefulness. The basic points, though, remain: first, that discourses, like sentences, can be analysed in terms of multiple layers, each layer providing detail about the unanalysed units of the layer above, and secondly, that the number of discourse patterns that can be built out of a finite set of relations signalled in a finite number of ways is indefinitely large. If these assumptions are correct, it would of course be a fool's errand to attempt to describe all discourse patterns, even if the field were narrowed primarily to the discourse patterns of written monologues only. The appropriate course of action would instead be one of two – either to describe in detail the nature of the lower-level familiar units, that is, the clause relations and their members, or to show how they typically combine to make up discourse patterns. A full description must properly include both. Since, however, the work of Winter is primarily directed towards the former objective and since this book is not aimed at a readership who would necessarily wish to wade through a magnum opus such as would be required to meet both objectives, the remainder of this work is devoted to the second objective only, namely, showing how discourse patterns are built up out of smaller, more familiar units.

This section has outlined our starting assumptions; in Chapter 8 we return to them in the light of the data analysed and attempt to formulate our position more exactly. For the moment though, we can summarise the purpose of the remainder of this and the next four chapters as being to discover some patterns typically built up in discourse and how they can be brought to view.

3   The Minimum Discourse

William Labov (1975) has drawn attention to some of the dangers of relying too heavily on made-up examples in linguistic study. If these dangers exist in work based on the sentence, still more must they exist for work based on the paragraph and beyond, where intuitions have not been sharpened by practice from school-days onwards. It would clearly be folly therefore not to use real examples on all possible occasions. On the other hand we must also be careful not to allow the size of our examples to lead us into the convenient neglect of important details or to untestable generalisation. For this reason, in this chapter alone, we permit ourselves the luxury of simplified made-up examples, much as a grammarian begins by examining the simple sentence before describing the intricacies of the compound or complex sentence.

We have chosen as our minimum discourse an example devised by Winter for teaching purposes and briefly discussed by him in Winter (1976), comprising the following four sentences:

> *I opened fire,*
> *I was on sentry duty,*
> *I beat off the attack,*
> and *I saw the enemy approaching.*

These four sentences can be sequenced in twenty-four ways. The degree of acceptability of the twenty-four possible sequence varies considerably; some sequences seem totally deviant, for example:

> **3.2** I beat off the attack. I opened fire. I saw the enemy approaching. I was on sentry duty.

Others seem somewhat less so if one or more of the sentences is given parenthetical intonation, for example:

> **3.3** I saw the enemy approaching. (I was on sentry duty.) I opened fire. I beat off the attack;

where, as the bracketing suggests, the second sentence is given special intonation. Only one sequence, however, is completely acceptable, given neutral intonation and equal emphasis on all sentences, namely,

> **3.4** I was on sentry duty. I saw the enemy approaching. I opened fire. I beat off the attack.

We would in fact appear to have (as in much linguistic analysis) a cline (that is, a gradation) from totally acceptable to totally unacceptable.

Apart from the variations in intonation mentioned above, no variation has been permitted among the twenty-four versions except that of sequence. It may be deduced therefore that the only non-phonological feature to affect the degree of acceptability of the twenty-four discourses is the particular sequence of the four sentences. Sequences would appear therefore to be capable of categorisation, on the same basis as sentences, into unmarked, marked, and unacceptable sequences. Just as we are able to accept 'It is not dull' as normal or unmarked, 'Dull it is not' as unusual but meaningful given an appropriate context, and 'Dull not is it' as unacceptable and meaningless, so we are able to recognise sequence **3.4** as normal (unmarked), sequence **3.3** as unusual but meaningful (marked) and sequence **3.2** as unacceptable and meaningless.

4   Sequence and Subordination

It is at this stage that the role of subordination becomes important. For the marked sequences become less marked or even unmarked if they are connected by appropriate subordinators. So, for example, sequence **3.3** may become,

> **3.5**   I saw the enemy approaching *while* I was on sentry duty. I opened fire. I beat off the attack.

Likewise, the marked sequence

> **3.6**   I was on sentry duty. I opened fire. (I saw the enemy approaching.) I beat off the attack.

can, when connected by subordination, become the less marked version:

> **3.7**   *While* I was on sentry duty, I opened fire, *because* I saw the enemy approaching. I (thereby) beat off the attack.

Perhaps more strikingly, sequences that were completely unacceptable without subordination, such as sequence **3.2**, become completely acceptable with subordination:

> **3.8**   I beat off the attack *by* open*ing* fire *when* I saw the enemy approaching *while* I was on sentry duty.

This suggests that once subordination is introduced, sequence becomes relatively unimportant, apart from the initial selection of the superordinate clause(s). So, of the twenty-four sequences of the four sentences, many more are now acceptable and our cline is no longer straightforward. Moreover, when the unmarked sequence, sequence **3.4**, is partially connected by subordination, the resultant discourse is in some respects no more probable than the original unconnected version:

> **3.9**   *While* I was on sentry duty, *because* I saw the enemy approaching, I opened fire. I (thereby) beat off the attack.[1]

From these facts it can be deduced that sequence and subordination are in part complementary. Indeed subordination can be seen as a means of making explicit in an altered sequence what was already implicit in the unaltered sequence. For example, if sequence **3.6** is selected (without special intonation or punctuation), it is necessary for the subordinators *while* and *because* (or paraphrases of these) to be introduced to counter the loss of the information which would have been provided by the unmarked sequence. This is a fact of crucial importance, for it assumes that sequence is, in itself, meaningful. The question then is: what are its meanings? To answer this, we must clearly examine more closely the means available for linking the various sequences.

5 Sequence and Conjuncts

We noted above that the relative improbability of the version of sequence **3.4** connected by subordination (that is, example **3.9**) arose from the fact that sequence and subordination are alternative methods for supplying the same meanings to a discourse. It might have been inferred from this that an unmarked sequence will normally have no such form of connection. This is not in fact the case. There are, as we saw in Chapter 2, other means available in English for making explicit the implicit meanings of sequence, that is, the conjuncts (to use the name Quirk *et al.*, 1972, give them). Thus we attest the following possibility among many:

> **3.10** I was on sentry duty. I saw the enemy approaching. *Therefore* I opened fire. *By this means* I beat off the attack.

In contrast to the subordinators, conjuncts require the sequence to be unmarked where they connect, and we will therefore not attest their use as connectives in the other sequences, except where those sequences retain part of the unmarked sequence. For example, when we rewrite **3.11**:

> **3.11** I opened fire. I saw the enemy approaching. I was on sentry duty. I beat off the attack.

so as to connect the clauses by either subordinators or conjuncts, we find we cannot use 'therefore' to connect the first two sentences because they are not in the unmarked sequence but we can use 'by this means' or 'thereby' to connect clauses 1–3 to clause 4, because clauses 1 and 4 are in the unmarked sequence:

> **3.12** I opened fire *because* I saw the enemy approaching *when* I was on sentry duty. *By this means* I beat off the attack.

The meanings of conjuncts and subordinators have been well described; they are therefore suitably well-established starting-points for our investigation into the meaning of sequence.

6   Sequence and Questions

A third method is available for elucidating the meaning of sequence, namely, questions. These can be used to connect either unmarked or marked sequences. The most effective way of utilising them is to project the discourse into dialogue form where the questions that each sentence is implicitly answering can be made explicit. Using this method we find for unmarked sequence the following possibility (among several):

3.13   D: I was on sentry duty.
      Q: What happened?
      D: I saw the enemy approaching.
      Q: What was your response?
      D: I opened fire.
      Q: How successful was this?
      or What was the result of this?
      D: I beat off the attack.

This type of interrogation might be termed narrative interrogation. It is only complete when the last answer is given. For the reverse sequence we find the following possibility (again among several):

3.14   D: I beat off the attack.
      Q: How ⟨did you beat off the enemy attack⟩?
      D: I opened fire.
      Q: Why ⟨did you open fire⟩?
      D: I saw the enemy approaching.
      Q: In what situation ⟨did you see the enemy approaching⟩?
      D: I was on sentry duty.

This type of interrogation might be termed elaborational interrogation. In at least one sense, it is complete at each stage.

Questions are a primary source of information about the meanings of sentences in sequence. When we convert a discourse into a dialogue (as above, in **3.13** and **3.14**) we are converting each sentence into an answer to a question; that question spells out explicitly the previously implicit communicative purpose of the sentence and, assuming this communicative purpose makes use of the language context, the question will spell out the context at the same time. On the other hand, as we saw in Section 8 of Chapter 2, questions must be handled with caution, because not only are various degrees of precision in their formulation possible but more than one question may be asked to elicit the same utterance (see for example **3.13**), reflecting the fact that many utterances serve several communicative purposes. This will become clearer in the course of this work.

There is one other method available in English for making explicit the meanings of a sequence, namely, lexical signalling, but this will not be taken into account at this stage. How lexical signalling may be used will be described in Section 19.

7   The Meanings of Sequence

Even without lexical realisation, we are now in a position to examine more closely the meanings of sequence in the case of our four-sentence example(s). Having collected three types of connector that can be used to make explicit the meanings of sequence, we now put these connectors together so as to give an overall picture (see Figure 3.1). Where the arrows point upwards, the items are used in reverse sequence (e.g. as in **3.14**). Where the arrows point downwards the items are used when the sequence is unmarked (e.g. as in **3.13**). Where arrows point in both directions, the direction of sequence is optional (e.g. 'while' in **3.7** and **3.8**). The number following each connector in the list indicates which sentence must follow it. So, for example, 'because', which connects sentence 2 with sentence 3, must be immediately followed by sentence 2 and not by sentence 3. There is no regular principle of symmetry operating in this area whereby 'a because b' entails 'b because a', or 'a in what situation b' entails 'b in what situation a'.

8   The Instrument–Achievement Relation

We find a useful degree of compatibility between the meanings of the paraphrasing connectors at each stage of the sequence. To begin with sentences 3 and 4, we have 'thereby', 'by-ing', 'by this means' and 'how?', all of which can be used to convey the meaning of instrument, and 'What was the result?' which can be used to convey the meaning of *result*. Winter has christened the type of relationship existing between sentences 3 and 4 Instrument–Achievement.

9   The Paraphrase Criterion

The criterion we will use for the existence of an Instrument–Achievement relationship will be either (1) the presence in the discourse of one

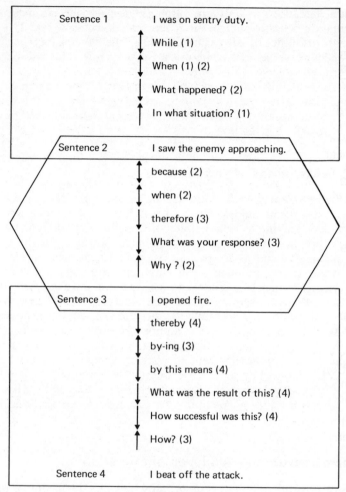

Figure 3.1

of the explicit features listed above (excluding the question 'How successful was this?') or (2) the reader's ability to paraphrase the relationship using one of those features. (The reason for the exclusion of 'How successful was this?' from the list will become apparent below.)

It is acknowledged that there are problems in deciding whether paraphrase can be said to exist or not, but it is not felt that these problems are serious enough to affect the validity of the criterion (2) as formulated above. It should be noted, however, that the context in which an utterance is produced will frequently prevent an otherwise synonymous utterance from being substituted for it in its place. For instance, **3.15**, **3.16** and **3.17** are all paraphrases in the sense that we mean in criterion (2):

3.15 I beat off the attack by opening fire.
3.16 I opened fire. By this means I beat off the attack.
3.17 The means by which I beat off the attack was by opening fire.

Nevertheless, placed in a context such as 'I expect you are wondering how I beat off the enemy attack', differences in the degree of acceptability of the resultant discourses appear. Utterance **3.18**, for example, is quite acceptable, if more emphatic than might normally be expected:

3.18 I expect you are wondering how I beat off the attack. I beat off the attack by opening fire.

Though unlikely in the extreme, **3.19**, also, seems acceptable:

3.19 I expect you are wondering how I beat off the attack. The means by which I beat off the attack was by opening fire.

However, **3.20** does not seem acceptable:

3.20 I expect you are wondering how I beat off the attack. I opened fire. By this means I beat off the attack.

This is very odd and could only be regarded as acceptable in quite exceptional circumstances. On the other hand, if the context provided is changed to 'I expect you are wondering how I reacted', both **3.15** and **3.16** become completely acceptable (as can be seen in **3.21** and **3.22**):

3.21 I expect you are wondering how I reacted. I beat off the attack by opening fire.
3.22 I expect you are wondering how I reacted. I opened fire. I (thereby) beat off the attack.

On the other hand **3.17** becomes unacceptable:

3.23 I expect you are wondering how I reacted. The means by which I beat off the attack was by opening fire.

That one paraphrase may be more appropriate in a particular context than another will become clearer when we look at real examples.

10 The Cause–Consequence Relation

If we now turn to the pair of sentences 'I saw the enemy approaching' and 'I opened fire', we find we can use the same method in describing the meaning of their sequence as we did in Section 8 to describe the meaning of the sequence of sentences 3 and 4. The sentences are connectable by 'because', 'therefore', and 'why?', all of which stand in a paraphrase relationship with each other (and, it is being suggested, with the simple sequence). This can be called the Cause–Consequence relation.

If a writer uses one of the connectors mentioned above to link a sentence of two or more clauses or if a reader can employ them in paraphrasing a sequence, then that sequence can be said to have Cause–Consequence meaning. (As we shall see, this need not preclude the possibility of other meanings as well.) To say that two clauses in sequence have a Cause–Consequence meaning is not, however, to say that such a relationship exists in fact. What the reader responds to is a combination of linguistic signalling (both between the clauses and in the larger context) and probability. If someone were to say

3.24   George killed my cat because he hates dogs.

he would be signalling with the connector 'because' that he regarded the two clauses as being in a Cause–Consequence relationship. Whether they really were or could be would not be a matter for the linguist to determine. Were the two clauses presented in simple juxta-position without context or intonation (outside the pages of linguistic research, an exceedingly improbable combination of circumstances), it would seem unlikely that the signal of simple sequence without the connector 'because' would be sufficient to override the improbability of the relation's being Cause–Consequence. In other words, the more improbable the truth of a relationship, or the less clear the nature of a relationship, the more explicitly it has to be signalled to the reader. In genuine discourses we often find that a potentially ambiguous juxta-position is made clear by means of an explicit connector.

11   Excluded Connectors

It will have been noticed that in our discussion of the meaning of the sentence pair 2 and 3 no mention was made of the connectors 'when' and 'what was your response?'. Similarly in our discussion of sentence pair 3 and 4, the connecting question 'How successful was this?' was ignored. The reasons for these omissions are varied. In the case of 'What was your response?' we have a question signalling a special type of subclass of Cause–Consequence relationship which we might want to call the Stimulus–Response relation. As such, it is compatible with the other connectors in meaning, but is not particularly well-suited for use as part of our paraphrase criteria for Cause–Consequence, as it would exclude pairs which in every other respect would qualify for inclusion. 'When', on the other hand, is too general. It links sentence 2 with sentence 3 in terms of time, but otherwise leaves the nature of the relation inexplicit. It is not therefore a suitable connector for use as a paraphrase criterion of Cause–Consequence.

The most important reason, however, for not handling 'when', 'What was your response?' and 'How successful was this?' with the other connectors is that they also signal at a different, though related, level – that of the discourse as a whole. What this means is that a relation may either be signalled as complete in itself or carry in it evidence that it is part of a larger set of relations. The distinction will become clearer in the course of the chapter and the relationship between the levels made explicit in Sections 21–2. In Section 6 above we remarked that caution is needed when handling questions on the grounds that more than one question might be used to elicit the same utterance, and the reason we gave was that many utterances serve several communicative functions. We have in these three connectors evidence of the truth of this statement.

12 Situation

Turning now to the sequence of sentences 1 and 2, we find 'while', 'when', 'what happened?' and 'in what situation?' as explicit connectors. Here there appears to be a less clearly defined sequential meaning. 'When' was noted in Section 11 to be a relatively inexplicit connector, and the same case can be made for 'what happened?'. It would be relatively uninformative to envisage our four-sentence sequence in a dialogue as follows:

3.25 D: I was on sentry duty.
     Q: What happened?
     D: I saw the enemy approaching.
     Q: And what happened?
     D: I opened fire.
     Q: And what happened?
     D: I beat off the attack.

Likewise we have an acceptable discourse if we use 'when' as a connector at each stage, as long as we separate the stages so as to avoid an accumulation of 'whens', that is,

3.26 When I was on sentry duty, I saw the enemy approaching. When I saw the enemy approaching, I opened fire. When I opened fire, I beat off the attack.

That 'when' and 'what happened?' are apparently very general connectors is not the only peculiarity of the sequence of sentences 1 and 2. The connector 'while' is also functioning in a different way from the connectors discussed so far. If **3.7** (on page 36) is re-examined, it will be seen that 'while' does not connect 'I was on sentry duty' with 'I saw the enemy approaching' but with 'I opened fire'; **3.7** can therefore be represented diagrammatically as in Figure 3.2. It is possible in fact to go further than this. 'While' will connect sentence 1 to any of the following three sentences:

> **3.27** I saw the enemy approaching while I was on sentry duty.
> **3.28** I opened fire while I was on sentry duty, because I saw the enemy approaching.
> **3.29** I beat off the attack while I was on sentry duty, by opening fire when I saw the enemy approaching.

Of course, the questions being answered in each case are different, but this does not affect the point that, given appropriate contexts, 'while I was on sentry duty' will enter into a similar relationship with each of the other three sentences. This is not true of the other sentences, whatever connector is selected.

If we now turn to the fourth connector listed in Figure 3.1 between sentences 1 and 2 – the question 'in what situation?' – we find a similar range of use to that of 'while'. 'In what situation?' does not exclusively link sentence 2 with sentence 1. It will just as readily link sentences 3 and 4 to sentence 1:

> **3.30** D: I beat off the attack.
> Q: In what situation?
> D: (while) I was on sentry duty.

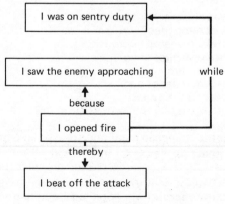

Figure 3.2

3.31   D: I opened fire.
Q: In what situation?
D: (while) I was on sentry duty.

It would seem therefore that Figure 3.2 is an oversimplification of the picture. Whereas 'when', 'because', 'therefore', 'what was your response?' and 'why?' connect sentences 2 and 3, and 'by-ing', 'thereby', 'by this means', 'how successful was this?' and 'how?' connect sentences 3 and 4, 'while', 'when', 'what happened?' and 'in what situation?' do not connect sentences 1 and 2 in particular but connect sentence 1 more or less equally with all three sentences.

This means that sentence 1's sequential meaning is not derived from its immediate proximity to sentence 2 but from its position in the overall discourse pattern. The explicit connectors associated with sentence 1 are therefore signals of its function in the whole discourse. Since one of these connectors is 'in what situation?', we can label that function Situation.

This is however only a label. As Longacre (1964) remarks, '[the linguist] should remember that his name-labels are but name-labels and will ultimately receive meaning only by virtue of usage in the description that he is producing'. In later sections and in the next two chapters it will become apparent that Situation can be properly defined only in terms of the complete discourse pattern. For the moment, we will simply note that if a reader can introduce into part of a discourse one or more of the above connectors, then that part of the discourse has 'situational features'. As we have seen, however, these are not synonymous with Situation, since two of the connectors – 'when' and 'what happened?' – can be used to connect sentences 2 and 3, and also sentences 3 and 4; moreover another – 'in what situation?' – can be used to connect sentences 2 and 3 (though not sentences 3 and 4). It follows that sentences 2 and 3 contain, to a varying extent, situational features. Only 'while' is exclusive to sentence 1, and even that can be used to connect sentences 2 and 3 if a change of meaning is tolerated:

3.32   While I saw the enemy approaching, I opened fire.

Indeed, sentences 3 and 4 can also be connected by 'while':

3.33   While I opened fire, I beat off the attack.

Here however the change in meaning is drastic and improbable, that is, 'at the same time that I opened fire, I beat off the attack by another unstated means'. In other words, 'while' modifies the other meanings of sequence. In **3.32**, 'I saw the enemy approaching' ceases to have the linguistic function of Cause though it retains some element of a common-sense reading of cause, and in **3.33** 'I opened fire' ceases to

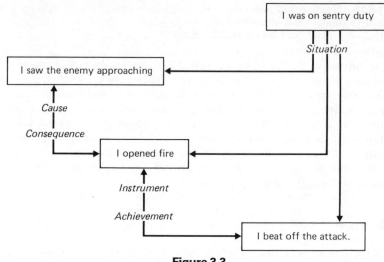

Figure 3.3

have the function of Instrument. (This ignores any interpretation of 'while' as meaning 'as long as'.)

We have seen that sentences 2 and 3 have situational features. It follows that sentence 1 is distinguished from them not in kind but in degree; sentence 1 alone has no other function within the discourse than that of providing Situation for the discourse. We can now redraw Figure 3.2, taking into account our analysis of the nature of the relations between sentences 2 and 3, and 3 and 4, and showing the special role we have given sentence 1, as in Figure 3.3.

13   Discourse Organisation

Although we have now accounted for all the sentences in the discourse, our analysis cannot be considered complete. We noted in Section 11 that the connectors 'What was your response?' and 'How successful was this?' (like 'when') signal at a different level; we have yet to justify such a claim. Secondly, and most importantly, there is nothing in our present analysis to indicate the incompleteness of **3.34** and **3.35**.

> **3.34**   I was on sentry duty. I opened fire. I beat off the attack.
> **3.35**   I was on sentry duty. I saw the enemy approaching. I opened fire.

The sequence **3.34** is incomplete because it leaves it fatally vague whether there was an assumed attack to which the opening fire was a rejoinder or whether it was the opening fire that provoked an attack in the first place. Sequence **3.35** is more obviously incomplete as a narrative; it has to be followed by a 'to be continued' tag. (It could, of course, occur in reply to the question 'How did it come about that you beat off the attack?', but then we would be entitled to treat the dialogue as the discourse, in which case the end of the story would be found presupposed in the question.) We have not, however, proposed a rule to suggest that the consequence of a Cause–Consequence relation must in turn be the Instrument of an Instrument–Achievement relation. The reason must lie therefore not with 'I opened fire''s relationship with its neighbours but with each sentence's relationship to the discourse as a whole. To identify those relationships, we must look again at the connectors we have so far ignored.

14 Evaluation

The connector we ignored with respect to sentences 3 and 4 was 'How successful was this?'. If we examine this question carefully, we find that it seeks to elicit a different type of answer to that of the other questions we have discussed or mentioned. Whereas 'What happened?', 'What was your response?', 'What was the result?', 'Why?' and How?' all normally elicit answers of fact, 'How successful was this?' seeks to elicit an opinion. It is asking the author/speaker to assess, or evaluate, his action described in sentence 3 in terms of its efficacy. We shall therefore tentatively describe the function of sentence 4 as that of Evaluation. What we are here proposing is that whereas Instrument–Achievement operates at adjacent clause level in this discourse, Evaluation is operating at discourse level in a pattern of the provisional type shown in Figure 3.4.

Situation–X–Y–Evaluation

Figure 3.4

The apparent discrepancy between sentence 4's answering the question 'What was the result?' which elicits a statement of fact and its answering the question 'How successful was this?' which elicits a statement of opinion will be resolved in Section 16 below after we have completed a provisional account of the organisation of our four-sentence discourse.

15 Response

In Section 11 mention was made of the greater degree of specificity of the question 'What was your response?' in connecting sentences 2 and

3. It was intimated at that time that this greater specificity was related to its operation as a connector at a different level to that of the other connectors of these two sentences. The reason for this should now be clearer. If the last sentence is seen as functioning as Evaluation in the discourse as a whole, then that Evaluation is of the response described in sentence 3 (which answers the question 'What was your response?'). The function of sentence 3 can therefore be characterised as that of Response. Response works therefore in two directions within this discourse: (1) the subrelations of Cause–Consequence – Stimulus–Response; (2) the discourse-functional pair Response and Evaluation of Response. Our putative pattern is therefore now as in Figure 3.5.

Situation–X–Response–Evaluation

Figure 3.5

If we adhere to the same principle that the sentence's function must be described in terms of the discourse as a whole, it follows that X must be a function that is related to both Situation and Response at one and the same time. We cannot use 'stimulus' to characterise X's function since it explains inadequately the link between sentences 1 and 2 (although it does of course explain quite satisfactorily the link between sentences 2 and 3). We must therefore expect to find another overlaid function. A clue as to its nature came in Section 12 when we discussed sentence 1. In our discussion in that sentence of the connectors that signal Situation, attention was drawn to the fact that sentence 2 could be connected to sentence 3 by 'when', 'what happened?' and 'in what situation?' (though not by 'while') and that it could therefore be said to contain situational features. Given this fact, a description of sentence 2 as also Situation would not be unreasonable; indeed if we do, we find ourselves with an analysis of our discourse which is neither unintelligible nor unintelligent (see Figure 3.6).

Situation–Response–Evaluation
(to Situation) (of Response to Situation)

Figure 3.6

But while this satisfactorily explains the completeness of the discourse, it leaves two (related) problems unsolved. First, sentence 1 (by this analysis, the first half of Situation) can stand moderately well on its own as a discourse (see **3.36** below), whereas sentences 1 and 2 together (the whole of Situation, according to this analysis) are palpably incomplete as a discourse (see **3.37**).

3.36 I was on sentry duty.
3.37 I was on sentry duty. I saw the enemy approaching.

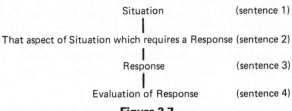

Figure 3.7

Secondly, 'Response (to Situation)' is clearly Response to the Situation contained in sentence 2 and not to the Situation contained in sentence 1. Unless therefore we regard sentence 1 as redundant, there must be a distinction in function between the two sentences. We can in fact use this selectivity of Response towards the two elements of Situation to make such a distinction. Sentence 1 can continue to be simply Situation; sentence 2 can become on the other hand that aspect of Situation which requires a Response. Not only does this explain why Response is Response to the Situation in sentence 2 but not to that in sentence 1 but it also explains why **3.36** does not seem incomplete whereas **3.37** does. The second sentence of **3.37** requires a Response which is, of course, not forthcoming.

Our putative description now becomes as in Figure 3.7. This in turn means that sentence 1's function can be defined more precisely as providing a context for the better understanding of subsequent sentences.

16 Evaluation Re-examined

In Section 14 we promised that we would return to Evaluation once a provisional analysis of our minimum discourse had been made. The problem there was that the sentence 'I beat off the attack' answered two questions, one, 'What was the result?', which appeared to elicit a statement of fact, the other, 'How successful was this?', which elicited an opinion. If we set out our discourse elements in pyramid form, as in Figure 3.8, we notice that the last line is not an accurate characterisation of sentence 4's discourse function. Sentence 4's Evaluation of Response is indirect; it evaluates the effectiveness of the Response by

Situation

Aspect of Situation requiring a response

Response to Aspect of Situation requiring a response

Evaluation of Response to Aspect of Situation requiring a response

Figure 3.8

giving the end Result of the Response. Notice that it has to be the end Result. A discourse such as we have in **3.38** below gives a Result which is not an end Result; consequently sentence 4 does not function as Evaluation nor is the discourse deemed complete (unless, of course, it is intended to answer a question such as 'How come these others are here?').

> **3.38** I was on sentry duty. I saw the enemy approaching. I opened fire. This brought other sentries to the spot.

This is readily seen if the last two sentences are projected into dialogue, thus:

> **3.39** D: I opened fire.
> Q: What was the result ‹of your opening fire›?
> D: [The result was that my opening fire] brought other sentries to the spot.
> Q: No, I mean, what happened in the end?

We can make clearer the relation between the Result and Evaluation aspects of sentence 4 if we use the same device of projecting the last two sentences into dialogue, thus:

> **3.40** D: I opened fire.
> Q: What was the result ‹of your opening fire›?
> D: [The result was that] I beat off the attack.
> **3.41** D: I opened fire.
> Q: How successful was this ‹i.e. opening fire›?
> D: [Very.]
> Q: On what do you base this evaluation?
> D: I beat off the attack.

So sentence 4 is end Result and, by implication, Evaluation, with the Result acting as the basis for Evaluation. That this is a valid analysis can be shown by considering what happens if we offer a discourse in which opening fire does not solve the sentry's problem:

> **3.42** I was on sentry duty. I saw the enemy approaching. I opened fire. I was captured within minutes.

This, though possible, seems less likely than the following:

> **3.43** I was on sentry duty. I saw the enemy approaching. I opened fire. Sadly this had no effect. I was captured within minutes.

In this discourse, the first, second and third sentences are, as before, respectively Situation, Aspect of Situation requiring a Response, and

Response, sentence 4 is Evaluation of Response, and sentence 5 is the Basis for the Evaluation, namely, the end Result of the Response. Thus the two functions of Result and Evaluation are kept separate in such a discourse. Only where the Evaluation is presumed self-evident does the Result carry an implied Evaluation, as in our original discourse.

17 Problem

Our final description then is shown in Figure 3.9. As such it could easily stand. However, for brevity's sake, it is convenient to replace the cumbersome phrase Aspect of Situation requiring a Response with the label Problem, since many real-world situations requiring a response are so called. The change of label involves no change in our description, however. The element of the pattern is defined in terms of the discourse as a whole and not in terms of real-world knowledge. The same degree of correlation exists between the discourse element Problem and real-world problems as exists between the noun as grammatical element and the names of things, that is, there is a high degree of correlation but we are not able to define the one in terms of the other. For example, suppose someone were to express his views as follows:

3.46 The trouble with this country's economy used to be that there were too many farthings being made. Once we stopped making them everything turned out all right.

Our opinion that the views are essentially wrong-headed would not prevent us from recognising that they have been encoded in a

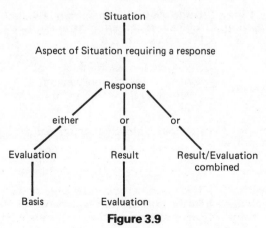

Figure 3.9

Problem–Response–Evaluation pattern. Yet real-world knowledge certainly would play little part in that recognition. We identify 'too many farthings' as a Problem only because of the linguistic evidence. Likewise the Evaluation in **3.44** is one which few in Britain in the 1960s and 1970s would wholeheartedly endorse; nevertheless no one would fail to identify it as an Evaluation. In Chapter 5 we shall similarly examine advertisements that claim to solve problems that no one realised he or she had. These are further examples of the complex relationship of linguistic Problem to real-world problem; it is often because A says that X is a problem that B sees it as such. In short, Problem is recognised in a discourse wherever it is linguistically signalled, or where the appropriate linguistic tests can be successfully employed.

Since most Responses are evaluated as successful, it has become normal to talk of the pattern as the Problem–Solution pattern. We shall not deviate from this practice when talking of the over-all pattern. When, however, we refer to the individual parts of the pattern we shall prefer the term Response to that of Solution as being neutral with regards to Evaluation.

18   Levels of Detail

For the sake of simplicity of presentation we have been using an artificial discourse with a one-to-one correspondence between sentence and function. No such correspondence exists in real discourses; if it did, no discourse would be longer than a handful of sentences. We could have, for example, an expansion of our original discourse as follows:

3.45

Situation
$\left\{ \begin{array}{l} \text{It was six o'clock in the evening.} \\ \text{All the rest of them were in the mess.} \\ \text{I was on sentry duty.} \end{array} \right.$

Problem
$\left\{ \begin{array}{l} \text{Suddenly I saw something move.} \\ \text{It was the enemy approaching.} \\ \text{I estimated that there were five hundred of them in all.} \end{array} \right.$

Response
$\left\{ \begin{array}{l} \text{I quickly sent a message for reinforcements.} \\ \text{At the same time I opened fire.} \end{array} \right.$

Result/
Evaluation
$\left\{ \begin{array}{l} \text{At first they kept on coming.} \\ \text{The machine gun, however, slowed them down.} \\ \text{By the time the reinforcements came, I had beaten off the attack.} \end{array} \right.$

In **3.45**, each of the elements of the pattern is made up of two or three sentences. In keeping with our assumptions about the quasi-hierarchical organisation of discourse, we find it is possible to have Problem–Solution patterns within larger Problem–Solution patterns as in **3.46**. These are further exemplified in Chapter 5.

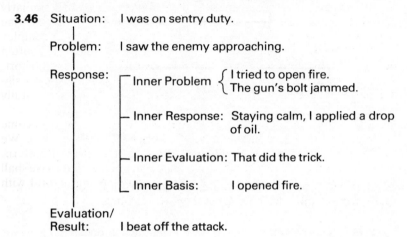

3.46 Situation: I was on sentry duty.

Problem: I saw the enemy approaching.

Response:

Inner Problem { I tried to open fire. / The gun's bolt jammed.

Inner Response: Staying calm, I applied a drop of oil.

Inner Evaluation: That did the trick.

Inner Basis: I opened fire.

Evaluation/Result: I beat off the attack.

19 Lexical Signalling

Up to now we have deliberately left out of account one of the most important means available for signalling discourse organisation–lexical signals. They had to be ignored because it was necessary to demonstrate the nature of discourse relations using only well-described and (relatively) well-understood phenomena such as subordinators, conjuncts and questions. Now, however, we can afford to introduce lexical signalling into our picture. We can rewrite our minimum discourse in a number of ways so as to show the clause relations in it by means of lexical signalling, for example:

3.47 The *means* whereby I beat off the attack was by opening fire. The *cause* of my opening fire was that I saw the enemy approaching. The *circumstances* of my seeing the enemy approaching was that I was on sentry duty.

Similarly, the overall discourse organisation can be made explicit in the same way:

3.48 My *situation* was that I was on sentry duty. I saw the enemy approaching. I *solved* this *problem* by opening fire. This *achieved* the *desired result* of beating off the attack.

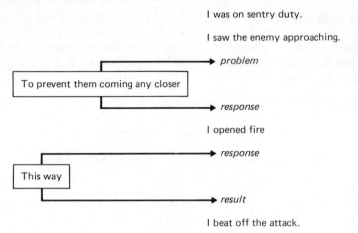

Figure 3.10

Such signals need not only to identify one part of the organisation. In **3.49**, for example, we have several two-way signals.

> **3.49** I was on sentry duty. I saw the enemy approaching. *To prevent them coming any closer*, I opened fire. *This way* I beat off the enemy attack.

The phrase, 'to prevent them coming any closer', is one of the two-way signals. It indicates that what follows is Response and that what precedes it is Problem; this is achieved by the lexical signal 'prevent', and the grammar of a purpose clause, 'to x'. 'This way' is also a two-way signal, indicating that what follows it is Result and what precedes it is Response. Thus in this version of our minimum discourse, Response is twice signalled. The discourse can be represented diagrammatically as in Figure 3.10.

Such signals are, as we shall see in the next chapter, an important aid to discourse analysis. An extension of their use exists in the form of the 'signalling sentence'. The 'signalling sentence', like the 'signalling clause' in **3.49**, does not itself enter directly into the pattern of organisation of the discourse but rather comments on that pattern. An example might be:

> **3.50** I was on sentry duty. I saw the enemy approaching. *This was a problem*. I opened fire. I beat off the attack.

The sentence 'This was a problem' makes explicit the discourse function of the previous sentence.

20 The Importance of Situation and Evaluation

Strictly speaking, all signals, whether in signalling sentences, clauses or phrases, are evaluative, though not at the level of the over-all organisation:

> **3.51** D: I saw the enemy approaching.
> Q: How did you evaluate this?
> or
> What did you feel about this?
> D: It (This) was a problem.

If we accept this, it follows that our paraphrase relations are also evaluative. This would result in a revised diagram of the pattern as in Figure 3.11. Such a diagram reflects a view that Situation and Evaluation are the fundamental units of discourse analysis, corresponding roughly to the questions 'What are the facts?' and 'What do you think of the facts?', and the other elements of the pattern, Problem, Response and Result, are 'molecular' forms built out of these two 'atomic' types of information. It should, though, be noticed that Situation and Evaluation are operating at a number of levels, first as elements in the over-all discourse pattern and secondly as elements at lower levels, including sentence levels. It is convenient not to change arbitrarily the labels we give them but the price of such convenience has to be vigilance in keeping the levels separate in analysis.

From the above, we can expect to find that smaller complete discourses are possible than our original four-sentence example. Discourse **3.52** demonstrates that this is the case:

> **3.52** I was on sentry duty. All was quiet.[2]

Here we have a simpler organisation still, consisting of only two parts – Situation and Evaluation of Situation as non-problem (see line 1 of Figure 3.11). That such a discourse is possible is further evidence for the claim made above that Situation and Evaluation are primary.

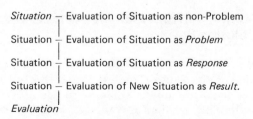

Figure 3.11

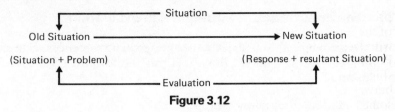

Figure 3.12

If we look at **3.53**, we find yet more evidence for this claim.

3.53   I was on sentry duty. I saw the enemy approaching. I opened fire. I beat off the attack. All was again quiet.

Here we have the four-part pattern plus a fifth element which is Evaluation of Response and of resultant Situation. We can represent how such a pattern is formed with Figure 3.12.

It should now be clear why sentence 3 was found earlier to have some situational features. It supplies one aspect of New Situation.

Finally, before we leave our minimum discourse for the more productive and enjoyable fields of short real examples culled from journals, textbooks and newspapers, we must demonstrate one more permutation on our long-suffering four-sentence example. In **3.54**, we see a case of Evaluation overruling an expected interpretation given no other information.

3.54   I was on sentry duty. I saw the enemy approaching. This was not serious.

Here we have a conflict between our real-world knowledge of approaching enemies as likely to cause problems and our linguistic evidence in the form of Evaluation of Situation as non-Problem. We would expect therefore such an Evaluation to be followed by a Basis for the Evaluation, for example, 'We had them covered on every side'. This resolves the conflict, and the final analysis would be Situation–Evaluation of Situation as non-Problem–Basis for Evaluation.

21   The Relationship between Clause Relations and the Problem–Solution Pattern

Up to now we have left unclear the relationship holding between clause relations such as Cause–Consequence on the one hand and the Problem–Solution pattern on the other. We noted in Section 11 that a relation may either be signalled as complete in itself or carry within it evidence of being part of a larger set of relations, yet this has not prevented us from using the signals of one set of relations as evidence of the existence of the other. For supplying connections to a discourse with subordination and conjuncts is a test not of the existence of the Problem–Solution pattern but of the existence of particular relationships (i.e. Cause–Consequence, Instrument–Achievement) holding between (normally) adjacent parts of a discourse. Unless therefore some rules are given to relate the one set of relations to the other, we cannot properly use evidence of the existence of Cause–Consequence, etc. as evidence of the existence of a Problem–Solution pattern.

We therefore propose four sets of mapping conditions to meet this need, two of which immediately follow:

(1) We will assume two parts of a discourse, *a* and *b*, in a Cause–Consequence relation. If (*i*) *a* has been independently established as Problem *and* (*ii*) *b* contains the role of agent, then *b* is Response.

(2) We will assume three parts of a discourse, *a*, *b* and *c*, of which *a* and *b* are in an Instrument–Achievement or Instrument–Purpose relation (Purpose being more or less equivalent to hoped-for achievement), and of which *a* has not been independently established as Problem.

Given these circumstances, *if* (*i*) *b* contains the role of agent *and* (*ii*) *c* prevents, reverses, avoids, avoids harm to, or seeks help in preventing, etc., some crucial aspect of *a*, then *a* is Problem and *b* is Response.

Let us look at how the two mapping conditions operate in practice. In the following trio of sentences (3.55) we will assume that 'unfortunately' (as a negative Evaluation of an aspect of the Situation) independently establishes the second sentence as Problem:

3.55 (1) My wife and I went to see *Citizen Kane*. (2) Unfortunately all the seats were booked. (3) So we went to the theatre instead.

The establishment of sentence 2 as Problem means that we can check sentences 2 and 3 against mapping condition 1. Since sentences 2 and 3 are in a Cause–Consequence relation and 'we' in sentence 3 has the role of agent, we are able to identify sentence 3 as Response.

Mapping condition 2 operates in a similar way. If we take three clauses linked together thus:

3.56 It was raining hard, so I shut the window to stop the rain blowing in

we find we have the first and second clauses in a Cause–Consequence relation and the second and third in an Instrument–Purpose relation.

Since the first clause has not been independently identified as Problem, we check the trio against mapping condition 2. Doing so, we find that the second clause does contain the role of agent ('I') and the third clause does contain an avoidance of some part of the first, i.e. 'stop the rain blowing in' versus 'raining'. We are therefore entitled to identify the first clause as Problem and the second as Response.

As they stand, however, our mapping conditions are not perfect. For instance, they exclude examples like **3.57**.

3.57   It was raining so I put my umbrella up.

where the Purpose of the action described in the second clause is so self-evident that it is not spelt out. It would clearly seem arbitrary to exclude this pair and include **3.56**. We therefore add a further two mapping conditions.

(3)   We will assume two parts of a discourse, *a* and *b*, in a Cause–Consequence relation and that *a* has not been independently established as Problem.
      If (*i*) *b* contains the role of agent *and* (*ii*) *b* also prevents, reverses, avoids, or avoids harm to some crucial aspect of *a*, or seeks help in preventing, etc. some crucial aspect of *a*, then *a* is Problem and *b* Response.
(4)   We will assume the same as for mapping condition 3.
      If (*i*) *b* contains the role of agent *and* (*ii*) *b* also can have attached to it a Purpose clause, *c*, which spells out a layman's understanding of what *b* means, and if (*iii*) the newly formed trio conforms to the conditions of mapping condition 2, then *a* is Problem and *b* Response.

We will now show how these work in practice. Let us take a pair of clauses such as

3.58   My daughter had taken the plug out, so I put it back

which are in a Cause–Consequence relation and the first clause of which has not been previously established as Problem. If we apply mapping condition 3, we find that the second clause contains an agent ('I') and reverses some aspect of the first ('take the plug out' versus 'put [the plug] back'). We can conclude that the first clause is Problem and the second, Response.

Similarly, if we take a pair of clauses such as the pair quoted in **3.57**, we find we can extend them thus:

3.59   It was raining, so I put my umbrella up to prevent the rain hitting me.

Such an extension creates an Instrument–Purpose relation between the second and third clauses and reflects any reader/listener's understanding of what is assumed in **3.57**. Awkward he would be indeed who claimed that **3.59** was saying something different. Since the attached Purpose clause 'prevents' a crucial aspect of the first clause, we may conclude that the first clause of **3.57** is Problem and the second Response.

In three of the mapping conditions, there is mention made of prevention, avoidance, and so on. These terms are not intended to be non-linguistic; rather, they are the characteristic vocabulary of Response. It is the presence of this vocabulary or its paraphrases, or in the case of mapping condition 4, the possibility of adding this vocabulary, that dictates our analysis. So in **3.56** and **3.59**, it is the presence of 'stop' and the possibility of 'prevent' that makes us analyse the examples as Problem–Response. The only exception to this is reversal whose characteristic vocabulary is that of opposites, e.g. push versus pull, give versus take, and also items like 'back' and 'again' (as in **3.58**).

22   The Scope of the Mapping Conditions

It might now be useful to give some examples of what is covered by the mapping conditions given in the last section and some examples of what is excluded. We will then give an example of a discourse covered by the mapping conditions which we would not necessarily expect to be so covered. Examples of discourses covered by the mapping conditions are:

3.60   The next-door neighbour's cat was scratching up my seed beds, so I threw a brick at it.
3.61   The book had fallen off the shelf, so I put it back again.

In both cases, a Cause–Consequence relation is signalled by the conjunct 'so'; likewise in both cases, there is no overt signal of Problem in the first clause. Discourse **3.60** can be shown nevertheless to be Problem–Response because of the possibility of adding a Purpose clause such as 'to prevent it scratching them up', thus utilising mapping condition 4. Similarly **3.61** can be shown to be Problem–Response by means of mapping condition 3, the second clause containing a reversal of a crucial aspect of the first, indicated by 'back again'.

On the other hand, the following examples, though both again in a Cause–Consequence relation, are not included as Problem–Response using our mapping conditions, though of course the application of other tests might result in their inclusion on other grounds in a larger context:

3.62   It was sunny, so I opened the window to let in the fresh air.
3.63   They started firing at me. I got scared.

Discourse **3.62** is not considered to be an example of Problem–Response because it fails to meet the second requirement of mapping condition 2, in that the Purpose clause contains none of the required reflections of the first clause (i.e. prevention, reversal, and so on). Discourse **3.63** on the other hand is not an example of Problem–Response because it fails to meet two of the requirements of mapping condition 4. It does not have an agent in the second clause and is not extendable by an appropriate Purpose clause.

In the above examples of what is and is not covered by the four mapping conditions, there are no surprises nor is any example offered that we would not want covered by those conditions. Consider, however, **3.64**:

3.64   The children were asleep, so I tiptoed away.

This meets all the requirements of mapping condition 4. The two parts of the discourse are in a Cause–Consequence, the second part contains an agent, and a Purpose clause, 'to avoid waking them', can be added which is a clear case of 'avoiding harm to' some crucial aspect of the first part. Yet in real-world terms, sleeping children are not a problem but a blessing fervently prayed for. How then can it conform to a Problem–Response pattern? The answer lies partly in the fact that linguistic Problem and real-world problem are not necessarily the same and partly in the fact that in **3.64** we have a border-line case. In terms of our analytical method not only does it conform to the requirement of our mapping conditions but the first clause is plausibly elicited by the question 'What aspect of the Situation required a Response [of a particular kind]?'. On the other hand, many of the lexical signals of Problem cannot operate here, for example, 'unfortunately', 'difficulty'. We shall treat examples such as **3.64** as forming a special subdivision of Problem which we shall term Delicate Situation. A real example of this subdivision of Problem will be found in Chapter 4.

23   Summary of Chapter 3

We have in this chapter made the following assumptions:

(1)   Discourses are seen as organised in part on a hierarchical basis.
(2)   Discourse organisation is to some degree perceived by listeners/readers.

(3)   There is something in the discourse itself that helps the listener/ reader perceive the organisation.

(4)   There are an infinite number of discourse patterns signalled by a finite number of clues.

We have also made the following claims:

(1)   There are three types of sentence sequence – unmarked, marked and unacceptable.

(2)   Sequence has functional meaning in itself.

(3)   The meaning of sequence can be paraphrased by means of subordinators and conjuncts, and highlighted by the projection of the sequence into question–answer dialogues.

(4)   Between clauses, sentences, or groups of sentences, there exist precise relationships that can be identified by the careful use of paraphrase criteria.

(5)   Each sentence in a complete discourse has a function in the discourse as a whole, either in itself or as part of a larger unit.

(6)   A common discourse pattern in English is that of Situation–Problem–Response–Result–Evaluation, of which a number of variants are possible.

(7)   The signals of clause relations such as Cause–Consequence and Instrument–Achievement can be used as signals of Problem–Response by the means of four mapping conditions.

Chapter 4

The Problem–Solution Pattern: Some Real Examples

1 Aims of This Chapter

In Chapter 3 we were using a simulated wave machine. It is time now to go out to sea. In this and subsequent chapters we abandon the use of concocted examples and develop our approach to discourse analysis with real discourses taken from a variety of sources. Our aims are threefold. First, we shall look at the ways in which our categories have to be elaborated and modified in the light of our examples. Secondly, we shall describe more fully than was possible in Chapter 3 those features that are responsible for signalling changes in function in a discourse. Thirdly, we shall demonstrate how the analysis of a discourse may be undertaken. Close analysis is never easy reading, but it is hoped that perseverance with the details of how to analyse discourse will stimulate readers to attempt analyses of their own. Two discourses are chosen, one brief but problematical unless analysed carefully, the other longer but more straightforward. Both are first given without analysis and then followed by a detailed discussion in which attention is drawn to any theoretical extensions made necessary by the example.

2 Methods of Analysis

In Chapter 3 we studied a number of ways of making explicit the meaning of the sequence and/or organisation of a discourse. These now have to be applied to fuller discourses. We will demonstrate how they are applied with reference to our first example, a self-contained passage from a larger article:

4.1 (1) All soft fruits are surface rooting with the root feeding areas extending several feet away from plants. (2) Any disturbance and breaking up of feeding roots by deep cultivation has a serious ill-effect on the cropping and health of the plants. (3) I limit cultivations between the rows to hoeing or a light going over with a three-pronged hand cultivator.[1]

Here, as in all the discourses we will be analysing throughout the book, each orthographic sentence is numbered for convenience of reference. The number is in no sense part of the text.

3 Method of Analysis: (a) Lexical Signalling

One of the first steps in the analysis of any discourse must be the identification of the lexical signalling present in it. Lexical signals are the author's/speaker's explicit signalling of the intended organisation and are therefore obviously of primary importance; it is probable that they are one of the main means whereby a reader/listener 'decodes' a discourse correctly. In some cases also they can interfere with the operation of some of the other steps in an analysis. For example, if sentence 3 of **4.1** read 'To avoid this I limit cultivations between the rows to hoeing or a light going over with a three-pronged hand cultivator', it would be impossible to apply the question test described in Section 6, Chapter 3, and in Section 4 below, successfully. So **4.2** forms an unsatisfactory dialogue:

> **4.2** Q: What is your response?
> D: To avoid this, I limit cultivation between the rows to hoeing or a light going over with a three-pronged hand cultivator

whereas, once the signalling phrase is removed (as in the original), a perfectly satisfactory dialogue ensues:

> **4.3** Q: What is your response?
> D: I limit cultivation between the rows to hoeing or a light going over with a three-pronged hand cultivator.

The reason for this is that question and signalling phrase duplicate each other's function; also the anaphoric 'this' is separated from what it refers to.

Lexical signalling can take the form of a sentence, clause or phrase and incorporates either one or more typical signals or an evaluation (as good or bad). We have already seen that there is strictly speaking no clear boundary-line between these two possibilities; both are ultimately evaluative. Nevertheless the distinction is a useful one in that it separates 'organising words' which are also evaluative from 'evaluative words' which happen to assist in organising. Examples of both can be found in sentence 2 of **4.1** in the phrase 'serious ill-effect'. 'Effect' is a lexical signal which functions as a link within the sentence; 'serious' and 'ill-' are negative evaluations. From the latter signals, we now can characterise sentence 2 as (in part) Evaluation of Situation as bad, i.e. Problem. Given that sentence 3 introduces a human element and contrasts 'deep cultivation' with 'limit[ed] cultivations', we have sufficient reason, on the strength of lexical signalling to guess (wrongly, as we shall see) that we may have a straightforward Situation–Problem–Response pattern.

4   Methods of Analysis: (b) Narrative Interrogation

The organisation of a discourse can also be identified by the use of questions. How these can be employed and the care that is needed in their use has been explained in several places. We begin by using narrative interrogation. In the case of **4.1**, we can apply the question test as follows:

> **4.4**   Q: What is the situation ⟨regarding the roots of soft fruits⟩?
> D: All soft fruits are surface rooting with the root feeding areas extending several feet away from plants.
> Q: What aspect of the situation requires a response?
> D: Any disturbance and breaking up of feeding roots by deep cultivation has a serious ill-effect on the cropping and health of plants.
> Q: What is your response to this problem?
> D: I limit cultivation between the rows to hoeing or a light going over with a three-pronged hand cultivator.

Such an interrogation does not really pass muster. A more acceptable one would involve replacing the second question with 'What aspect of the situation requiring a response arises out of this situation?'. Our question test has therefore partly confirmed our tentative analysis based on lexical signalling and partly complicated it.

5   Methods of Analysis: (c) Elaborating Interrogation

We now apply the test of elaborating interrogation. Before we can apply this test, however, we must note two difficulties in its application. First, since the test requires that the discourse be given in reverse order, we must be prepared to flesh out nominal groups referring back to earlier parts of the discourse and similarly provide the reference for all pronouns. For example, sentence 3 of **4.1** must become:

> **4.5**   I limit cultivations between [the] rows [of soft fruit plants] to hoeing or a light going over with a three-pronged hand cultivator

where inserted material is in square brackets and deleted material in square brackets with a line through them.

Secondly, the larger the discourse, the less well the test is likely to operate. Beyond a certain point, it only becomes practicable if key sentences in the discourse are used; care has to be taken not to distort the material in such circumstances. Only the first of these difficulties is relevant, however, to the application of elaborational interrogation to **4.1**. When applied, **4.1** looks as follows:

4.6   D: I limit cultivations between [the] rows [of soft fruit plants] to hoeing or a light going over with a three-pronged hand cultivator.
       Q: Why ⟨do you limit cultivation, etc.⟩?
       D: [Because] any disturbance and breaking up of feeding roots [of soft fruit plants] by deep cultivation has a serious ill-effect on the cropping and health of [the] plants.
       Q: In what situation ⟨does any disturbance and breaking up of feeding roots have a serious ill-effect⟩?
       D: [When] All soft fruits are surface rooting with the root feeding areas extending several feet away from the plants.

In this dialogue, the last question and answer pair are clearly faulty and must be replaced by something of the nature of:

4.7   Q: Why ⟨does any disturbance and breaking up of feeding roots have a serious ill-effect⟩?
       D: [Because] All soft fruits are surface rooting with the root feeding areas extending several feet away from the plants.

According to the revised dialogue as reflected in the first half of **4.6** and **4.7** the relationship between the three sentences appears to be as in Figure 4.1. From what we find in Figure 4.1, we can confirm the characterisation of sentence 2 and 3 as Problem and Response, since they are shown there to be in a Cause–Consequence relation and it is possible to add on to sentence 3 a Purpose clause such as 'to prevent any disturbance and breaking up of feeding roots', which clearly 'prevents' some crucial aspect of sentence 2. On the other hand, Figure 4.1 does not confirm any characterisation of sentence 1 as Situation. Instead it confirms what we first found in Section 4, when we used narrative interrogation on the discourse, namely, that the relationship between sentences 1 and 2 is not that found between 'I was on sentry duty' and 'I saw the enemy approaching' in Chapter 3. We shall return to sentence 1 at the end of the next section.

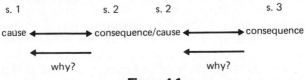

Figure 4.1

6   Methods of Analysis: (d) Subordination and Conjuncts

Whereas with narrative and elaborating interrogation we converted one type of discourse – a written monologue – into another type of discourse – a written dialogue – subordination and/or conjuncts can be added to a discourse without its status as a discourse being affected. Consequently, we find that the statements in our discourses are frequently already linked by subordinators and conjuncts, whereas the use of questions in a discourse is comparatively infrequent. Our first step must therefore be to identify all subordinators and conjuncts already present in the discourse. Those sentences not linked in this way can then have appropriate connectors inserted, as in Chapter 4. It should be noted however that connectors found in the discourse are more reliable than those inserted subsequently as part of a paraphrase test, simply because the former are the writer/speaker's own explicit comments on the relations holding between his or her sentences whereas the latter are our (perhaps faulty) attempts to make explicit what the writer/speaker chose to leave implicit. Sometimes it is not possible to insert connectors; this is of as much interest as when we can.

The qualifications on the use of this method of analysis are the same as on method (c). Using reverse order involves supplying missing detail. Likewise, the size of the discourse affects the ease of applicability. Especially with subordination, key sentences have to be selected for the method to apply.

A sample result of applying this method of analysis to **4.1** is the following:

> **4.8** I limit cultivations between [the] rows [of soft fruit plants] to hoeing or a light going over with a three-pronged hand cultivator, *because* any disturbance and breaking up of feeding roots by deep cultivation has a serious ill-effect on the cropping and health of [soft fruit] plants *as a consequence of* all soft fruits being surface rootings with the root feeding areas extending several feet away from plants.

This result and other parallel results confirm the analysis of **4.1** presented in Figure 4.1 in the last section. The status of the first sentence has now therefore to be settled. It has met none of our criteria for identification as Situation except that of answering the question (in Section 4) 'What is the situation?'. We have three separate sets of results which suggest a Cause–Consequence relation between sentences 1 and 2, namely, the question 'What aspect of Situation requiring a Response arises out of this?' in Section 4, the connection by 'why?' in Section 5, and the connection by 'as a consequence of' in this section. One way out of this would be to say that whereas the Problem 'I saw the enemy approaching' in Chapter 4 arose in one particular Situation, the Problem in this passage arises in all Situations concerning soft fruit. But although this is true, if we allow it as an explanation, our system of analysis as so far presented will not have worked. A clue as to how to handle the question can instead be found in the notion of Delicate Situation, raised in the handling of **3.66**. If we omit sentence 2 of our discourse, we get the following perfectly coherent and complete discourse:

> **4.9** All soft fruits are surface rooting with the root feeding areas extending several feet away from plants. I [therefore] limit cultivations between the rows to hoeing or a light going over with a three-pronged hand cultivator.

As we shall see in other instances as well, the omission of some sentences from a discourse frequently highlights remaining relations holding in the discourse. In this case, the omission of sentence 2 highlights the fact that sentences 1 and 3 also hold in a Cause–Consequence relation. Applying mapping condition 4 to them, we find that sentence 3 can be extended to include a Purpose clause such as 'to avoid harming the root feeding areas'. (We have already established it as having an agent.) This Purpose clause is of the 'avoid harm to' type which makes sentence 1 that border-line category of Problem which we called Delicate Situation. This aptly sums up all our analysis so far. Our final analysis of **4.1** is given in Figure 4.2.

Passage **4.1** is in many ways an extreme case in its brevity and simplicity. It has been used here to demonstrate each of the main methods of analysis in turn. Normally, of course, we do not use each method separately but rather bring all types of method to play at the same time. How this works will be seen in the next sections.

Passage **4.1**'s simplicity also prevents us bringing into play several other supplementary forms of analysis. They will each be described in their separate places when they are introduced.

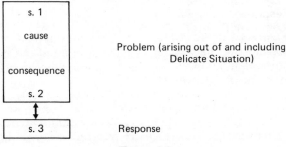

Figure 4.2

7   The Analysis of a Fuller Discourse

Up to now we have analysed either simplified made-up examples or the briefest of real examples. In this and the next sections we will bring to play all the methods so far described on a complete eleven-sentence discourse from the *New Scientist* 'Technology review'. The discourse is presented first without comment (**4.10**) and then a general analysis is given (**4.11**). A detailed justification of that analysis will then follow.

4.10   *Balloons and Air Cushion the Fall*

(1) (*a*) Helicopters are very convenient for dropping freight by parachute, (*b*) but this system has its problems. (2) Somehow the landing impact has to be cushioned to give a soft landing. (3) The movement to be absorbed depends on the weight and the speed at which the charge falls.

(4) Unfortunately most normal spring systems bounce the load as it lands, sometimes turning it over. (5) (*a*) To avoid this, Bertin, developer of the aerotrain, has come up with an air-cushion system (*b*) which assures a safe and soft landing. (6) It comprises a platform on which the freight is loaded with, underneath, a series of 'balloons' supported by air cushions. (7) These are fed from compressed air cylinders equipped with an altimeter valve which opens when the load is just over six feet from the ground. (8) The platform then becomes a hovercraft, with the balloons reducing the deceleration as it touches down.

(9) Trials have been carried out with freight-dropping at rates from 19 feet to 42 feet per second. (10) (*a*) The charge weighed about one and half tons, (*b*) but the system can handle up to eight tons. (11) At low altitudes freight can be dropped without a parachute.[2]

This can be analysed as:

4.11

Situation:	(1) (*a*)	
Problem:	(2)–(4)	
Response:	(5) (*a*)	
Evaluation:	(5) (*b*)	
Response: (continued)	(6)–(8)	
Basis for Evaluation:	(9)–(10) (*a*)	
Evaluation (continued):	(10) (*b*)–(11)	

As before, each sentence is numbered; where a major discourse division occurs within a sentence, as it does within sentences 1, 5 and 10, the two halves of the sentence are referred to as *a* and *b* (e.g. 1*a*, 1*b*).

8   The Multiple Nature of Sentence 1a

Discourse **4.10** begins with a short Situation clause which is couched in Evaluative terms. By this we mean that sentence 1*a* ('Helicopters are very convenient for dropping freight by parachute') can be paraphrased as follows:

> **4.12**   Helicopters are used for dropping freight by parachute. They are very convenient for this

where the first sentence of **4.10** is Situation and the second sentence is Evaluation of Situation as non-Problem. For discussion of this possibility, see Section 20 and Figure 3.11 in Chapter 3. In the original sentence, 1*a* combines both elements; depending on context, therefore, either Situation or Evaluation could become its dominant meaning. It takes little imagination, for example, to recognise the possibility of a discourse occurring in which helicopters are put forward as a Response to some Problem; in such a discourse, sentence 1*a* could become part of the general Evaluation of the Response as in **4.13**:

> **4.13**   These tests show that helicopters are very convenient for dropping freight by parachute.

In this type of context, previous mention would have been made of helicopters and freight-dropping, thus focusing attention on what would be the new material in the sentence – i.e. the Evaluative item 'convenient'. In the context of **4.10**, however, the dominant meaning is Situation for reasons that are spelt out immediately below. It is not uncommon to have an Evaluative element within a Situation, as was pointed out in Chapter 3. Its function is to put the Problem – which is a 'bad' aspect of the Situation – into the larger context of 'good' aspects of Situation.

9   Analysis of 4.10: (i) Situation

Sentence 1*a*'s function can be identified as that of Situation by the following means.

(a)   Lexical Signalling

Sentence 1*b* ('but this system has its problems') contains anaphoric reference to 1*a* in the phrase 'this system'. 'System' is a lexical signal which is used to signal either Situation or Response, and in this case can be taken as retrospectively characterising sentence 1*a* as Situation, since there is no other evidence to justify treating 1*a* as Response.

(b)   Narrative Interrogation

Sentence 1*a* answers the question 'What is the situation?'; as has already been stated, it will not answer the question 'What is your evaluation?' because such a question requires a context – What is your evaluation *of x?* – which has not been provided in this discourse.

(c)   Elaborating Interrogation

The reverse order question test is productive. We need, however, to ignore sentence 1*b* for this purpose, as its sole role is to signal the function of what precedes and follows it. It is in fact a signalling clause, in some respects like a conjunct in operation. We also need to ignore the Evaluative element of sentence 1*a* and use the non-Evaluative form as in **4.12**. This is quite reasonable, as we have already shown that the non-Evaluative version of sentence 1*a* is contained within the Evaluative version. Having made the above adjustments, we attest the following:

> **4.14**   D: Somehow the landing impact has to be cushioned to give a soft landing.
> Q: In what situation *or* circumstances?
> D: (When) Helicopters are used for dropping freight by parachute.

(d) Subordination/Conjuncts

With the same adjustments as above, we attest the following, among several:

> **4.15**   When helicopters are used for dropping freight by parachute, somehow the landing impact has to be cushioned to give a soft landing.

10   Analysis of 4.10: (ii) Problem

Sentences 2–4 can be identified· as constituting the 'Problem'. The grounds for this analysis are given below.

(a)   Lexical Signalling

The signalling clause 1*b* anticipates what follows as problems. ('This system has its problems.') Clause 1*b* is a Preview statement and as such will normally be followed by Details. (The relationship will be discussed in detail in Chapter 7.). In the absence of any further evidence for a contrary reading, therefore, sentences 2–4 will be read as providing the Details to the Preview statement that the system has its problems. Were no other signals present, this would normally be sufficient to signal Problem function.

The verb phrase 'has to' in sentence 2 is another lexical signal of Problem. It indicates a need; indeed it is possible to paraphrase the sentence using 'need to' in place of 'have to'

4.16 Somehow the landing impact needs to be cushioned to give a soft landing.

In the context of 1*b*, the equation of this need with one of the details of Problem is natural. Furthermore, one definition of 'need' might be 'an aspect of situation requiring a response', our alternative formulation of Problem. Where 'need' differs from the other signals of Problem, however, is that it specifies some of the characteristics necessary for a Response to be a Response. It is not the statement of a bad, positive situation but of a bad, negative Situation. Problem is often divided into negative Evaluation + Need.

Another relevant lexical signal in the same sentence is the indefinite adjunct of Instrument 'somehow'. This indicates that we have an as yet unfulfilled Instrument–Purpose relationship. This can be shown (in colloquial terms) by the following dialogue.

4.17 D: The landing impact has to be cushioned to give a soft landing.
Q: How?
D: Somehow.
Q: Yes but how?

In Chapter 3 we saw how Instrument–Purpose could be mapped onto the Response part of a Problem–Solution pattern. Purpose is hoped-for result and relates to the 'prevention, reversal, avoidance, avoidance of harm to, or the seeking of help in preventing, reversing, etc. the Problem'. Purpose specifies, in other words, what a Response is intended to do. If therefore no Instrument is given except the unspecific 'somehow', the Purpose clause becomes a statement of need that has not been met, that is, a Problem. The existence of the signal 'problems' in the previous sentence makes it inevitable that the need for a way of cushioning the landing impact will be interpreted as one of the problems foreshadowed. It is worth noticing, though, that even if no mention were made of 'problems' in 1*b*, the missing instrument would still operate as a signal of 'Problem':

4.18 Helicopters are very convenient for dropping freight by parachute, but somehow the landing impact has to be cushioned to give a soft landing.

The 'but' left over from 1*b* has a part to play in this; it indicates that the second independent clause (formerly sentence 2) contains material that is incompatible with the positive Evaluation of the first (formerly sentence 1*a*).

A fourth relevant signal is the attitudinal disjunct 'unfortunately' in sentence 4. This indicates a negative Evaluation of the content of sentence 4 in contrast to the positive one of sentence 1*a*. As a disjunct, however, it does not convert the whole sentence into an Evaluation but remains a comment on the information carried in the clause to which it is attached. The whole sentence can be paraphrased thus:

> **4.19** Most normal spring systems bounce the load as it lands, sometimes turning it over. This is unfortunate.

A parallel can be seen with our paraphrase of sentence 1*a* as **4.12**. We saw in Chapter 3 that when an aspect of Situation is negatively evaluated, we have a signal of Problem (unless other factors intervene). It should be noted that if sentences 1*b*, 2 and 3 were all removed, we would still have an acceptable Situation–Problem pair:

> **4.20** Helicopters are very convenient for dropping freight by parachute. Unfortunately most normal spring systems bounce the load as it lands, sometimes turning it over.

Nor is this pair dependent upon the positive Evaluation contained in sentence 1*a*; this is demonstrated by **4.21** below where sentence 1*a*'s Evaluation element is removed:

> **4.21** Helicopters are used for dropping freight by parachute. Unfortunately most normal spring systems bounce the load as it lands, sometimes turning it over.

As if the items 'problems', 'has to', 'somehow' and 'unfortunately' were not sufficient lexical signalling of Problem, there is a fifth lexical signal to be considered. In sentence 5, the phrase 'to avoid this' refers anaphorically to sentence 4 and retrospectively characterises it as 'something to avoid'. This is a two-armed signpost pointing to both Response and Problem, where what is avoided is categorised as Problem and the action adopted as a means of avoidance is categorised as Response. Moreover we have met all the conditions of mapping condition 2. We have three parts of a discourse: *a* (sentence 4); *b* (the main clause in sentence 5: 'Bertin, developer of the aerotrain, has come up with an air-cushion system'); and *c* (the clause 'to avoid this'). Parts *a* and *b* are in a Cause–Consequence relation, as will be shown below; *b* and *c* are in an Instrument–Purpose relation as is shown (among other means) by the special grammatical form of the purpose clause ('to' +

predicate). Even if we ignore the fact that sentences 2–4 are already established as Problem, we may note that b has an agent, Bertin, and that c 'avoids' some crucial aspect of a, and thereby conclude that sentence 4 is Problem and the main clause of sentence 5, Response.

(b) Narrative Interrogation

Sentences 2–4 answer the high-level broad question 'What is the problem?' or 'What aspect of this situation requires a response?'. As before, the non-evaluation form of sentence 1a is used. Since 1b is a signalling clause, it is of course ignored (see Section 3).

4.22 D: Helicopters are used for dropping freight by parachute.
Q: What aspect of this situation requires a response?
D: Somehow the landing impact has to be cushioned to give a soft landing. The movement to be absorbed depends on the weight and the speed at which the charge falls. Unfortunately most normal spring systems bounce the load as it lands, sometimes turning it over.

(c) Elaborating Interrogation

The reverse order question test is similarly productive. We need however to ignore the clause 'to avoid this' when making the dialogue for the same reasons that we ignored sentence 1b in applying the question and paraphrase tests:

4.23 D: Bertin, developer of the aerotrain, has come up with an air-cushion system.
Q: Why ⟨has he come up with such a system⟩?
D: (Because) Somehow the landing impact has to be cushioned to give a soft landing. The movement to be absorbed depends on the weight and the speed at which the charge falls. Unfortunately most normal spring systems bounce the load as it lands, sometimes turning it over.

This provides evidence that the two parts of the passage are in a Cause–Consequence relation; the demonstration that this leads us to an analysis of the two parts as Problem and Response is given above under (a) *Lexical Signalling*.

(d) Subordination/Conjuncts

The paraphrase tests outlined in Chapter 3 are productive. It will be remembered however that one restriction of the paraphrase tests lies in the fact that they can only connect limited stretches of language. To make the tests workable, therefore, it has been necessary to select representative sentences from each of the groups. Omitting the clause 'to avoid this' and the disjunct 'unfortunately', we attest a number of paraphrase possibilities of which **4.24** and **4.25** are typical:

> **4.24** Because the landing impact has to be cushioned to give a soft landing, Bertin, developer of the aerotrain, has come up with an air-cushion system . . .
>
> **4.25** Most normal spring systems bounce the load as it lands, sometimes turning it over. Therefore Bertin, developer of the aerotrain, has come up with an air-cushion system . . .

These paraphrase tests confirm the Cause–Consequence relation holding between the two parts of the passage which was used in the operation of mapping condition 2.

(e) Other Points of Analysis

It has perhaps been noticed that sentence 3 has been ignored in our analysis so far. No lexical signal is present in it, and in the paraphrase tests, it is the only sentence that will not connect with the main clause of the sentence 5. The reason for this is that its function is to provide a context for the better understanding of the nature of the Problem, to supply additional information about what is required of a freight-dropping system. It does not in fact have any role at the level of the whole discourse but functions at the level of the internal organisation of Problem. It can be omitted without substantially affecting the meaning or meaningfulness of the discourse:

> **4.26** Helicopters are very convenient for dropping freight by parachute, but this system has its problems. Somehow the landing impact has to be cushioned to give a soft landing. Unfortunately most normal spring systems bounce the load as it lands, sometimes turning it over.

11 Analysis of 4.10: (iii) Response

Sentences 5–8 (excluding the Evaluative clause in sentence 5) comprise our next main function within the discourse, that of Response. Many of the reasons for regarding these sentences as Response also serve to provide evidence for treating sentences 2–4 as Problem. For simplicity's sake, we handled all such reasons under Problem.

(a) Lexical Realisation

The phrasal verb 'come up with' is a typical signal of Response to a problem, probably most frequent in journalism and advertising. It is commonly used in phrases such as 'come up with a solution', 'come up with an answer', and 'come up with an idea'. By itself it would not be conclusive evidence of sentences 5–8 having the function of Response, but in conjunction with the fact that sentences 2–4 have been shown to have the function of Problem, it provides valuable support for so identifying sentences 5–8.

(b) Narrative Interrogation

Sentences 5–8 (excluding the evaluative clause in 5) answer the high-level broad question 'What response has been made?' as is shown in **4.27**:

> **4.27** D: Somehow the landing impact has to be cushioned to give a soft landing. The movement to be absorbed depends on the weight and the speed at which the charge falls. Unfortunately most normal spring systems bounce the load as it lands, sometimes turning it over.
> Q: What response has been made to this problem?
> D: Bertin, developer of the aerotrain, has come up with an air-cushion system, [which] comprises a platform on which the freight is loaded with, underneath, a series of 'balloons' supported by air cushions. These are fed from compressed air cylinders equipped with an altimeter valve which opens when the load is just over six feet from the ground. The platform then becomes a hovercraft, with the balloons reducing the deceleration as it touches down.

Another possible formulation of the question used in the above dialogue is 'What solution has been offered?'. This alternative is very often available as a signal of Response; indeed, its availability explains why most linguists choose to call this part of the pattern Solution.

(c) Elaborating Interrogation

The reverse order question test has already been shown to be productive in the last section. Dialogue **4.23** demonstrated not only that sentence 5*a* was (part of) Response. We can further demonstrate this by projecting into dialogue form sentences 5–8 (see **4.28**), this time including sentences 6–8 under Response. To do this, however, it is necessary to convert sentence 5*b* into its equivalent passive form so that we lose the need to specify the Instrument (represented in the active form by 'which'). Otherwise our initiating sentence would presuppose its answer.

> **4.28** D: A safe and soft landing [for freight] is assured.
> Q: How ⟨ has a safe and soft landing been assured⟩?

D: Bertin, developer of the aerotrain, has come up with an air-cushion system [which] comprises a platform on which the freight is loaded with, underneath, a series of 'balloons' supported by air cushions. These are fed from compressed air cylinders equipped with an altimeter valve which opens when the load is just six feet from the ground. The platform then becomes a hovercraft, with the balloons reducing the deceleration as it touches down.

Thus elaborating interrogation confirms our analysis of sentences 5*a* and 6–8 as Response.

(d)   Subordination/Conjuncts

The same is true of the subordination and conjunct paraphrase tests as was true of the elaborating interrogation test. They have already been applied successfully in the previous section. (See **4.24** and **4.25**.) Further paraphrase tests can however be employed linking putative Response and putative Evaluation, as in **4.29** and **4.30**. Again, the clause 'which assures a safe and soft landing' has to undergo permutation, in **4.29** to allow the main clause to have the same subject as the subordinate clause, and in **4.30** for the reasons given for (*c*).

4.29   By coming up with an air-cushion system [which] comprises a platform on which the freight is loaded . . ., Bertin [has] assure[d] a safe and soft landing for freight.

4.30   Bertin, developer of the aerotrain, has come up with an air-cushion system [which] comprises a platform on which the freight is loaded with, underneath, a series of 'balloons' supported by air cushions. These are fed from compressed air cylinders equipped with an altimeter valve which opens when the load is just over six feet from the ground. The platform then becomes a hovercraft, with the balloons reducing the deceleration as it touches down. A safe and soft landing is thereby assured.

(e)   Other Points of Analysis

Two further features help signal sentences 5–8 (excluding 5*b*) as Response. The first of these is the verb form. The verb of sentence 5*a* is in the form traditionally known as the present perfect, that is, have-ed. This verb form is used to describe happenings that either began or took place wholly in the past but that continue or have consequences of interest in the present. As such, it is ideally suited for the description of Response since real-world solutions (typically represented as Response) are normally achieved at a definite time in the past and by their nature have consequences for the present. This verb form appears however to be reserved primarily for the description of other people's real-world solutions, not normally for the writer/speaker's own unless, as in advertising, an element of boasting is present in the discourse. Once the Response has been thus signalled, the verb form normally reverts to the simple non-past, since the real-world solution continues to be valid over a period of time extended beyond the present. Thus after 'has come up with', we find 'comprises', 'is loaded', 'are fed', 'opens', 'is', 'becomes' and 'touches', all of which are in the simple non-past ('assures' is excluded from this list for reasons given in Section 12 below). This is compatible with Response's being regarded as providing new situation (see Figure 3.12, Chapter 3). A common pattern for Response is 'have-ed' followed by simple non-past. (For further discussion of and some explanation of the reasons for this, see Chapter 5, Section 9 and Chapter 7, Section 5.)

The second feature that indicates that sentence 5*a*, etc., is Response is the repetition in the discourse. This is best demonstrated by showing sentences 2 and 5 (including 5*b*) together thus:

4.31 Somehow the landing impact has to be ‌cushioned‌ to give a ‌soft landing.‌ Bertin, developer of the aerotrain, has come up with an air ‌cushion‌ system which assures a safe and ‌soft landing.‌

The reason for this closeness of connection lies in the omitted adjunct 'somehow'. It will be remembered that we identified the function of 'somehow' as indicating an unfulfilled Instrument–Purpose relation, where the Purpose was specified but the Instrument left indefinite. The items repeated in sentence 5 are those items constituting the specified purpose of sentence 2. They are repeated to provide an explicit context for 'an air-cushion system' which replaces the indefinite 'somehow'. If we alter the verb phrase 'has to be cushioned' to 'is cushioned' and insert an instrument phrase containing 'an air-cushion system' in the place of 'somehow', we get a sentence that summarises the discourse.

4.32 Using an air-cushion system, the landing impact is cushioned to give a soft landing.

In this analysis we had to use the putative Evaluative clause 'which assures a safe and soft landing' because we could not otherwise assume that Purpose had necessarily been converted into Achievement. (The close relationship between Achievement and Evaluation was discussed in Chapter 3.) The evidence for treating sentence 5*b* as (part of) Evaluation is given immediately below.

12   Analysis of 4.10: (iv) Evaluation

We noted in Chapter 3 that Evaluation may take one of three forms – Evaluation accompanied by Basis, Result accompanied by Evaluation, or combined Result/Evaluation optionally accompanied by Basis. In this discourse our claim is that the first form is followed, with sentences 9 and 10*a* providing the Basis for sentence 5*b*'s Evaluation. Sentences 10*b* and 11 return to Evaluation proper. Since there are two segments to the Evaluation, each is justified separately.

(a)   Lexical Realisation

'Assures' is an item used to express Evaluation: assurance can never be a matter of fact, only of assessment. Otherwise there is no other direct lexical realisation of Evaluation.

(b)   Narrative Interrogation

All the typical broad questions for eliciting Evaluation can be asked: 'How successful is this response?', 'What is your evaluation of this response?', 'What is the result of this response?' or, most simply, 'Does it work?'. (All these questions either were or could have been used to elicit the sentence 'I beat off the enemy attack' in Chapter 3, allowing of course for a change of tense in each case.) One such dialogue is given:

> **4.33**   D: Bertin, developer of the aerotrain, has come up with an air-cushion system which comprises a platform on which the freight is loaded with, underneath, a series of 'balloons' supported by air cushions. These are fed from compressed air cylinders equipped with an altimeter valve which opens when the load is just over six feet from the ground. The platform then becomes a hovercraft, with the balloons reducing the deceleration as it touches down.
> Q: How successful is this [system]?
> D: [It] assures a safe and soft landing [and] [the system] can handle up to eight tons. At low altitudes freight can be dropped without a parachute.

(c)   Elaborating Interrogation, Subordination and Conjuncts

The subordination and conjunct tests and the test of projecting the discourse into reverse order dialogue have already been shown to work, in Section 11.

(d) Other Points of Analysis

A further feature that helps identify the function of sentence 5*b* and sentences 10*b* and 11 as Evaluation is the fact that sentence 5*b* can change position within the discourse. It is possible to permute sentences 2–4 in several ways; we can have the orders 2–3–4, 4–2–3 and 4–3–2, though not with equal probability, all of which permutations occur within the discourse element Problem. No other sentence or clause, however, has any flexibility of position within the discourse, except for sentence 5*b*; readers are invited to test this for themselves. Sentence 5*b*, with 'which' spelt out as 'the air-cushion system', can move to one of two positions – either immediately before sentence 9 at the head of the last paragraph (or at the end of the middle paragraph) or, rather less certainly, immediately after sentence 9 between 9 and 10. That this is possible reinforces our suggestion that 5*b* belongs with 9–11 as a single element of the discourse organisation.

13 The Arguments for Basis

Sentences 9 and 10*a* are regarded as Basis for the Evaluation in 5*b* for the following reasons:

(*a*) They answer the broad questions in narrative interrogation 'What makes you say that?':

> **4.34** D: The air-cushion system assures a safe and soft landing.
> Q: What makes you say that?
> D: Trials have been carried out with freight-dropping at rates of from 19 feet to 42 feet per second in winds of 49 feet per second. The charge weighed about one and a half tons.

(*b*) They contain some of the special vocabulary of Basis, namely 'trials' and 'carried out', though these can in other contexts also signal Response.

(*c*) The predicators are either present perfect or simple past in form. This indicates that the facts described took place in the past, though they may have consequences for the present. Here we have 'have been carried out' and 'weighed'.

(*d*) As we would expect from the flexibility of position of sentence 5*b* vis-à-vis sentences 9 and 10*a*, elaborating interrogation produces two results:

> **4.35** D: Trials have been carried out with freight dropping at rates of from 19 feet to 42 feet per second in winds of 49 feet per second. The charge weighed about one and half tons.

Q: EITHER What evaluation did this lead to?
OR What evaluation does this support?
D: (That) the air-cushion system assures a safe and soft landing.

The former question would connect the order 9, 5*b*, 10*a*; the latter question connects the order 5*b*, 9, 10*a*. This result supports the categorisation of 9 and 10*a* as Basis.

14   A Skeleton Summary of 4.10

A point worthy of note about **4.10** is that a reasonable skeleton summary of the discourse can be achieved by the simple expedient of taking the first sentence of each element of the pattern as long as we exclude the signalling clauses, 'but this system has its problems' and 'to avoid this' and either exclude the Evaluative element of sentence 1*a* or include the conjunction 'but' that follows it:

> **4.36** Helicopters are used for dropping freight by parachute. Somehow the landing impact has to be cushioned to give a soft landing. Bertin, developer of the aerotrain, has come up with an air-cushion system which assures a safe and soft landing. (Trials have been carried out with freight-dropping at rates of from 19 feet to 42 feet per second in winds of 49 feet per second.)
>
> **4.37** Helicopters are very convenient for dropping freight by parachute but somehow the landing impact has to be cushioned to give a soft landing. Bertin, developer of the aerotrain, has come up with an air-cushion system which assures a safe and soft landing. (Trials have been carried out with freight-dropping at rates of from 19 feet to 42 feet per second in winds of 49 feet per second.)

In both the above summaries, the first sentence of the Basis of the Evaluation has been added in brackets to show one possible extension.

Hutchins (1977a) has warned against the use of such a method to produce abstracts, noting that though it may produce an admirable précis, it leaves out too much of the essential new information to make a good abstract. Nevertheless, from a pure linguist's point of view rather than that of one interested in information retrieval, it is of considerable interest that the system of analysis here proposed can be used to produce satisfactory skeleton summaries. It seems to demonstrate that the analysis is getting to the communicative core of the discourse.

Chapter 5

Some Modifications to the Problem—Solution Pattern

1 Preview of Modifications

In the last two chapters, we have outlined the basic criteria for identifying Problem—Solution patterns in English discourses. So far, however, apart from the artificial examples of Chapter 3, we have analysed only two short discourses – a passage from an *Amateur Gardening* article and a report from the 'Technology review' of the *New Scientist*. Inevitably, therefore, some oversimplifications have resulted. In this chapter we consider two important facets of discourse organisation that we have not yet discussed and in so doing take the opportunity of broadening the range of discourse varieties from which we draw our illustrations.

The two modifications to our description both result in more complex analyses, but they are not complex in themselves. The first involves the concept of multilayering, the existence of more than one Problem—Solution pattern within the same discourse. Building on this, we consider a rather special type of multilayering as generated by a computer, which leads us onto our second modification – the role of participants and audience in the analysis of discourse – which will be shown to affect the analysis of fiction, scientific writing, and advertisements.

2 Evaluation – Positive and Negative

The Problem—Solution pattern as we have described it in the past two chapters can be represented as in Figure 5.1. These categories have proved adequate for the description of the discourses we have so far examined and would indeed prove adequate for the description of many more. Nevertheless they contain a simplifying assumption that would prevent us from applying them in many cases where they might be expected to be of use. This assumption is that the Evaluation of the Response will always be positive.

Despite its currency in discourse work, the label 'Solution' is in some respects unfortunate in that the word is a lexical signal that signals not only Response but also a positive Evaluation of the Response. If our simplifying assumption that all Evaluations are positive were in truth

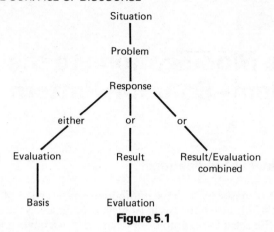

Figure 5.1

correct, the fact that the label 'solution' contains a positive Evaluation would be an advantage, not an argument for its disuse. The truth of course is that it is quite common for Evaluations to be negative, and we have allowed for that in our terminology.

Nevertheless, it is also true that in the vast majority of cases a Problem–Solution pattern ends with a positive Evaluation. A discourse that does not so end often reads like an interim report or simply seems incomplete. One of Kafka's short stories, 'The Burrow', achieves much of its impact from its unusual use of the Problem–Solution pattern. The first third of the story is spent on describing, from a burrowing animal's viewpoint, the comfortable home that the animal has built itself (the Situation). One day, inexplicably, a high-pitched continuous whistle disrupts the peace of the burrow (the Problem). The animal makes several attempts at locating the source of the whistle (the Response) but fails (a negative Evaluation). And there ends the story. Because of our expectation that a Problem–Solution pattern will end with a positive Evaluation, the effect is that we share the disruption of the animal's contentment. In other words, the disturbance to the burrow is mirrored by the disturbance to the discourse organisation. (There is a case for arguing that many of Kafka's effects are achieved by sabotaging discourse expectations.)

3   Multilayering

How are these two facts to be reconciled? On the one hand, we have asserted that it is common to have negative Evaluations and on the other we have claimed that so powerful is the expectation that a Problem–Solution pattern will end with a positive Evaluation of a

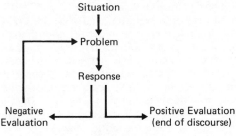

Figure 5.2

Response that if it is undermined in any way the effect is to discompose a reader quite markedly. The answer lies in the phenomenon of multilayering.

Multilayering is based on a simple fact of signalling that has already been discussed, namely that a negative Evaluation is a signal of Problem. We had a number of illustrations of this in Chapter 4. It remains true that negative Evaluation is a signal of Problem even when the Evaluation is not local but the Evaluation of a Response. Thus whenever a Response is negatively Evaluated, another Problem is normally signalled, except where the Negative Evaluation does not allow for any further Response (e.g. 'This killed him'). In other words, a principle of recursiveness is introduced (see Figure 5.2). (Figure 5.2 of course oversimplifies greatly the possibilities.) There is no particular reason why the pattern should not be repeated several times.

There are several types of multilayering which overlap with each other. At the one extreme we have a type that we may call chained multilayering where each Response results in a different Problem. Some comedy is built on this pattern; so is the traditional nursery-rhyme 'There was an old woman who swallowed a fly'. At the other extreme we have a type which we may call spiral multilayering where there are repeated attempts to solve the same Problem, all but the last of which fail, leaving the Problem exactly or largely as it was: **5.6**, discussed later on, exemplifies this type of multilayering. In between these, there is a type that shares features of both, which we may call progressive multilayering, where each Response solves part of the Problem but leaves part of it still requiring solution. This is the most common type, and an example follows below.

4 Examples of Multilayering: An Advertising Discourse

The first example we have chosen to look at is drawn from a large class of advertisements that attempt to focus on a medical or quasi-medical need:

5.1   (Heading and picture omitted)

(1) Over 20 million people in Britain wear dentures. (2) Often the major cause of losing teeth is poor oral hygiene, leading to gum disease.

(3) Regular toothbrushing helps, but it's only one part of the answer. (4) A toothbrush simply cannot clean the spaces in between the teeth. (5) If these spaces aren't cleaned, plaque builds up in them. (6) Plaque is a sticky film that clings to teeth, causing decay and the unhealthy gum conditions that dentists call gingivitis. (7) To avoid this condition, use Inter-dens Gum Massage Sticks regularly. (8) They massage the gums whilst cleaning the interdental spaces, removing plaque and promoting firm, healthy gums.

(9) Use Inter-dens – and help keep your natural teeth for life. (10) *Ask your dentist!* (11) *Inter-dens Gum Massage Sticks – from your chemist.* (12) Nicholas – Inter-dens products for oral hygiene.[1]

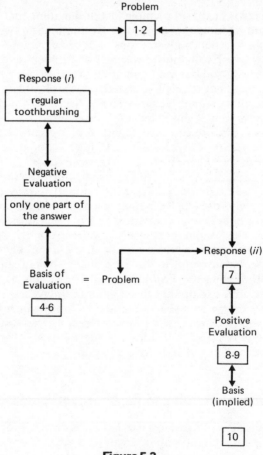

Figure 5.3

Although apparently simpler in language than the discourses so far analysed, this advertisement conceals several complicating features, the most important of which for our purposes is that it is multilayered. This can be represented diagrammatically, as in Figure 5.3.

Our analysis of this and subsequent examples will be highly selective, as it is assumed that by now our method of arriving at a description has been adequately demonstrated. We briefly note therefore only sufficient features to help us identify the phenomena under consideration.

Sentences 1–2 comprise the first statement of Problem, there being no Situation. A number of signals of Problem are present. To begin with, in sentence 2 we have a negative Evaluation: 'poor' (reinforced by the reader's real-world knowledge of 'disease' as something to be avoided). This negative Evaluation affects the previous sentence because of a complex chain of consequences, of which 'poor oral hygiene' is a part. This chain can be represented as in Figure 5.4. It will be seen that the negative Evaluation implicates the whole chain.

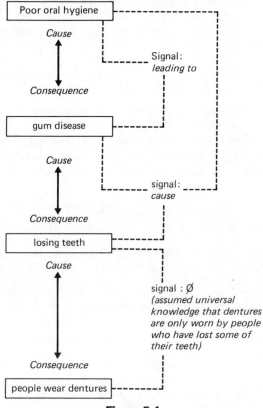

Figure 5.4

A signal of both Problem and Response is 'helps' in sentence 3. This leaves unstated what exactly is helped, but it will be recalled that in Section 21, Chapter 3, 'help' was listed as one of the typical vocabulary of Response in such contexts as 'help avoid/prevent/overcome this'. Since no other reading is possible here, we are entitled to regard 'helps' in this instance as an example of the same use. As such it functions as a signal both of Problem (sentences 1–2) and Response ('regular toothbrushing').

In the same way, 'answer' in sentence 3 is a clear signal that 'regular toothbrushing' is Response; what it is a (partial) answer to is therefore simultaneously signalled as Problem.

This then is our first layer, with sentences 1 and 2 as Problem and the subject of sentence 3 as Response. What needs to be added now is the paradoxical fact that 'helps' and 'answer', although signalling Problem and Response, are themselves neither Problem nor Response but Evaluation. They answer the question 'How successful is regular toothbrushing?'. As such they technically complete the pattern. But though the pattern may be complete in terms of the analytical system we have been hitherto employing, there can be no question that it is informationally incomplete:

5.2 (1) Over 20 million people in Britain wear dentures. (2) Often the major cause of losing teeth is poor oral hygiene, leading to gum disease.
(3) Regular toothbrushing helps, but it's only one part of the answer.

There are three reasons for its seeming incomplete. The first is that the Basis is missing. However, although once this is added the discourse is marginally improved, the improvement is not sufficient to make the discourse whole:

5.3 (1) Over 20 million people in Britain wear dentures. (2) Often the major cause of losing teeth is poor oral hygiene, leading to gum disease.
(3) Regular toothbrushing helps, but it's only one part of the answer.
(4) A toothbrush simply cannot clean the spaces in between the teeth. (5) If these spaces aren't cleaned, plaque builds up in them. (6) Plaque is a sticky film that clings to teeth, causing decay and the unhealthy gum conditions that dentists call gingivitis.

The second reason is that only one part sets up an expectation of 'another part of the answer'; the nature of such expectation-creators is discussed in Chapters 7 and 8. For the present, we need only note that it is not the sole or even the main reason for the sense of incompleteness evinced by **5.2** or **5.3**. This is simply demonstrated by substituting another negative Evaluation in its place:

5.4 (1) Over 20 million people in Britain wear dentures. (2) Often the major cause of losing teeth is poor oral hygiene, leading to gum disease.

(3) Regular toothbrushing helps, but it is generally speaking an inadequate answer. (4) A toothbrush simply cannot clean the spaces in between the teeth. (5) If these spaces aren't cleaned, plaque builds up in them. (6) Plaque is a sticky film that clings to teeth, causing decay and the unhealthy gum condition that dentists call gingivitis.

Since the absence of Basis and the presence of 'only one part' are insufficient to account for the sense of incompleteness by themselves, the third reason must be given the greatest weight – that a negative Evaluation is not felt to be an appropriate completion point because it is itself a signal of Problem. Kafka aside, we expect completion of the pattern with successful Response. (It should perhaps be pointed out that the Evaluation is strictly speaking in two balanced parts, 'helps' being positive and 'only one part of the answer' being negative. We have encountered such balancing before, in Chapter 4, Section 8; it is quite characteristic of Evaluation. It is the second, negative, half of the Evaluation that creates the sense of incompleteness. Had the two Evaluations been reversed and greater stress thereby placed on the positive Evaluation, the sense of incompleteness would have been more muted.)

The second layer of the Problem–Solution pattern begins, as we have seen, at sentence 3. The two layers therefore substantially overlap. The relationship between sentences 3 and 6 can be clearly shown if they are projected into dialogue:

5.5 D: Regular toothbrushing helps, but it's only one part of the answer.
    Q: What is the basis of your evaluation?
           or
    Why is that?
           or
    What (part of the) problem does it not solve?
    D: A toothbrush simply cannot clean the spaces in between the teeth.
    Q: What is the consequence ⟨of not cleaning the spaces between the teeth⟩?
    D: If these spaces aren't cleaned, plaque builds up in them.
    Q: Can you give the details (or a definition) ⟨of plaque⟩?
           or
    What is plaque?
    D: Plaque is a sticky film that clings to teeth, causing decay and the unhealthy gum condition that dentists call gingivitis.

It can be seen from **5.5** that another chain of consequences has been set up in sentences 4–6, which can be diagrammed as in Figure 5.5. It will

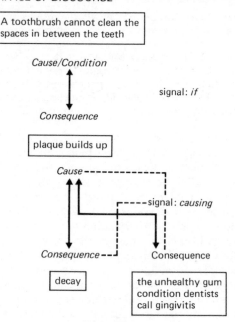

Figure 5.5

be seen that there is a correlation between 'gum disease' on the first chain (Figure 5.4) and 'the unhealthy gum condition' on the second (Figure 5.5). 'Disease' and 'unhealthy condition' are near paraphrases. Indeed the *Concise Oxford Dictionary* defines disease as an 'unhealthy condition of body, etc.'. Consequently the two chains are clearly to be identified at that point. Since the first chain was shown to be Problem, this means that the second is also. It also means that we have an example here of progressive multilayering. The Problem has not changed but has narrowed as a result of the first Response.

Further evidence that sentences 4–6 are Problem is provided by the subordinate purpose clause of sentence 7 – 'to avoid this condition'. 'Avoid' has been fully discussed elsewhere (Section 10, Chapter 4); it simultaneously signals of course that sentence 7 is Response. Sentence 8 answers two questions – 'Does it work? (Evaluation) and 'How does it work?' (Details of Response). The two functions are not separable; 'cleaning the interdental spaces is both a statement of how it works and a positive Evaluation of its success. Figure 5.6 compares sentence 4, restatement of Problem left by toothbrushing, with this part of sentence 8. The only important changes are from 'a toothbrush' to 'Inter-dens Gum Massage Sticks' and from negative to positive, that is, this Response meets the need that the former Response did not. Likewise, 'removing plaque' is both a statement of what it does and a claim of

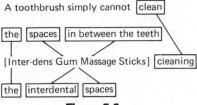

Figure 5.6

success, since plaque is near the head of the two chains that lead to wearing dentures. In the last clause, 'promoting firm healthy gums', the double function disappears. This is purely Evaluative and matches the positive Evaluation 'healthy gums' against the Problem-signalling negative Evaluation 'unhealthy gum condition' in sentence 6. Sentence 9 continues the positive Evaluation with a re-use of 'help', this time not counterbalanced by a negative Evaluation. We now have a sense of completeness and would now be as disturbed by the offer of another Response as we would have previously been if no further Response had followed.

5 Examples of Multilayering: A Scientific Discourse

In Section 4, we considered an example of multilayering which, though complex to describe, was in essence simple in its organisation. Multilayering is by no means limited to advertising, however, nor is it always as simple as the example we have analysed. The following passage from a piece of technological writing shows a more complex organisation, employing a combination of progressive and spiral multilayering (footnotes and headings have been omitted):

5.6 (1) A difficult problem associated with the construction of large parabolic-reflector antennas is that of maintaining the surface profile of the reflector to a high accuracy under all operating conditions. (2) Profile inaccuracies introduce phase errors across the antenna aperture, and such errors reduce the gain, spoil the side-lobe structure of the antenna directional pattern and determine the upper frequency limit of operation.

(3) Although high accuracies have been achieved with some large steerable parabolic reflector antennas, the economic problems involved in the reflector construction and the maintenance of the reflector profile under operational conditions, which may include variations in wind, temperature and gravitational loads, still present a major problem.

(4) Considerable improvement in the performance of large steerable paraboloids has been achieved by improved structural design and

alignment techniques. (5) The British Post Office modified Goonhilly antenna and the Australian CSIRO Parkes antenna are examples of such improvements. (6) Both antennas operate without radomes, relying on their rigid structure to reduce the effects of meteorological variations. (7) In the class of radome-protected antennas, the MIT Haystack facility represents an outstanding example of the application of modern design techniques to achieve a high profile accuracy for all elevation angles. (8) In general, however, antennas of both types involve very high initial costs; and, while the latter system gives the best approach to profile maintenance, it is still prone to the effects of temperature variations, and considerable controversy still exists over the amount of performance deterioration introduced by the radome cover.[2]

Detailed analysis of this passage would be inappropriate at this stage. It will be noticed, however, that sentence 3 gives one Response and a negative Evaluation of it, and that sentences 4–7 also give two other Responses which are then negatively Evaluated in sentence 8. In each case, the statement of the Response also includes a positive Evaluation; the negative Evaluations signal the Problems left over, whereas the positive Evaluations tell the extent to which the Problems have been solved.

So Response 1 in sentence 3 solves the Problem 'of maintaining the surface profile of the reflector to a high accuracy' but does not solve the Problems of doing it 'under all operating conditions', nor of doing it economically. Responses 2 and 2*a* in sentences 4–7 describe attempts to solve the latter Problem for large steerable paraboloids. They both succeed in 'considerable improvement in [their] performance' and the latter in achieving 'a high profile accuracy', but fail to solve the Problem of doing it economically ('antennas of both types involve very high initial costs') and the Problem of achieving accuracy 'under all operating conditions'. (The latter system 'is still prone to the effects of temperature variations'.) So we have a triple-layered discourse with an organisation that may be represented as in Figure 5.7.

This is an instance of progressive and spiral multilayering combined. In so far as the first and subsequent Responses solve the Problem of high accuracy, it is an instance of progressive multilayering. In so far as all the Responses leave largely unsolved the Problems of maintaining the surface profile of the reflector under all operating conditions and economically, however, it is an instance of spiral multilayering. Complex as the organisation of this passage may seem, the principles underlying the organisation are simple. A parsing analysis of a long and complex sentence can give the impression that sentence grammar is unmanageable, yet when the component parts are examined it is found to be constructed on essentially the same principles as much shorter and simpler sentences. Likewise a passage such as **5.6** might

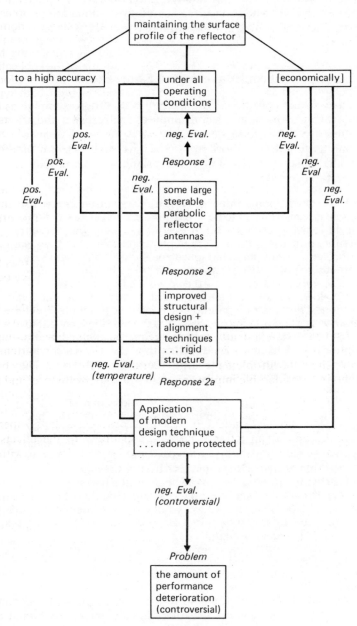

Figure 5.7

daunt the would-be discourse analyst into doubting the practicability of the method, yet when considered carefully it is found to be built out of components as simple as those used to construct much less complex discourses.

6   Examples of Multilayering: A Short Story

We have so far considered the examples of progressive and spiral multilayering as manifested in examples of advertising and scientific discourse. In this section we consider an example of chained multi-layering as found in a short story by Hans Andersen translated by Reginald Spinks. (The fact that it is translated is of no consequence for the point to be made.)

5.7   (1) Once upon a time there was a prince and he wanted to marry a princess, only she had to be a *real* princess. (2) So he went all over the world looking for one. (3) But every time there was something the matter: princesses there were in plenty, but whether they were real princesses or not, he could never really make out, there was always something not quite right about them. (4) So he came home again and was so very sad, because he did so want a real princess.

(5) Now, one night there was terrible storm. (6) It thundered and lightened and the rain poured down – it was frightful! (7) All at once there was a knock at the city gate, and the old king went out to open it.

(8) There, standing outside, was a princess. (9) But dear me, what a sight she looked, in the wind and the rain! (10) The water was running down her hair and her clothes, and it was running in at the toes of her shoes and out again at the heels. (11) And then she said she was a real princess.

(12) 'We'll see about that!' thought the old queen. (13) But she didn't say anything; she went into the bedroom, took off all the bedclothes, and put a pea in the bottom of the bed. (14) Then she took twenty mattresses and put them on top of the pea, and then again twenty featherbeds on top of the mattresses.

(15) That was to be the princess's bed for the night.

(16) In the morning they asked her how she had slept.

(17) 'Dreadfully!' said the princess. (18) 'I hardly got a wink of sleep all night! (19) Goodness knows what can have been in the bed! (20) There was something hard in it, and now I'm just black and blue all over! (21) It's really dreadful!'

(22) So now they were able to see that she was a real princess, because she had felt the pea right through the twenty mattresses and the twenty featherbeds. (23) Only a real princess could be so tender as that.

(24) So the prince took her for his wife, now he knew he had a real princess. (25) And the pea was placed in the museum, where it may still be seen – if nobody has taken it.

(26) There, now that was a real story![3]

'The Princess and the Pea' is constructed with two Problem–Solution patterns. One of them consists of sentences 1–3, the other the rest of the story. Sentences 1–3 can be projected into dialogue as follows:

5.8 Q: What was the situation?
D: Once upon a time there was a prince . . .
Q: What was the problem?
D: [and] he wanted to marry a princess, only she had to be a *real* princess.
Q: What response did he make?
or (more naturally)
What did he do about it?
D: [So] he went all over the world looking for one.
Q: How successful was this?
D: [But] every time there was something the matter.
Q: What was the matter? That is, What was the Problem with the Response tried?
D: Princesses there were in plenty, but whether they were real princesses or not, he could never really make out, there was always something not quite right about them.

The rest of the discourse is concerned with the solution of the second Problem. For reasons that will be discussed in Section 8, the negative Evaluations in sentences 9–10 do not establish a Problem and sentences 5–10 instead all function as Situation. Sentence 11 re-establishes at a particular level the Problem left in general form by sentence 4. The princess claims to be a *real* princess, and a method is needed to test her claim in the light of the prince's previous experience. Sentences 12–15 provide that method, thereby fulfilling the function of Response; the story's point derives partly from the fact that though we have linguistic evidence that this is Response (' "We'll see about that!" thought the old queen') we are unable to see how the actions described will meet the required Need. Sentences 16–21 provide the Result, answering the question 'What was the result of the old queen's response?' and sentences 22–3 evaluate that Result. Sentence 24 provides the Response to the first Problem of wanting to marry a *real* princess. As was

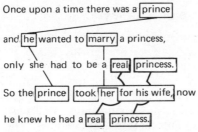

Figure 5.8

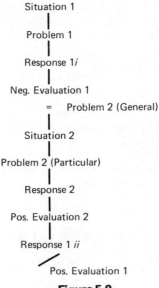

Figure 5.9

the case with the Inter-dens advertisement (see Figure 5.6), the original Problem and final Response are related by repetition. Since the first Problem is couched in the form of a Need to be met and the Response is the complete fulfilment of the Need, an Evaluation would be redundant; the pattern is complete.

As far as the overall organisation of the story is concerned, sentence 25 plays no role, providing an answer only to the jokey question 'What finally happened to the pea?' Likewise sentence 26, an Evaluation of the story as story that would normally be supplied by the reader rather than the writer, plays no necessary or important function within the discourse. Both can be omitted; if we do so, we can represent the discourse's organisation in simplified form (see Figure 5.9).

7   A Special Case of Multilayering

Although there are significant differences between the three types of multilayering so far discussed and illustrated, all three share much in common. To begin with, they all require only one successful Response to be complete. Likewise all three have Problems that are clearly relatable to each other; in the case of the spiral multilayering the Problems are identical. Most significantly, all three are organised from one viewpoint only. This feature they share with the examples already discussed in Chapters 4 and 5. But it is not a feature universal to discourses organised in a Problem–Solution way. This can be seen by examining a special case of multilayering which considers two viewpoints. Discourse **5.9** is computer-generated. The computer is describing the moves of a game of noughts and crosses. Though generated on non-relational criteria (Davey, 1978), the computer's discourse reflects the organisational features we have been discussing. It is chosen not as an aberration but as an interestingly marked example of a common discourse pattern. The moves made are given in diagrammatic form alongside the commentary:

5.9 (1) The game began with my taking a corner, and you took an adjacent one.

(2) (*a*) I threatened you by taking the corner adjacent to the one which you had just taken, (*b*) but you blocked my diagonal and threatened me.

(3) I blocked yours and forked you.

(4) Although you blocked one of my edges and threatened me, I won by completing the other.[4]

Many of the typical signals of Problem and Response are present in this discourse but it cannot be analysed in the way we have been describing without making an important modification to our descriptive system as so far laid down. We have up till now referred to Problem or Response or Evaluation as if they have an absolute existence within the discourse. This is not, however, the case. A Problem can only be a Problem for someone; a Response can only be a Response by someone for someone. Consequently if there are two participants, there are potentially not one but two Problems possible, and if there are more than two, the possible number of Problem–Solution patterns increases by the same amount.

Thus **5.9**, having two main participants – the protagonist computer and his human and fallible antagonist – has two Problem–Solution patterns running alternately throughout. The first Problem is signalled by 'threatened' in sentence 2*a*, a key signal of an Aspect of Situation requiring a Response. By itself, indeed, 'threatened' conveys little other than Problem and needs to be made specific in some way. This is done in the present case by means of an Instrument–Achievement relation (signalled by 'by-ing'), the Achievement being the general 'threatened' and the Instrument the specific nature of the threat. The threat is not to the narrator, however, but to the opponent. It is the opponent, therefore, of whom report of a Response must be expected. This comes in sentence 2*b*. It is signalled by 'but' (which shows that there is a Contrast between the expected result of a threat and what happened instead), by the reversal of agent and patient, and by the usual question and paraphrase tests. (It is instructive to note that the Cause–Consequence paraphrase works once 'but' is removed, highlighting the fact that 'but''s function is to signal unexpectedness and not to override logical connections.) Once again the relation between the parts is an Instrument–Achievement relation with the Achievement the general Problem.

This time, however, the Problem is for the narrator, so a Response is expected from 'him'. This comes in sentence 3 which is as before in an Instrument–Achievement relation. The difference is that the Problem is now 'forked you', a technical term for a penultimate move by a certain victor in noughts-and-crosses. There is no adequate Response possible to that, so the antagonist's Response and consequent 'Problem' for the protagonist, built as before on the Instrument–Achievement pattern, can be subordinated as of little consequence, thereby focusing attention on the protagonist's Response and Evaluation as successful: 'I won'. It should be noted that though it is necessary to know the meaning of 'forked' to appreciate the reasons for subordinating the antagonist's move in sentence 4, it is not necessary for establishing the Response/Problem nature of sentence 3. That can be done by the usual tests.

The organisation of the discourse can be represented as in Figure 5.10.

8   The Role of Participants in Problem–Solution Patterning

As was said before, 5.9 was not chosen as curious in this respect. Such interweaving of Problem–Solution patterns is common in fiction, where several participants may jostle for the reader's attention. To take one simple example, consider the following passage from a popular children's book:

5.10 (*a*)   (1) [Mr Noisy] walked into the baker's shop. (2) CRASH went the door as he opened it. (3) BANG went the door as he shut it. (4) 'I'D LIKE A LOAF OF BREAD,' boomed Mr Noisy to Mrs Crumb the baker's wife.
(5)   Mrs Crumb trembled, and sold him a loaf. (6) Then Mr Noisy walked along the street to the butcher. (7)   CLUMP! CLUMP! CLUMP!

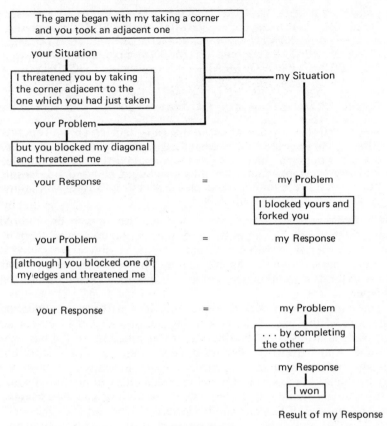

Figure 5.10

(8) He walked into the butcher's shop. (9) CRASH went the door as he opened it. (10) BANG went the door as he shut it! (11) 'I'D LIKE A PIECE OF MEAT,' boomed Mr Noisy to Mr Bacon the butcher. (12) Mr Bacon trembled, and sold him some meat. (13) Afterwards, Mrs Crumb met Mr Bacon in the street. (14) 'We really must do something about Mr Noisy being so noisy,' she said.[5]

Mrs Crumb has an answer which is revealed to Mr Bacon but not to the reader. The story continues:

5.10 (*b*) (15) The following day Mr Noisy again went shopping down to Wobbletown. (16) CLUMP! CLUMP! CLUMP! (17) He went into Mr Crumb's shop. (18) 'I'D LIKE A LOAF OF BREAD,' he boomed. (19) 'Sorry! What did you say?' asked Mrs Crumb, pretending not to hear. (20) 'I'D LIKE A LOAF OF BREAD!!' Mr Noisy shouted. (21) 'Sorry,' said Mrs Crumb, putting her hand to her ear. (22) 'Can you speak up, please!' (23) 'I'D . . . LIKE . . . A . . . LOAF . . . OF . . . BREAD!!!' roared Mr Noisy. (24) 'Can't hear you,' replied Mrs Crumb. (25) Mr Noisy gave up, and went out. (26) Mr Noisy went into Mr Bacon's shop. (27) 'I'D LIKE A PIECE OF MEAT,' he boomed. (28) Mr Bacon pretended not to notice. (29) 'I'D LIKE A PIECE OF MEAT!!' Mr Noisy shouted. (30) 'Did you say something?' asked Mr Bacon. (31) 'I . . . SAID . . . I'D . . . LIKE . . . A . . . PIECE . . . OF . . . MEAT!!!' roared Mr Noisy. (32) 'Pardon?' said Mr Bacon. (33) Mr Noisy gave up. (34) And went out. (35) And went home. (36) And went to bed. (37) Hungry! (38) The day after Mr Noisy tried again. (39) He went into Mrs Crumb's shop. (40) 'I'D LIKE A LOAF OF BREAD,' he boomed. (41) 'A what?' asked Mrs Crumb. (42) Mr Noisy started shouting at the very top of his voice. (43) 'A . . . LOAF . . . OF . . .' and then he stopped. (44) And then he thought. (45) And then he said quietly, 'I'd like a loaf of bread please Mrs Crumb.' (46) Mrs Crumb smiled. (47) 'Certainly,' she said.

Mr Noisy then visits Mr Bacon's shop and attempts to use the old noisy methods of buying meat once more without success; learning from his experience with Mrs Crumb, he tries a quieter voice and is promptly served. Finally, having acquired the habit of quietness, Mr Noisy extends it to other areas of his life, learning even to tiptoe and whisper.

The story is essentially a simple one. It is perhaps an indication therefore of the size of the task facing the discourse analyst that no complete analysis could be offered, at this juncture, of the passages quoted. Apart from the obvious difficulty that not all the story has been given because of the exigencies of space and copyright, there are also problems in accounting for dialogue elements within a monologue. A full analysis would require reference to something like the exchange structure model of Sinclair and Coulthard (1975) and Coulthard and Brazil (1979) and to the rules of interaction proposed by Labov and Fanshel (1977). Furthermore, it could not be taken for granted that approaches to the analysis of conversation suitable for real dialogue would be necessarily appropriate to a simulated re-creation. Consequently a careful transference and adaptation would have to take place before any use could be made of them. Since the focus of this work has throughout been on monologue, we have taken the opportunity of side-stepping these problems and concentrating only on those matters of organisation that most concern the argument we are developing.

We can divide the passages quoted into three sections – sentences 1–14, sentences 15–37 and sentences 38–47 – which represent three stages in the development of the plot. In the first stage Mr Noisy has no Problem but he is one to Mrs Crumb and Mr Bacon, signalled among other ways by the Need ('must') to 'do something about' the noise he makes, and (in a sentence omitted from the quoted passages) by reference to Mrs Crumb's idea as 'the answer', a classic two-way signal of Problem and Response.

In the second stage, a Problem is created for Mr Noisy as a Response to the Problem of Mr Noisy's noisiness. As yet, however, no positive effect has been achieved; we have now therefore two unresolved Problems. For Mrs Crumb and Mr Bacon, Mr Noisy remains a Problem, while Mr Noisy has the Problem of making himself heard so as to buy food. The latter is signalled in several ways. First his Need to buy food (shown by his repeated 'I'd like') is not met (he goes to bed *hungry*). Secondly, sentences 25 and 33 inform us that he 'gave up'; 'give up' is a signal of negative Evaluation of an action as unsuccessful and thereby (re-)signals Problems. (The *Concise Oxford Dictionary* gives as one of its definitions of 'give up': 'to pronounce . . . insoluble'). Thirdly, 'tried again' in sentence 38 signals that the previous attempt was unsuccessful.

The above analysis is loose in so far as it merges the sequence of incidents in the second stage into one. Let us now tighten it up slightly. In sentence 18 we have a statement of a Problem (wanting a loaf of bread) and the normal Response by Mr Noisy to that Problem of asking a shopkeeper for what he wants. In sentence 19, the Response is seen to have been unsuccessful, thereby instating 'getting heard' as a Problem. Sentence 20 sees Mr Noisy attempt to solve that Problem by raising his voice, symbolised by an additional exclamation mark and the replacement of 'boomed' by 'shouted'. This is likewise unsuccessful. Sentence 23 describes Mr Noisy's attempt to solve his Problem by raising his voice still more; 'shouted' is replaced by 'roared' and a further exclamation mark is added together with the separation of each word of his utterance by three stops. Sentence 24 shows this Response to have been no more successful, at which point Mr Noisy, in the words of the *Concise Oxford*, 'declares' his Problem 'insoluble' and leaves the shop. The same pattern is repeated in sentences 26–34 with the same progression of boomed–shouted–roared, the same increment of orthographic signals of loudness, and the same outcome.

So much for Mr Noisy's Problem. We must now turn to that of Mrs Crumb and Mr Bacon. We are shown that their behaviour in pretending not to hear Mr Noisy is their Response to the Problem of Mr Noisy's noisiness in two main interrelating ways. First, since 'must do something about' and 'answer' are both two-way signposts pointing forward to Response as well as back to Problem, a strong expectation is set up for a following Response. In the absence of an explicit statement of Response, we interpret any variation in the behaviour of those who are expected to respond as (part of) the waited-for Response. Mrs Cumb's and Mr Bacon's newly acquired deafness meets that criterion.

The second way in which Response is signalled is by the use of the word 'pretend' in sentences 19 and 28. There are two important elements to the meaning of this word: it denotes a conscious action and one which is a deviation from the customary (or at least desirable) mode of behaviour of people in their dealings with each other. The latter element reinforces the variation in behaviour interpreted as Response; the former, an essential component of its meaning (one cannot unintentionally pretend), carries with it the assumption of a purpose behind it. Since no purpose is explicitly mentioned, we read the earlier stated need to 'do something about Mr Noisy being so noisy' as the purpose. This inevitably leads us again in an interpretation of their actions as Response.

In the third stage, we have a complex resolution of both Mr Noisy's and Mrs Crumb and Mr Bacon's Problems. That we are about to have described another Response by Mr Noisy is signalled, as has already been noted with reference to his previous failure, by 'tried again' in sentence 38. Sentence 47 shows the Problem of not being heard to have been successfully resolved, and a later sentence (not quoted) refers to Mr Noisy 'carrying his bread and his meat' showing that the Problem of getting food has as a consequence also been successfully resolved. That Mrs Crumb and Mr Bacon's Response has likewise met with success is shown by the contrast between 'noisy' and 'quiet'(ly) in sentence 14 where the Problem is stated and sentence 45 where Mr Noisy is shown to use a different method to make himself heard. It is also shown in two general Evaluations not included in the passages quoted, to the effect that Mr Noisy 'isn't anything like as noisy as he used to be' and that 'the people of Wobbletown are delighted – especially Mrs Crumb and Mr Bacon'.

As before, it is possible to break down further the parts of our analysis. Sentence 40 shows Mr Noisy responding as before to his Problem with the same lack of success (sentence 41). He responds by raising his voice as high as he can (sentence 42), abandons this Response mid-way and employs instead an alternative (sentence 45) which meets with success. An identical sequence of events is then described as happening in Mr Bacon's shop (omitted from the passages cited) culminating in the same alternative Response and the same profitable outcome.

The organisation of this discourse can be represented as in Figure 5.11. Again, it should be noted that the diagram is basically simple, built as it is out of a number of recurring elements.

In the discussion that has preceded, it may at times have appeared that our analysis was no longer of the language but of the actions of the fictional characters. This is not, however, the case. Every statement made was translatable into an unambiguously linguistic form. The linguistic evidence for each Problem and Response (of which of course only a representative sample was given) was of the same kind as that used and discussed in Chapters 3 and 4. The difference lay in the clear connection of those signals with the characters. Thus 'must do some-

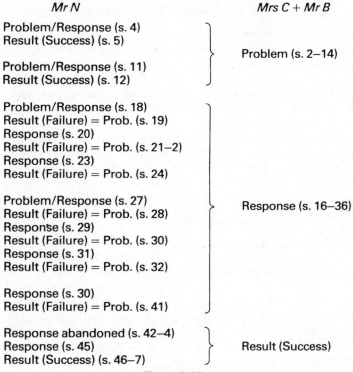

Figure 5.11

thing about' and 'answer' are signals placed in the mouths of Mrs Crumb and Mr Bacon, and 'I'd like', a signal placed in the mouth of Mr Noisy. Similarly 'gave up', 'tried again', 'boomed', 'shouted', 'roared', 'said quietly', and 'carrying his bread and his meat' all have as their agent Mr Noisy, as does 'pretend' Mrs Crumb and Mr Bacon. In short, the signals are linguistically related to a participant or participants within the discourse.

We are now in a position to explain why we said that the negative Evaluations in sentences 9 and 10 of 'The Princess and the Pea' do not signal Problem. In one sense they do – but for the princess, not the prince whose Problem has hitherto been the focus of attention. Since we are primarily interested in the solution to the latter Problem, we do not look for (and do not get) a clearly marked Response to the princess's Problem, though one is assumed in sentence 15.

9 The Nature of Attribution in Discourse

Our method of presentation may have given the impression that the participant-linking of Problem–Solution elements is a feature limited to fictional (or quasi-fictional) discourses only. This is not, however, the case. All discourses organised on a Problem–Solution pattern have participant-linking to some degree, though it is not always apparent. One reason for its invisibility is that narrative accounts are frequently written exclusively from one point of view. Thus our made-up sentry example in Chapter 3 is strictly speaking a Problem–Solution pattern in which, as told, the Problem is 'my' Problem and the Response 'my' Response. The questions that elicit the sentences as offered should really be:

What was the situation that I was in?
What was the problem I faced?
What was my response?
What was the result of my response?
or
How successful from my point of view was it?

Where, however, no ambiguity can arise, nor organisational knots otherwise occur, there is nothing lost in omitting references to the sole or dominant participant. Another example, this time a real one, of a discourse organised on (a variant of) the Problem–Solution pattern with one main participant is the Kafka story, 'The Burrow', discussed in section 2 of this chapter.

Another reason for the inconspicuousness of participant-linking in many discourses is that the Problem elements of such discourses are often couched in general terms. Examples of this can be found in **4.1**,

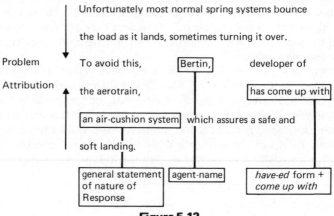

Figure 5.12

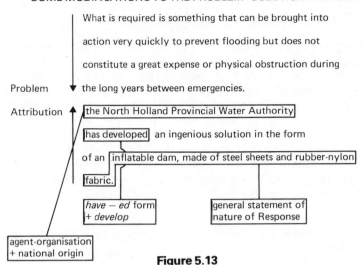

Figure 5.13

4.10, **5.1** and **5.6**. Whereas the Problems may be presented generally, however, Responses are usually specific to one participant or group of participants. This manifests itself, particularly in scientific discourses and advertisements, as attribution. Attribution introduces the Response element of a discourse where the Response is not the author's own. It is used to assign responsibility for some suggested or adopted Response.

It is signalled in a number of ways. First, its position is normally immediately adjacent to that of Problem. Secondly, the sentence contains an agent which is either a person's name or the name of an organisation (or both). This is usually coupled with a statement of national origin or place-name (or both). Thirdly, the verb of an attribution sentence is normally of the 'have-ed' form and is one of a set of items including 'develop', 'build', 'construct', 'introduce', 'invent' and 'come up with'. As noted above, attribution regularly introduces the Response part of the discourse and very often contains a general statement of the nature of the Response to be described. In Figures 5.12 and 5.13 the attribution elements of **4.10** and another scientific report[6] are indicated and the various typical features circled.

Attribution normally occurs only where the developer(s) of the solution described is (are) either different from the author or a group of people of whom the author is but one. Except in advertising copy, we will not usually find an author introducing his own Response with an attribution sentence. (And even in advertising, the copywriter and the advertiser are not strictly identical.) Attribution sentences answer the question 'Who has made a response?' or more naturally, 'Who has developed a solution?'.

10   Participant-Linking in Advertisements

As was remarked in the previous section, attribution can occur (though not all that frequently) in advertisements. An example is seen in Figure 5.14.[7] The only feature that separates this example from those discussed in Section 9 is the absence of a personal name or a name of an organisation in agent role in the attribution sentence. (Subsequent paragraphs do not supply the reference for 'we'.)

Though these examples are far from isolated, most advertisements do not however introduce their product as Response with an attribution. In many cases, we have instead a formulation of Response such that the reader is advised/instructed by means of an imperative or interrogative clause. We had an example of this in **5.1**, repeated here for convenience:

> **5.11**   To avoid this condition, use Inter-dens Gum Massage Sticks regularly.

Other examples are:

> **5.12**   Too many things in life cause tension, creating headaches, aches, pains and fatigue. Come home to, lean on, relax with the one thousand soothing fingers inside our simulated fur Vibrelax cushion.[8]
> **5.13**   When you've a film to be developed and you're wondering where to take it [Aspect of Situation requiring a Response] – take it to Boots.[9]

The important point to notice about these Responses is that they answer a slightly different question to those answered in earlier discourses. Instead of answering questions such as 'What response has been made?' or 'What response can be made?' they answer the question. 'What response can I make?'. In other words there is participant-linking in the Response element. The Response is not general but a

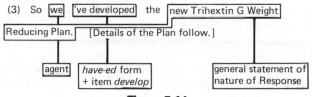

(1)   Many people have a weight problem at some time or other.

(2)   And it takes a lot of willpower to enjoy a stick of celery

as much as a plate of chips.

(3)   So we 've developed the new Trihextin G Weight Reducing Plan.   [Details of the Plan follow.]

agent   *have-ed* form + item *develop*   general statement of nature of Response

Figure 5.14

particular Response for 'you', the reader. In **5.12**, for example, we have a very general statement of Problem followed by a Response couched in imperative form which answers the specific question 'What can I do about the tension caused by so many things in life?'. It should be noted that the second sentence of **5.12** is incapable of answering a general question such as 'What can be done about the tension caused by so many things in life?'.

Sometimes the personalisation of advertisements is not restricted to Response only. On occasion, the Problem also is linked to the reader as potential participant. Thus in **5.13**, the Problem is worded 'When you've a film to be developed and *you*'re wondering where to take it'; the question it answers is (excluding the 'when') 'What is sometimes a problem for me?' thus leading naturally into the personal Response in imperative form.

We have seen that both Problem and Response are always implicitly or explicitly participant-linked. There is thus a stylistic choice to be made in each discourse as to whether the linking should be made explicit or not. The knack of the advertisement is to make the Response personal to the reader even though the formulation of the Problem may be quite impersonal. The imperative form is one way in which this can be economically achieved.

11 Summary of Chapter 5

In this chapter the following modifications have been made to the generalisations about Problem–Solution patterns given in previous chapters:

(1) Only a positive evaluation of a Response will satisfactorily 'round off' a discourse unless the Response is projected or recommended rather than a past fact.

(2) Multilayering is a common phenomenon in the organisation of discourse and is built upon the fact that a negative evaluation is a signal of Problem.

(3) There are three types of multilayering that overlap with each other: chained multilayering where each Response results in a different Problem, spiral multilayering where each Response leaves the same Problem unsolved, and progressive multilayering where each Response solves part of the Problem but leaves another part of it unsolved.

(4) A Problem or a Response may be linked to a particular participant by linguistic means; that is, a Problem for x, a Response by x (or y) for x.

(5) In principle there may be as many Problem–Solution patterns as there are participants.

(6)   In some discourses participant-linking to a Response may take the special form of attribution which answers the question 'Who has made a response?'

(7)   In advertisements participant-linking to a Response may take the special form of an imperative.

Chapter 6

Matching Patterns

1 Other Types of Discourse Pattern

In the last three chapters we have concentrated almost all of our attention on discourses organised on the Problem–Solution pattern. Although the Problem–Solution pattern is of considerable importance in discourse analysis and, as we have seen, is a popular form for a wide range of types of written discourse, it does not apply to all discourses equally well nor does it account for all the material in those discourses to which it does apply. In this and the next chapter we shall examine several other important types of pattern that can be used to organise discourses and we will show how these explain the existence of some discourses and flesh out our understanding of others.

We began our discussion of the Problem–Solution pattern in Chapter 3 by considering a simple, short example. In the same way the patterns introduced in this chapter are discussed with the assistance of short passages only. During the chapter, however, the principles are established whereby the patterns may be identified and the means suggested whereby they may be used in combination to build up larger stretches of discourse. In Chapter 7 we will then consider their applicability to longer and more complex passages and discourses.

2 Types of Repetition

Repetition was discussed in Chapter 2 as one of the key signalling devices available for the setting up of relations and thereby for the patterning of discourse. Yet we have made very little use of it in our description so far. Lexical signalling, questions and paraphrases have all been extensively employed to reveal Problem–Solution patterns but repetition has been used only in a minor supportive role at best. Repetition is however an important signalling device of Matching and General–Particular relations and must therefore be considered in some detail.

There are several types of connection between parts of a discourse that we shall want to subsume under the general heading of repetition.

(a)   Simple Repetition

By simple repetition is meant the straightforward repeating of a lexical item that has appeared earlier in a discourse, with no more alteration than is explicable by reference to grammatical paradigms. For example, in 6.1 below, 'fluctuation' and 'trend' are both instances of simple repetition, since the only alteration in the repeated form is the loss of the plural suffix -s.

> **6.1**   In circumstances such as these, fluctuations and trends are apt to become confused. How can one tell if an apparent pre-seasonal fluctuation is in fact the beginning of an expected fluctuation occurring earlier than usual or whether it is evidence of a new trend?[1]

Similarly, in **6.2** the repetition of 'tearing' as 'tore' is simple, since the difference in form is explainable entirely in terms of the grammatical difference between a non-finite and a finite verb-phrase.

> **6.2**   There it remained in the darkness, the great pain, tearing him at times, and then being silent. And when it tore him he crouched in silent subjection under it, and when it left him alone again, he refused to know of it.[2]

We exclude from the category of simple repetition any instance of accidental repetition, that is, where there is neither co-reference nor any discernible relation. So, for example, in the following made-up example, the second use of 'reason' is not a repetition of the first:

> **6.3**   No faculty of the mind is more worthy of development than the reason. It alone renders the other faculties worth having. The reason for this is simple.

(b)   Complex Repetition

Not all instances of lexical repetition are as straightforward as those we have just examined. If two items apparently share a morpheme and can be paraphrased in context in such a way that a paraphrase of one of the words contains the other, we can say that the second item is a complex repetition of the first. An instance is given in **6.4**.

6.4   Edith had danced herself into that tired, dreamy state habitual only with debutantes, a state equivalent to the glow of a noble soul after several long highballs. Her mind floated vaguely on the bosom of her music; her partners changed with the unreality of phantoms under the colourful shifting dusk and to her present coma it seemed as if days had passed since the dance began.[3]

It is apparent in this example that 'danced' and 'dance' share a morpheme, but it is also apparent that the difference between them is not explicable in terms of a grammatical paradigm. 'Dance' can, however, be defined in this context as a 'gathering at which one dances', and is therefore a complex repetition of the verb 'danced'.

Complex repetition frequently involves a change of grammatical class, so, for instance, in **6.4** 'dance' (noun) repeats 'danced' (verb). It is possible, however, to have complex repetition without such a change in class, for example, 'fool' (noun) might be repeated by 'foolishness' (noun); or 'wise' (adjective) might be repeated as 'unwise' (adjective).

(c)   Substitution

Up to this point, our discussion of repetition has not differed significantly from that of Halliday and Hasan (1976). They, however, treat substitution as a different type of cohesive feature from repetition, whereas we here treat it as a subclass of repetition. The reason for this is simple. Halliday and Hasan are concerned to classify the variety of means available for providing cohesion to a discourse, whereas we are concerned to bring together any cohesive features which serve the same organisational and relational functions. The difference of presentation should be seen therefore as representing little more than a difference of purpose.

Under the heading substitution we include personal pronouns (he, she, it, one, etc.), demonstrative pronouns (this, that, etc.), demonstrative adverbs (there, then, etc.), and the proverb 'do' with or without 'so'. Since all these features are fully discussed in other works, one example will suffice.

6.5   Parallel action, reminding the spectator of the simultaneous development of two or more events, is a familiar method of dramatic *intensification* possible only in cinema. Like close-up, it was first fully exploited by D. W. Griffith.[4]

(d)   Ellipsis

Ellipsis (or deletion) occurs when the structure of one sentence is incomplete and the missing element(s) can be recovered from a previous sentence unambiguously. It is more common in speech than in writing. An example is the following, from a taped conversation:

> **6.6**   A: What would you do if you learnt you had won a thousand pounds?
> B: ∅ Think about it a lot.[5]

The ellided elements indicated by the ∅ are unambiguously 'I' derived from 'you' and the change of role in the interaction, and 'would' derived from the 'would' of the question.

(e)   Paraphrase

Finally, we treat as repetition all instances of paraphrase. It is possible to subdivide paraphrase in a number of ways. We are concerned primarily with simple and complex paraphrase. Simple paraphrase can be said to occur whenever one of two items can substitute for another in a particular context with no discernible change in meaning. If this works only one way, that is, *a* can replace *b* but *b* cannot replace *a*, then we call it simple partial paraphrase; if it works both ways in a context, then we call it simple mutual paraphrase. An example of the latter is the following:

> **6.7**   The Transport and General Workers' Union, which represents over 70 per cent of the workforce at Leyland, is opposed to centralised wage bargaining, because it would end local plant bargaining and open up pay differentials between skilled workers and the production workers, most of whom are in the TGWU. It is highly unlikely that a majority of the TGWU will change their minds on pay bargaining by Tuesday.[6]

Although in other contexts the criterion of mutual (or even partial) interchangeabilty for this pair of lexical items might not be met, in this context there can be no doubt that it is met.

Complex paraphrase occurs in similar circumstances to complex repetition, and, as with complex repetition, often involves a change in grammatical class. It can be said to exist whenever one of the items can be paraphrased within the context in such a way as to include the other; in this respect it can be compared with complex repetition, the difference lying in the absence of a shared morpheme. As with simple paraphrase, it can be mutual or partial.

An example of complex partial paraphrase can be found in **6.8**:

6.8 There will, indeed, always be a theory, since man is a theory-making animal; but the theory is always something invented ⌐afterwards⌐ to fit the facts; it is not the reason which directed their production. It is rather like the 'rationalizations' which psychologists speak of when a man who has performed an action from irrational, perhaps unconscious, motives seeks to justify to himself what he has done by ascribing it to a rational purpose. In such a case the reasoning seems to be the motive which has produced the act, but in reality the act has given birth to the reasoning. According to the Marxian doctrine, the political theories are 'rationalizations' of a similar kind, being secondary and ⌐subsequent⌐ to the political facts they pretend to justify.[7]

In this example, 'afterwards' can be paraphrased as 'at a subsequent time', but no shared morpheme is present, and 'subsequent' cannot be paraphrased by any phrase containing 'afterwards'.

Examples of complex mutual paraphrase on the other hand can be found in **6.9**:

6.9 (1) Fred and Ted were friends.

(2) Fred was ⌐big⌐.

(3) Ted was ⌐little⌐.

(4) Ted ⌐was⌐always⌐broke⌐.

(5) Fred always ⌐had money⌐.

(6) When they walked in the rain, Fred ⌐got wet⌐but Ted⌐stayed dry⌐.

(7) They both like music.

(8) Fred played the flute.

(9) Ted played the tuba.

(10) When they had dinner, Fred ate the spinach ... and Ted ate the beetroots.

(11) When they painted the house, Ted used red paint.

(12) Fred used green.

(13) One day Fred and Ted took a trip.

(14) Fred went in his green car.

(15) Ted went in his red car.

(16) Fred drove his car ⌐slowly⌐.

(17) Ted drove his car ⌐fast⌐.[8]

'Big' and 'little' have no morpheme in common but can be paraphrased in terms of each other: 'big' – 'far from little', 'little' – 'not at all big'. Likewise 'slowly' and 'fast' can be respectively paraphrased as 'far from fast' and 'far from slowly'. Other examples of complex mutual paraphrase from this passage are 'was . . . broke' and 'had money', and 'got wet' and 'stayed dry'. Most true antonyms can be handled in this way; cultural opposites, however, such as 'red' and 'green', cannot be so treated. (We will return to **6.9** in Section 4.)

Up to this point we have discussed paraphrase as essentially operating at word or phrase level. We shall have occasion elsewhere, however, to refer to paraphrase at clause or multiple clause level. For example, take the two sentences 'The way things appear to one man is the truth for him' and 'If one sees things in one way, then that is the way they are for him'.[9] In the original context these two sentences are intended by the writer to be rewordings of each other. A technique must therefore be used to show the extent to which they are equivalent. The method to be used here is interchangeability discussed above. If two sentences or clauses are interchangeable in both directions, then we have mutual paraphrase, and if they are interchangeable without alteration (for example, without the addition or removal of negation), then we have simple paraphrase. In the example above, we can show the two sentences to be close in meaning as follows:

6.10   A: (the first original sentence) The ways things appear to one
man . . .
B: If things appear to one man one way, that way is . . .
C: If one man sees things one way, that way is . . .
D: (the second original sentence) If one sees things in one way,
(then) that (way) is . . .

It is not maintained that the main clauses of both sentences are identical, nor is it maintained that the subordinate clauses discussed above would be identical in all contexts. It is however maintained that in this context they are. In short, we make no distinction between paraphrase at word or phrase level (as illustrated in **6.8** and **6.9**) and paraphrase at clause or sentence level (as in **6.10**). Where two clauses are mutually interchangeable, we treat them as mutual paraphrases. Where the changes involve some alteration to the grammatical shape of the sentences we treat them as complex paraphrases. The presence of some repetition between the two clauses is not taken to affect their status as paraphrases.

3   The Matching Relation

The reason that we have dwelt in so much detail on the various manifestations of repetition in English is that repetition is a key signal of the Matching relation, and the Matching relation is essential for a fuller understanding of discourse organisation. As was briefly mentioned in Chapter 2, Matching is what happens when two parts of a discourse are compared in respect of their detail. Sometimes they are matched for similarity, in which case we call the resulting relation Matching Compatibility, and sometimes for difference, in which case we call the resulting relation Matching Contrast. Whether the differences are highlighted or the similarities depends on a number of factors, many of which will be noted in this and subsequent sections.

Repetition is not the only means used to signal a Matching relation. In the course of our discussion of Matching we will find examples of signalling by conjuncts, syntactic and semantic parallelism, lexical signals and parallelism of questions answered. Nevertheless, repetition is perhaps the clearest signal of Matching, and it is therefore with repetition that we begin our discussion of this relation.

In **6.11** below we have a good example of the use of systematic repetition:

> **6.11** It is interesting to note that iconic models only represent certain features of that portion of the real world which they simulate. For example, a map will only contain those features which are of interest to the person using the map. Similarly, architects' models will be limited to include only those features which are of interest to the person considering employing the architect.[10]

The repetition in this example, though heavy, is not superfluous; its function is to focus attention on the new information in the sentence by putting it in the context of known information. In other words, the repetition is used to show what the information in one sentence has in common with that in previous sentences. This becomes clearer if we set out the second and third sentences of **6.11** as in Table 6.1.

We have here a demonstration of the interlocking functions of repetition and 'replacement'. The repetition acts as a frame for highlighting the new information which 'replaces' the old information. In

Table 6.1

For example	a map	will only contain	those features which are of interest to	the person using the map
Similarly	architects' models	will be limited to include only	those features which are of interest to	the person considering employing the architect
	replacement	repetition (paraphrase)	repetition	replacement

Table 6.2

(For example)	a map	will only contain	those features which are of interest to	the person using the map
(Similarly)	architects' models	will be limited to include only	those features which are of interest to	the person considering employing the architect
constant	iconic model	repetition (paraphrase)	repetition	person with purpose in mind
variable	type of iconic model			nature of purpose

this case, 'architects' models' replaces 'a map', and 'the person considering employing the architect' replaces 'the person using the map'. (The term 'replacement' does not imply, of course, that the old information necessarily ceases to be valid.)

Although the information 'architects' models' and 'the person considering employing the architect' is in one sense new and replaces that in the previous sentence, in another sense it is by no means entirely different from what it replaces. An architect's model is different from a map but they are both iconic models. A person using a map and a person considering employing an architect are alike not only in their 'person-ness' but also in their desire to make use of something. We may conclude that every replacement is made up of a constant (what it shares with the information it replaces) and a variable (where it differs from the information it replaces). Repetition of course is constant without variable. We can now redraw Table 6.1 as Table 6.2.

One of the uses of systematic repetition in speech and writing is to connect sentences in such a way that they are understood as sharing a particular meaning. In Table 6.2 we see that the latter sentence's function is the dual one of on the one hand pointing up the differences between the two types of iconic model and on the other hand revealing the similarities between them. The two sentences are said in such a situation to be 'matched'.

In the case of **6.11**, a number of factors show that the similarities between sentences 2 and 3 are being highlighted, not the differences. We have the presence of the conjunct 'similarly'. We have the influence of the context which shows that sentences 2 and 3 are both illustrations of the same point and therefore obviously compatible. (We shall return to this point in much more detail in Chapter 7.) We have the ability to insert comparative affirmation paraphrases such as 'The same is true of x' or 'What was true of y is true of x'; thus we can have (omitting conjuncts and slightly altering verb forms):

6.12 A map only contains those features which are of interest to the person using the map. The same is true of architects' models. Architects' models are limited to include only those features which are of interest to the person considering employing the architect.

We are able also to project the sentence pair into dialogue form employing either the broad request 'Compare *x* with *y* in respect of *z*' or the broad question 'Is what is true of *x* also true of *y*?'.

> **6.13** D: A map only contains those features which are of interest to the person using the map.
> Q: Compare architects' models with maps in this respect.
> D: Architects' models are [likewise] limited to include only those features which are of interest to the person considering employing the architect.

All these factors make the relation between sentences 2 and 3 in **6.11** unmistakably one of Matching Compatibility, not Contrast. Further examples of Matching Compatibility will be found later in this chapter.

Tables such as Table 6.2 are invaluable for demonstrating the existence of Matching relations of either type. Many Matching relations, however, cannot be represented in this form because of a lack of grammatical parallelism or because the two parts of the relation are each longer than a sentence. In such cases, the key clues to the relation are of the sort illustrated above:

(i) Do they answer the same question *vis-à-vis* a previous sentence in the discourse?

(ii) Does the second part answer the broad requests/questions 'Compare/contrast *x* with *y* in respect of *z*' or 'Is what is true of *x* (not) also true of *y*?' or 'Is what is true of *x* at one stage (not) also true of *x* at another stage?'

(iii) Can they be connected by the appropriate conjuncts or comparative affirmation/denial paraphrases? (More details of the latter will be found in the next section.)

On some occasions, of course, paraphrase can remove the problem of lack of grammatical parallelism; see our discussion of sentences 13 and 14 in **6.14** below, for example.

4 Some Examples of Matching Contrast

The only example of Matching we have looked at so far is that of a Compatibility relation. In **6.14** below will be found three examples where Contrast rather than Compatibility is indicated. The passage is comparing potassium with sodium (which has just been described) and is contrasting the behaviour of the two elements with that of the other elements. Sentences, as always in long passages, are numbered for convenience of reference, and the contrasts we shall be discussing are in italics.

6.14   (1) Potassium is a soft metal, so light that like sodium it floats on water. (2) It is even higher than sodium in the electromotive series, so while sodium decomposes in water with great energy and rusts very quickly, potassium surpasses it in both these respects.

(3) After sodium has acted upon water, the hydroxide (NaOH) remains in solution. (4) The result with potassium is similar, the hydroxide in this case having the formula KOH. (5) We have already noted that *while the hydroxides of most metals are either insoluble in water or slightly soluble, those of both sodium and potassium are extremely soluble.* (6) The solutions feel soapy, and are strongly alkaline to litmus. (7) *Carbonates are usually decomposed by heat, carbon dioxide being evolved and the oxide of the metal remaining behind.* (8) Thus with calcium carbonate –

$$CaCo_3 = CaO + CO_2$$

(9) Here again sodium and potassium stand apart. (10) *Their carbonates are not decomposed even when heated in the electric furnace.* (11) Let us next glance at the bicarbonates, $NaHCO_3$ and $KHCO_3$. (12) The unusual feature here is *that these bicarbonates are sufficiently stable to exist in the solid condition* [also italicised in original]. (13) *Other bicarbonates are so unstable that they exist only in solution.* (14) Calcium bicarbonate is an example, and *many metals are unable to form a bicarbonate even in a solution.*[11]

There are a number of means available for demonstrating the existence of a Matching Contrast relation. These include, as has already been mentioned, the presence or potential presence of an appropriate conjunct (for example, however, by contrast, on the other hand), the presence of antonyms or appropriate negation, and the presence of signalling in the immediate context. A further means of demonstrating Contrast is to use what Winter (1974) calls the denial paraphrase. In his words, 'this means denying an attribute or action of x for the compared y'. There are a number of ways in which the denial of an attribute or action can be paraphrased. Among the versions Winter (1974) employs are, for the pair of sentences 'She is nice. He is nasty',

(i)   She is nice. *He is not nice.* He is nasty.
(ii) She is nice. *The same is not true of him.* He is nasty.
(iii) She is nice. *The opposite is true of him.* He is nasty.

In each the denial paraphrase is placed between the two sentences in such a way as to spell out the relation that holds between them. The form of the denial paraphrases is not the same in each case, however. In (*i*) the denial repeats the lexical items of the first sentence with the addition of a negative element. There is therefore a Matching relation between 'she is nice' and 'he is not nice'. On the other hand, in (*ii*) and (*iii*) the denial paraphrase takes the form of a signalling sentence such as we discussed and found examples of in Chapters 4, 5 and 6. More particularly, it takes the form of an Evaluation of the truth of what is said about the first sentence when applied to the subject of the second. That the denial paraphrases do not function in quite the same way can be demonstrated by placing both types of denial between the two sentences:

(*iv*) She is nice. The same is not true of him. He is not nice. He is nasty.

Although (*iv*) is heavily marked, it is not impossible, thus showing that the two denials function in slightly different ways.

In the discussion that follows we shall use denial paraphrases, conjuncts, antonyms and negation to identify the Matching relations as Contrast. We shall not however use context at this point, as the importance of context will be discussed separately.

In **6.14** we find our first Matching Contrast within sentence 5, within the matrix clause 'we have already noted that . . .' (In the larger context, the matrix clause signals the repetition of information from earlier in the book.) We can represent the Matching of the two clauses within the matrix clause in tabular form as in Table 6.3.

That this Matching relation is one of Contrst is indicated in several ways. First, the first clause is subordinated by 'while' which in one of its uses is an indication of Contrast. (For other uses, see Chapter 3.)

Table 6.3

(while)	the hydroxides of	most metals	are	(either) insoluble	in water
				(or) only slightly soluble	∅
	those of	both sodium and potassium	are	extremely soluble	∅
constant:	repetition	metals	rep.	solubility	repetition
variable:		nearness to top of electromotive series		degree of solubility	

Secondly, we have the antonyms 'insoluble–soluble' and near-antonym 'only slightly–extremely' in the 'solubility' column. Thirdly, it is possible to insert a denial paraphrase between the two clauses, thus:

> **6.15** While the hydroxides of most metals are either insoluble in water or only slightly soluble, *the same is not true of those of sodium and potassium.* They are extremely soluble.

It should be noted that this paraphrase discounts the fact that sentence 5 is recapping information from earlier in the book; it would of course be most unusual to find an emphatic form such as that of **6.15** in the circumstance of a recap. It should also be noted that the paraphrase has converted part of one sentence into two complete sentences. This is further confirmation of the fact already noted in Chapter 3 that clause relations are no respecters of sentence boundaries. There we saw that one way of demonstrating the relations holding between four simple sentences was to convert them by means of subordinators into one complex sentence. Here we see the same process in reverse; to demonstrate the relation holding between the parts of (part of) a complex sentence, we have converted that sentence into two, one of them simple.

A Matching Contrast of a different type is represented by sentences 7 and 10. Here not only is the Contrast between two separate sentences and not two clauses of the same sentence, but the two sentences are not immediately adjacent. Again, we can represent the Matching of the two sentences in table form (see Table 6.4). The material in brackets does not enter into the Matching relation as such. The bracketed material in the first row gives the Consequence part of a Cause–Consequence relation, the Cause being the decomposition by heat.

Table 6.4

	Carbonates	are usually decomposed	by heat	(carbon dioxide being evolved and the oxide of the metal remaining behind)
	Their [ref. to sodium and potassium] carbonates	are not decomposed	when heated	(even . . . in the electric furnace)
constant	carbonates	decomposability	repetition (complex)	
variable	which metal the carbonate is derived from	whether decomposable		

(Sentence 8, omitted from the table, gives an example of this Consequence.) The bracketed material in the second sentence eliminates a potential exception to the preceding generalisation.

As before, we can demonstrate the Matching relation to be one of Contrast in several ways. Although we cannot insert a conjunct such as 'however' between the two parts of the Contrast because of the intervening sentences 8 and 9, if we remove these such a conjunct can be added so as to spell out the relationship between the two sentences. Furthermore, while there are no antonyms or near-antonyms in the sentence in the sentence pair, there is the equally significant presence of a direct negation in the second sentence of a part of the first. In other words the denial of an attribute of x for the compared y, elsewhere artificially introduced as a paraphrase test, here exists naturally. This is not unusual. In this case the attribute of 'decomposability by heat' which 'carbonates in general' have is denied for 'the carbonates of sodium and potassium' which are being compared with them.

All this would be sufficient by itself to show that the Matching relation between sentences 7 and 10 is one of Contrast. We have however one more piece of evidence that such is the case. Sentence 9 is a signalling sentence of a type similar to those discussed earlier in this section and elsewhere. We are told 'sodium and potassium stand apart'; 'stand apart' is a lexical signal of Exception (a subclass of Contrast). In the context it is a near-paraphrase of the denial types described earlier, differing from them only in specifying the Contrast as one of Exception. Little change occurs in the passage if we substitute denial paraphrase (*iii*) for sentence 9:

6.16 (7) Carbonates are usually decomposed by heat, carbon dioxide being evolved and the oxide of the metal remaining behind.

(8) Thus with calcium carbonate –

$$CaCO_3 = CaO + CO_2$$

(9) The opposite is true of sodium and potassium. (10) Their carbonates are not decomposed even when heated in the electric furnace.

As we have it both in 6.16 and in the original, sentence 7 is followed by a denial paraphrase of the signalling sentence type (sentence 9) and then by a denial of the repetition type (sentence 10). In other words, the original is a real example of pattern (*iv*) given above, without the final affirmative sentence.

It should be noticed that one change has occurred to sentence 9 in the substitution we have made; we have lost the adjunct/conjunct pair 'here again'. This is important because it has the function of indicating that the Contrast under discussion is in a Matching Compatibility

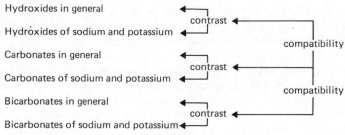

Figure 6.1

relation with the earlier Contrast in sentence 5. Informally, the pattern being set up can be shown as in Figure 6.1. There are a number of oversimplifications in this diagram, both because of omitted material and because the last pair, which we have yet to discuss, is in reverse order. Nevertheless in essence the diagram represents the organisation of the passage accurately, and 'here again' is an important signal of that larger organisation. The organisation represented in Figure 6.1 occurs quite frequently. For instance, the passage from 'Big Dog . . . Little Dog' cited as containing examples of complex mutual paraphrase (6.9) is organised on the same basis, statements being Compatible about the two dogs because always Contrastive by opposites (universal or cultural).

The third instance of Matching contrast in 6.14 is in the pair of sentences 12 and 13. As before we can demonstrate how they match in tabular form (see Table 6.5). A number of factors help identify the Matching relation as one of Contrast. To begin with, 'stable' and 'unstable' are clear-cut antonyms. Secondly, 'solid condition' and 'solution' are mutually exclusive alternatives out of a set of three. Thirdly, we can insert a denial paraphrase between the sentences

Table 6.5

(The unusual feature here is that)	these bicarbonates [i.e. $NaHCO_3$ and $KHCO_3$]	are sufficiently stable	to exist	in the solid condition
	other bicarbonates	are so unstable	that they exist	only in solution
Constant	bicarbonates	stability	repetition (complex)	physical state of existence
Variable	which metals the bicarbonates are formed from	degree of stability		which physical state

(The circled words in the table anticipate and are linked up with the material that follows.)

without affecting the relation between them. Fourthly, the first half of the Contrast is characterised as unusual and this unusualness is further emphasised by the italicising in the original of the relevant clause. The presence of the Evaluation 'unusual' signals a Contrast with the usual; it can be said to 'anticipate' the Contrast (Winter, 1974). Because of the presence of this signal, it is impossible to insert a conjunct of Contrast with any plausibility.

5 Contrast and Compatibility in Combination

In our discussion of the last pair in Section 4 we ignored an important fact about that part of the chemistry passage. Sentence 12 is not only in Matching Contrast with 13; it is also in Matching Contrast with the second half of sentence 14 – '*many metals are unable to form a bicarbonate even in a solution*'. Obviously the Matching cannot be shown by means of a table without some adjustment to one or other sentence, there being no clear parallelism between the two sentences. An adjustment can however be made quite easily; a complex paraphrase holds in this context between '*these bicarbonates are sufficiently stable to exist in the solid condition*' and '*These metals are able to form bicarbonates sufficiently stable to exist in the solid condition*'. Once we allow this paraphrase, sentences 12 and (the second half of) 14 can be compared in table form as before (see Table 6.6).

Contrast is shown by the antonyms 'able/unable' and the 'solid condition' versus 'solution' opposition, among other means. It is also possible to insert 'On the other hand' between the juxtaposed pair even in the original, as long as intervening clauses are omitted. We now have a position that can be represented as in Figure 6.2. As Figure 6.2 shows, this is not the complete story. For we must now consider the relationship that holds between 13 and the latter part of 14. A complex paraphrase is capable of bringing the two 'sentences' together more

Table 6.6

	These metals [i.e. sodium and potassium]	are able	to form bicarbonates	sufficiently stable to exist	in the solid condition
	Many metals	are unable	to form bicarbonates	[that can exist]	even in solution
Constant	metals	ability	repetition	repetition	physical state of existence
Variable	which metals	whether exists or not			which physical state

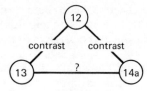

Figure 6.2

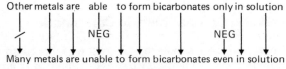

Figure 6.3

closely. '*Other bicarbonates are so unstable that they exist only in solution*' can be paraphrased in the context as 'Other metals are able to form bicarbonates only in solution'. This paraphrase loses some of the attention on the instability of 'other bicarbonates' but otherwise it is accurate. In Gopnik's (1972) terms, the latter is an included paraphrase of the former. (All sentence paraphrases interfere of course with the meanings conveyed by theme, focus, etc.; for our present purposes such interference can be ignored.) The test of the paraphrase's accuracy is as before interchangeability in the context; no claims are being made for the accuracy of the paraphrase out of context.

If we place the paraphrased sentence 13 next to the original 14 (second part), we see that the second is the direct opposite of the first, apart from the replacement of 'other' by 'many' (see Figure 6.3). 'Even' is the negation of 'only' because 'only' signals an exception. On the face of it, it looks as though we have a Contrast. If so, our diagram looks like that of Figure 6.4. In some contexts they might have been in Contrast; in this one, however, they are not. The main reason is the limiting quality of 'only' in 13. Sentence 13 tells us of a solitary condition under which some metals can form bicarbonates and sentence 14 of the absence of even that condition for other metals. Both sentences are therefore negative, the difference between them being one of degree, and they are therefore in a Compatibility relation. This can be further shown by the fact that a typical conjunct of Compatibility

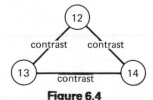

Figure 6.4

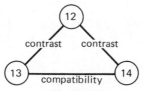

Figure 6.5

such as 'moreover' can be inserted between the two sentences as long
as the example that begins sentence 14 is first removed.

Of course, in addition to being in a Compatibility relation with each
other, sentences 13 and 14 are both in Contrast with sentence 12. Thus
we have a complex of relations that can be shown in diagram form (see
Figure 6.5).

As we have seen, the presence of 'only' in sentence 13 makes the
analysis of the relations of the three sentences clearer. Often however
where we have three sentences of this type together, the analysis is
more complex. A few years back there was a celebrated series of
comedy sketches shown on TV featuring three men, one upper-class
and tall, one middle-class and medium-sized, and one working-class
and short. The humour of the sketches came from the three men
comparing themselves with each other. In one sense, the middle-sized
man contrasted himself with both the taller and the shorter man. In
another, he was compatible with both. The reason is best explained in
a simple double diagram (see Figure 6.6). The same complexity of
relationships can and does occur in written language. So we have, for
example:

6.17 (1) There was a big bed, a middle-sized bed, and a teeny-tiny
bed in the corner.
  (2) 'Oh, how sleepy I am,' yawned Goldilocks and flung herself
on the big bed.
  (3) It was far too hard, however, so she climbed down and tried
the middle-sized bed. (4) That was far too soft, so Goldilocks
tried the teeny-tiny bed in the corner. (5) That was just right
and Goldilocks was soon fast asleep.[12]

Here the three Evaluations of the three beds can be said to set up a
complexity of relations similar to that in Figure 6.6. The independent

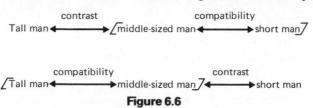

Figure 6.6

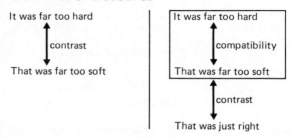

Figure 6.7

clauses that begin sentences 3 and 4 contrast by means of the antonym pair 'hard–soft', and they both contrast with the independent clause that begins sentence 5 by virtue of the negative Evaluations in the first two and the positive Evaluation in the last. We can represent them as in Figure 6.7. In short, sentence 4 answers the question 'In what respect did this bed differ from the other?'; sentence 5 answers the same questions but assumes a similarity between sentences 3 and 4. In the first case, the degree of hardness is contrasted; in the second, the degree of discomfort found to be alike.

6   Parallelism Without Repetition

Not all Matching relations are signalled by as much repetition as there has been in the examples we have examined so far. Occasionally they are not signalled by repetition as such at all but by grammatical and lexical parallelism. An example of a passage so signalled is the following:

> **6.18**   (1) Many simple observations in physics may be made by the naked eye, by touch or by ear. (2*a*) A blacksmith judges the temperature of hot iron by the colour of glowing metal, knowing that there is a relation between brightness of glow and degree of hotness; (2*b*) a railway mechanic tests for flaws in the metal of carriage wheels by the sound of his hammer blows; (2*c*) the piano tuner can tell the pitch of a musical note by ear; (2*d*) the photographer often judges lighting conditions by eye; (2*e*) and the spinning wheel worker judges the thickness of threads with great skill by touch.[13]

There are a number of points of difference between this passage and the others we have examined. The most striking of these is perhaps that already mentioned – the relative absence of lexical repetition. The Matching Compatibility relation is instead conveyed by paraphrase, syntactic repetition (that is, by the retention of the same grammatical shape for each sentence) and by the constants underlying the differ-

Table 6.7

	A blacksmith	judges	the temperature of hot iron	by the colour of the glowing metal,	(knowing that there is a relation between brightness of glow and degree of hotness);
	A railway mechanic	tests	for flaws in the metal of carriage wheels	by the sound of his hammer blows;	
	the piano tuner	can tell	the pitch of a musical note	by ear;	
	the photographer	(often) judges	lighting conditions	by eye;	
	the spinning wheel worker	gauges	the thickness of threads	(with great skill) by touch.	
constant	skilled workers	repetition (paraphrase)	the physical state of something	the use of a sense	
variable	types of skilled worker		types of physical state	types of sense	

ences. Because of the parallelism created by these means, the passage is amenable to analysis of the same kind as used in previous sections, as can be seen in Table 6.7.

Strictly speaking, we have oversimplified in the column with the constant 'use of a sense'. The material in this column subdivides into two, the first two rows having as their constant 'sensory impressions' and the last three having 'the use of a sense'. These constants have in turn the constant 'concerned with sensory impressions' and the variable 'emitter or receiver of sensory impressions'. However this subdivision adds little to our understanding of the way the passage holds together, so we may usefully ignore it.

7   Discourses Organised Using Matching Contrast

Matching relations are not used by themselves with anything like the same frequency as the Problem–Solution pattern to organise long complete discourses. One of the reasons for this is that the pressure is great when matching information to preface the information thus matched with a generalisation to make sense of the 'match'. Thus where we find Matching playing a significant role in the organisation of a discourse, we usually find it in conjunction with one of the General–Particular relations. The use of Matching in conjunction with General–Particular is discussed in the next chapter. Occasionally, however, short discourses such as letters and poems are organised by one of the Matching relations. The examples that follow are mostly of this sort.

The following poem is an example of a complete discourse structured by a Matching Contrast relation:

6.19

'Love seeketh not itself to please,
Nor for itself hath any care,
But for another gives its ease
And builds a Heaven in Hell's despair.'

5 So sung a little Clod of Clay,
Trodden with the cattle's feet;
But a Pebble of the brook
Warbled out these metres meet:

10 'Love seeketh only self to please,
To bind another to its delight,
Joys in another's loss of ease,
And builds a Hell in Heaven's despite.'[14]

Table 6.8

	A little Clod of Clay, Trodden with the cattle's feet,	sung	so: [anaphoric to lines 1–4]	Love	seeketh	not itself	to please
(But)	a Pebble of the brook	warbled out	these metres (meet) [cataphoric] to lines 9–12)	Love	seeketh	only self	to please
Constant	inanimate part of earth's surface	repetition (paraphrase in context)	repetition (both refer to verses)	rep.	rep.	object of pleasing	repetition
Variable	type of part					whether self or others	

Table 6.8 shows how the Matching is signalled by repetition: the Contrast is shown both by the 'but' that begins line 7 and by the negation in lines 1 and 9. Although strict symmetry disappears after the first lines of verses 1 and 3, Blake has further emphasised the Contrast by placing opposites in the same place in each verse. So we have (1. 3 and 1. 11) 'ease' and 'loss of ease', and (1. 5 and 1. 12) 'builds a Heaven' and 'builds a Hell'. This is further supplemented by the false opposition (1. 4 and 1. 12) of 'Hell's despair' and 'Heaven's despite'.

The example we have just been looking at is unusually symmetrical. Often one half of the structuring Contrast will dominate the other as in **6.20**:

6.20

I was angry with my friend:
I told my wrath, my wrath did end.
I was angry with my foe:
I told it not, my wrath did grow.

5 And I watered it in fears,
Night and morning with my tears;
And I sunned it with smiles,
And with soft deceitful wiles.

And it grew both day and night,
10 Till it bore an apple bright;
And my foe beheld it shine,
And he knew that it was mine,

And into my garden stole
When the night had veiled the pole:
15 In the morning glad I see
My foe outstretched beneath the tree.[15]

Because the two parts of the Matching relation are much larger than those we have hitherto analysed, we place the sentences of each paragraph side by side according to the questions they answer. The Contrast again stems from negation and near-opposites ('end'/'grow') (see Table 6.9). As presented in Table 6.9, the organisation is made to seem far less complex than it in fact is. A fuller stylistic analysis would for example note that the consequences of 'telling not his wrath' are such that 'telling it not' becomes (for the first-person 'persona') a full solution; not responding is in other words a Response. Furthermore a full analysis would discuss lines 5–9 as a Response to the problem 'my wrath did grow', the point being that this poem, like many others, is multi-patterned. Nevertheless, for our purposes, Table 6.9 clearly shows the Matching Contrast that holds between the first two lines and the remaining fourteen.

Letters are another type of discourse that sometimes are patterned

Table 6.9

What was the problem?	I was angry with my friend	I was angry with my foe
What was my response?	I told my wrath	(None) I told it not
What was the result?	My wrath did end	My wrath did grow. And I watered it in fears, Night and morning with my tears; and I sunned it with smiles, and with soft deceitful wiles. And it grew both day and night, Till it bore an apple bright; And my foe beheld it shine, And he knew that it was mine, And into my garden stole When the night had veiled the pole: In the morning glad I see My foe outstretched beneath the tree.

by a Matching Contrast relation. Winter (1974; 1979) has discussed their typical organisation. The reader should refer to those works for a more detailed method of analysis. Here a simple example will suffice to illustrate the type:

6.21   Sir,

(1) William Mann, in his review (January 30), of a concert from Manchester, wrote that I had the singer Ella Lee in mind when composing my Third Symphony. (2) I gather he heard this announced during the radio prologue to the broadcast.

(3) May I beg the courtesy of your columns to set the record straight? (4) The announcement was incorrect. (5) Indeed, rarely, if ever, have I had a particular performer in mind when composing a major work.

Yours,
Michael Tippett[16]

The contrast in this passage is between the claim made by William Mann in sentence 1 and Tippett's denial of the truth of that claim in sentence 5. The Matching can be shown as in Table 6.10. In addition to the open Contrast between 'I had in mind' and 'I have had rarely if ever in mind', there is a hidden Contrast between the overtly stated 'William Mann wrote that' and the implicit 'I write that'. This hidden Contrast between the originators of the statements is what Winter refers to as a Hypothetical-Real relation, so called because in the case of the first sentence the author (Tippett) merely reports what has been written and does not give it his assent as the truth. It remains therefore

Table 6.10

(William Mann, in his review [January 30] of a concert from Manchester wrote that)	I had in mind	the singer Ella Lee	when composing	my Third Symphony
(indeed)	I have had, rarely, if ever in mind	a particular performer	when composing	a major work
constant	I had in mind	a particular performer	repetition	a major work
variable	whether had or hadn't	example or not		example or not

Hypothetical. In the case of sentence 5, however, we are offered what the author himself believes to be the truth; this then, for the author, is the Real (and in this instance, who better to know?). This is a common pattern in letters and articles.

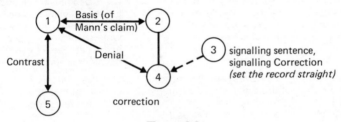

Figure 6.8

The overall organisation of Tippett's letter is shown in Figure 6.8, where 3 is outside the pattern, 2 provides a basis for Mann's claim, 4 denies the basis and by implication the claim, and 5 is a Correction of the denied claim. The trio Statement–Denial–Correction is of course essentially the same as that arrived at using the paraphrase test in Section 3; the only difference is that there x was contrasted with y in respect of z whereas here A's claim x in respect of z is being contrasted with B's claim y in respect of z.

8 Two Promises Fulfilled

Astute readers with long memories will perhaps have noticed that two promises made in Sections 2 and 4 of Chapter 1 have yet to be fulfilled. First, in Section 2 we described an experiment conducted by Winter using a jumbled ten-sentence discourse, and we promised to return to the discourse at a later stage to explain (*a*) the consensus about its organisation shown by the students who successfully unscrambled it, and (*b*) why a small number of wrong variants regularly occurred where almost all the several million other possibilities never occurred.

Secondly, we described an experiment by Young and Becker in which they showed a considerable measure of agreement amongst informants as to where paragraph breaks should come in a deparagraphed passage. The question that was left only partly answered was what it was that informants were responding to in the passage that led them to paragraph in a similar way. We are now in a position to fulfil both promises; we begin with the paragraphing passage.

The almost universal desire to place a paragraph break at line 13 of that passage was in part the result of a change of topic at that point, as was pointed out in Chapter 1. Another factor, however, that can only now be discussed, was that the passage was organised by matching. This can be seen clearly in Table 6.11, where it will be seen that the

Table 6.11

Was Grant/Lee the greatest general of the Civil War?	Grant was, judged by modern standards, the greatest general of the Civil War.	Lee is usually ranked as the greatest Civil War general, but this evaluation has been made without placing Lee and Grant in the perspective of military developments since the war.
How was Grant/ Lee as an over-all strategist?	He [Grant] was head and shoulders above any general on either side as an over-all strategist, as a master of what in later wars would be called global strategy. His Operation Crusher plan, the product of a mind which had received little formal instruction in the higher area of war, would have done credit to the most finished student of a series of modern staff and command schools.	Lee was interested hardly at all in 'global' strategy, and what few suggestions he did make to his government about operations in other theatres than his own indicate that he had little aptitude for grand planning.
How was Grant/ Lee as a theatre strategist?	He was a brilliant theatre strategist, as evidenced by the Vicksburg campaign, which was a classic field and siege operation.	As a theatre strategist, Lee often demonstrated more brilliance and apparent originality than Grant, but his most audacious plans were as much the product of the Confederacy's inferior military position as of his own fine mind.

same questions are answered for Grant and Lee (see Table 6.9). Clearly Table 6.11 oversimplifies the nature of the comparison between Grant and Lee, in particular obscuring the complex Evaluation–Basis relations between its component parts, but it does show why almost everyone makes a paragraph break at line 13 in the deparagraphed version.

The original version of the jumbled discourse experiment described in Section 2 of Chapter 1 was written by Winter as part of the course material for a communications class at the Hatfield Polytechnic, illustrating as it does the organisational features of both Problem–Solution and Comparison. Its brevity and simplicity subsequently made it a suitable choice for the jumbled discourse experiment.

The discourse is an interesting instance of the phenomenon where

Table 6.12

What is the situation?	(8) Whenever there is snow in England . . .	In Norway where there may be snow and ice for nearly seven months of the year . . .
What is the problem?	some of the country roads may have black ice. (10) Motorists coming suddenly upon stretches of black ice may find themselves skidding off the road.	∅
What method of solution is adopted?	(2) Road maintenance crews try to reduce the danger of skidding by scattering sand upon the road surfaces.	. . . the law requires that all cars be fitted with special steel spiked tyres.
How successful is this for the country concerned?	(7) Such a measure is generally adequate for our very brief snowfalls. (5) Its main drawback is that if there are fresh snowfalls the whole process has to be repeated, and if the snowfalls continue, it becomes increasingly ineffective in providing some grip for tyres.	(6) These tyres prevent most skidding and are effective in the extreme weather conditions as long as the roads are regularly cleared of loose snow. (4) Their spikes grip the icy surfaces and enable the motorist to corner safely where non-spiked tyres would be disastrous.
How successful would it be for England?	∅	(1) In England, however, the tungsten-tipped spikes would tear the thin tarmac surfaces of our roads to pieces as soon as the protective layer of snow or ice melted.

two compatible but separate descriptions of its organisation are possible at the same time. In the first place, it is a Matching Comparison, and as such can be set out as in Table 6.12. This table 12 oversimplifies the picture to some extent in that sentence 4 also answers the question *How does it work?*; furthermore, it disguises the fact that the Evaluation is in both cases 'good' followed by 'bad', in the case of Norway, however, 'bad' being 'bad for England'. It nevertheless adequately demonstrates both the comparison and the double Problem–Solution patterns. It can be seen from this that each of the variants reported in Chapter 1 are faithful to both basic patterns. Thus variant 1.7 provides the same answers to the same questions in the same order but reverses the order of the comparison, putting the second column before the first; 1.8 on the other hand intermingles the two halves of the comparison, moving from England to Norway and back to England again, but preserving the same order to the questions answered within the columns.

This first description is sufficient to account for the regularly occurring wrong answers. It does not explain why the right answer is better than these. There are three reasons why 1.6 is the best version. The first is the most basic, namely, that some of the cohesive elements are disrupted if 1.6 is not adopted. So, for example, in both 1.7 and 1.8 'therefore' in sentence 3 mis-signals the relationship of what precedes it to that sentence. The second reason is that given by Winter (1976), namely, that it is expected that new information will be provided in the context of given information. Both 1.7 and 1.8 flout that expectation

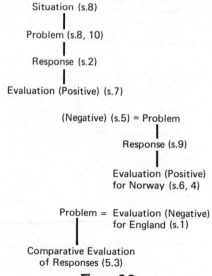

Figure 6.9

(for a Briton) in that they provide new information about Norway's Solution before providing familiar information about England's. For a Norwegian, on the other hand, the order would be reversed. The third reason why 1.6 is the best version is that, as already has been mentioned, it can be analysed in another way. Not only is it organised by Matching but it is also in fact an example of a spiral mutltilayered discourse which can be represented as in Figure 6.9.

9 Summary of Chapter 6

The following points have been made in this chapter:

(1)   Repetition takes a number of forms including substitution, ellipsis, and paraphrases.
(2)   Systematic repetition is a signal of Matching and can often be represented in table form so as to show what is repeated and what replaced. Other signals include syntactic parallelism, affirmation/denial paraphrases and parallel answering of same/similar questions.
(3)   Matching can be either Contrast or Compatibility depending on

   (*a*)   The use of antonymy, negation, etc., in the sentence or clause-pair, and
   (*b*)   context.

(4)   Matching Contrast sometimes supplies the organisation for short discourses such as poems and (more frequently) letters to the press, either with equal weight to each member of the relation or with extra weight on the second member.

Chapter 7

General–Particular Patterns

In Chapter 6 we concentrated almost exclusively on short passages. Only a few of the examples were longer than ten sentences, and we analysed no complete discourse at all. From this it might have been concluded that the relations discussed in that chapter are never used to organise long passages or complete discourses. Such a conclusion would, however, be erroneous; in this chapter, we shall examine how the Matching relations we have considered combine with two types of General–Particular relations – the Generalisation–Example relation and the Preview–Detail relation – to organise long passages or complete discourses. We shall also consider passages organised by each of the relations on its own.

1 The Generalisation–Example Relation

In the last chapter we treated each Matching relation as self-contained and did not consider its place in the larger pattern of the discourse. In many cases, however, a full description demands that attention be paid to the role of the context. Our description of both **6.11** and **6.18** has been deficient in this respect. Sentences 2 and 3 of **6.11** and the five parts of sentence 2 in **6.18** can be shown to be in a Matching Compatibility relation by all the means discussed; nevertheless the crucial factor in showing the relations to be Matching is that of the context. In both cases the context has a very specific role to play. It not only enforces an interpretation of the relation between the parts that follow as Matching, but it places these parts in a subservient role to itself. If we look again at **6.11**, discussed in Section 3 of Chapter 6, we find that the Matched pair is preceded by the sentence 'It is interesting to note

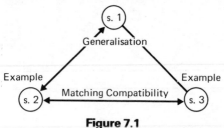

Figure 7.1

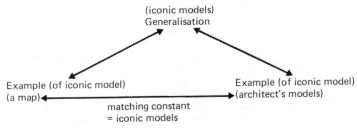

Figure 7.2

that iconic models only represent certain features of that portion of the real world which they simulate'. This sentence is a Generalisation for which the subsequent two Matching sentences provide Examples. That this is the case is indicated by the conjuncts 'for example' and 'similarly', 'for example' self-evidently showing that the sentence it belongs to has the same function as the one before it. In diagram form, then, we have the interlocking of two relations, Generalisation—Example and Matching Compatibility, as in Figure 7.1.

Furthermore, the same network of relationships occurs in this case between the parts of the sentences. The Generalisation talks about 'iconic models' for instance, and as we saw in Table 6.2, iconic model was one of the constants between the two Examples. In the same way, the Generalisation talks of 'features' which is the noun head in column 3 of that table. These sets of relationships can be represented as in Figures 7.2 and 7.3.

As noted above, Generalisation—Example is one type of a more comprehensive relation which Winter calls General—Particular; we shall return to this more comprehensive relation and its manifestations later in this chapter. For the moment, we should simply note that the Generalisation in this case is an important part of the evidence for deciding that the Matching relation between the two Examples is one of Matching Compatibility and not of Contrast. If we change the Generalisation, as in 7.1 below, and replace the second conjunct with the subordinator 'while' and the conjunct 'on the other hand', we find that the two Examples are now in a Matching Contrast relation:

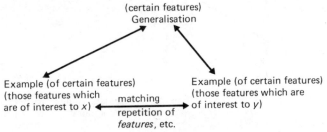

Figure 7.3

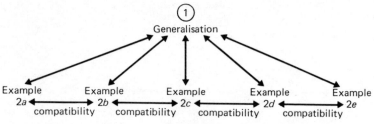

Figure 7.4

7.1 Maps and architects' models, although both types of iconic model, are very different in a number of important respects. For example, a map will only contain those features which are of interest to the person using the map, while architects' models, on the other hand, will be limited to include only those features which are of interest to the person considering employing the architect.

There is a sense in which the two examples could even now be said not to be in a Matching Contrast relation. Both sentences give particulars of the 'difference' referred to in the Generalisation; they spell out what 'different' means. So **7.2**, though odd, is interpretable in the same way as **7.1**:

7.2 Maps and architects' models, although both types of iconic model, are very different in a number of important respects. For example, a map will only contain those features which are of interest to the person using the map. Similarly, architects' models will be limited to include only those features which are of interest to the person considering employing the architect.

In this case, for most people, the Generalisation's signal of expected Contrast over-rides the signal given by the conjunct, of Compatibility.

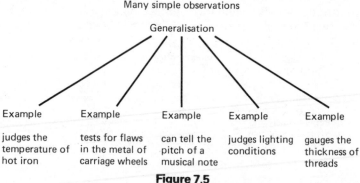

Figure 7.5

by naked eye, by touch or by ear (1)

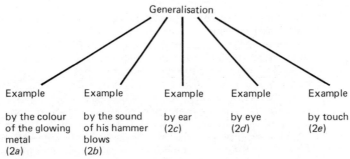

Figure 7.6

This type of conflict between signals is a fertile source of confusion in speech and writing.

Passage **6.18** is built on a Generalisation–Example relation in exactly the same way as **6.11**. The five parts of sentence 2 are in a Matching Compatibility relation fundamentally because they are all Examples to sentence 1's Generalisation. In other words, their Compatibility arises out of their sharing the same function within the larger organisation. The passage can therefore be diagrammed as in Figure 7.4.

The relationship between sentence 1 and the parts of sentence 2 can be shown to be that of Generalisation–Example by inserting 'for example' in 2a. As was the case with **6.11**, we find that the components of sentences 1 and 2 reflect the same pattern as that shown in Figure 7.4 (see Figure 7.5).

Similarly we find (subject to the oversimplification already mentioned) the pattern shown in Figure 7.6.

The Generalisation–Example relation is, as has already been said, a subtype of the General–Particular relation. It occurs whenever a passage can be projected into dialogue in such a way as to include the reader's broad request 'Give me an example or examples'. For instance, **6.11** can be projected into dialogue as follows:

7.3 D: It is interesting to note that iconic models only represent certain features of that portion of the real world which they simulate.

Q: Give me some examples ⟨of iconic models only representing certain features of that portion of the real world which they simulate⟩.

D: (For example) a map will only contain those features which are of interest to the person using the map. Similarly, architects' models will be limited to include only those features which are of interest to the person considering employing the architect.

Passage **6.18** can be projected into dialogue form in the same way:

7.4   D: Many simple observations in physics may be made by the naked eye, by touch or by ear.
　　 Q: Give me some examples ⟨of simple observations in physics being made by the naked eye, by touch or by ear⟩.
　　 D: A blacksmith judges the temperature of hot iron by the colour of the glowing metal, knowing that there is a relation between brightness of glow and degree of hotness; a railway mechanic tests for flaws in the metal of carriage wheels by the sound of his hammer blows; the piano tuner can tell the pitch of a musical note by ear; the photographer often judges lighting conditions by eye; and the spinning wheel worker judges the thickness of threads with great skill by touch.

The ability to project a passage into dialogue using the request form employed in both the above examples and the ability to insert between the two sentences a conjunct such as 'for example' or 'for instance' (if one is not already present as an indication of the relation) are the two main tests of a Generalisation–Example relation.

2   The Preview–Detail Relation

The Generalisation–Example relation is not the only type of General–Particular relation, although it is a very important one. Another, as mentioned in Section 1, is the Preview–Detail relation. A test of the existence of a Preview–Detail relation is whether or not the passage can be projected into dialogue using the broad request 'Give me some details of x' or 'Tell me about x in greater detail'. The Detail member of the relation supplies information about (part of) the Preview member that would otherwise typically be placed as postmodification to the appropriate noun (where postmodification is taken to include all *wh*-clauses whether restrictive or non-restrictive) or as adjunct to the clause.

The Preview member may contain no clues that it is part of a relation with a subsequent Detail member, or it may contain a clue in the form of listing, the extreme form of the latter being enumeration, which normally demands Detail to follow. Examples of all three are:

7.5   (1) A man writes a letter to *The Times* and the result is the Hampstead Murder . . . (2) You may not recall the Hampstead Murder. (3) There is no special reason why you should. (4) It created no excitement whatever. (5) A woman – a lady if you like – was found strangled in a drawing room.[1]

where there are no clues in the first sentence, apart from its being couched in general form, that Detail will follow;

7.6 (1) It [the harpoon] consists of a 'socket', 'shank', and 'mouth'. (2*a*) The shank, which is made of the most pliable iron, is about two feet long; (2*b*) the socket is about six inches long, and swells from the shank to nearly two inches in diameter; (2*c*) and the mouth is of a barbed shape, each barb or wither being eight inches long and six inches broad, with a smaller barb reversed in the inside.[2]

where the first sentence contains a list which predicts but does not demand that Detail will follow; and

7.7 (1) I think then that the language of verse may be divided into three kinds. (2) The first and highest is poetry proper, the language of inspiration . . . (3) The second kind I call Parnassian. (4) It can only be spoken by poets, but is not in the highest sense poetry . . . (5) The third kind is merely the language of verse as distinct from that of prose, Delphic, the tongue of the Sacred Plain, I may call it, used in common by poet and poetaster.[3]

where the first sentence contains an enumeration which demands that Details of each follow. In each of these cases it should be noticed that the Preview is more exactly not the whole sentence but a nominal group within the sentence. So the Detail of **7.5** is related to the nominal group the 'Hampstead Murder', that of **7.6** to the three nouns 'socket', 'shank', and 'mouth', and that of **7.7** to the nominal group 'three kinds of language of verse'.

The Details of a Preview–Detail relation may be Matched, partially Matched, or Unmatched. An example of a Preview–Detail relation where the Details are Matched is **7.8**.

7.8 (1) The physical reactions of gases and metals are much less apparent than the chemical reactions, but often are more important. (2) Gases act on metal in two ways – by *ad*sorption and by *ab*sorption. (3) These terms are often confused because of their similarity in spelling and punctuation. (4) Therefore, clarification of their meaning is important if one is to fully comprehend how gases affect metals.

(5) *Adsorption* occurs at the surface of the metal in contact with the gas, and may be looked upon as a physical condensation of the gas in a layer one or more molecules thick. (6) It can be readily seen that the amount of gas retained in such a manner is directly proportional to the total surface area of the metal exposed to the gas. (7) This quantity of gas is also a function of both pressure and temperature. (8) As the pressure is decreased, the amount of adsorbed gas correspondingly decreases, but as the temperature is raised, the amount of gas adsorbed by the metal surface increases.

(9) *Absorption* is the term applied to the phenomenon by which gas is taken up by the inner structure of the metal exposed to the atmosphere. (10) Apparently, molecules of the gas penetrate into the molecular lattice of the metal and are retained there by molecular forces. (11) The terms 'occlusion' and 'occluded gases' mean *absorbed* gases, as differentiated from gases held on the surface by adsorption. (12) The amount of a given gas retained by a given metal by absorption is function of the mass of the metal involved, rather than the surface area exposed. (13) Hence, solid metallic masses can absorb gas in large quantities, whereas finely divided metal powders, porous metals, or metal shapes having a large ratio of surface area to mass will adsorb large amounts of gas. (14) Absorption of gases also changes with temperature and pressure; higher temperature and lower pressure tend to reduce the amount of gas absorbed by a given mass of metal.[4]

Several factors lead us to analyse this passage as organised by a Preview–Detail relation. First, we have a signalling sentence (sentence 4) which tells us we are to have clarification of the meanings of the terms introduced in sentence 2; this is accompanied by a reason for such clarification (sentence 3). Definition is one of the most typical types of Detail to be provided in a Preview–Detail relation. Secondly, if we omit the signalling sentences, sentence 2 and the two subsequent paragraphs can be converted into dialogue using the high-level request form outlined above:

7.9   D: Gases act on metals in two ways – by *ad*sorption and *ab*sorption.

Q: Give me some details ⟨of how gases act on metals by *ad*sorption⟩.

D: *Adsorption* occurs at the surface of the metal in contact with the gas, and may be looked upon as a physical condensation of the gas in a layer one or more molecules thick, etc.

Q: Give me some details of how gases act on metal by *ab*sorption .

D: *Absorption* is the term applied to the phenomenon by which gas is taken up by the inner structure of the metal exposed to the atmosphere, etc.

It will be noticed that the details provided flesh out part only of the original sentence. So, although Details of the ways gases act on metals

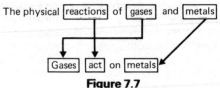

Figure 7.7

are provided, they are linguistically incidental in that the main purpose of the Detail is to clarify the meaning of the two terms in sentence 2. This is shown both by the signalling sentence and by the beginning of paragraph 3 – absorption *is the term applied to* the phenomenon . . .' Thus the relation is between paragraphs 2 and 3 and the latter part of sentence 2.

Table 7.1

What is adsorption/ absorption? Where does it take place?	(5) Adsorption occurs at the surface of the metal in contact with the gas, and may be looked upon as a physical condensation of the gas in a layer one or two molecules thick.	(9) Absorption is the term applied to the phenomenon by which gas is taken up by the inner structure of the metal exposed to the atmosphere. (10) Apparently, molecules of the gas penetrate into the molecular lattice of the metal and are retained there by molecular forces.
What do the terms *occlusion* and *occluded gases* mean?		(11) The terms 'occlusion' and 'occluded gases' mean *absorbed* gases, as differentiated from gases held on the surface by adsorption.
How can one calculate the amount of gas retained?	(6) It can be readily seen that the amount of gas retained in such a manner is directly proportional to the total surface area of the metal exposed to the gas.	(12) The amount of a given gas retained by a given metal by absorption is function of the mass of the metal involved, rather than the surface area exposed.
What are the consequences of this difference?		(13) (Hence), solid metallic masses can absorb gas in large quantities, whereas finely divided metal powders, porous metals, or metal shapes having a large ratio of surface area to mass will adsorb large amounts of gas.
In what respects is the amount retained affected by pressure and temperature?	(7) This quantity of gas is also a function of both pressure and temperature. (8) As the pressure is decreased the amount of adsorbed gas correspondingly decreases, but as the temperature is raised, the amount of gas adsorbed by the metal surface increases.	(14) Absorption of gases also changes with temperature and pressure; higher temperature and lower pressures tend to reduce the amount of gas absorbed by a given mass of metal.

The first part, 'Gases act on metals in two ways', merely recaps in independent clause form information in noun phrase form from sentence 1 (which itself recaps part of a distinction between chemical and physical reactions of gases and metals made several paragraphs earlier). The lexical relationship between the subject of sentence 1 and the first part of sentence 2 can be represented diagrammatically as in Figure 7.7. All that is added is the number of ways in which they act; these are then specified in the second part of the sentence. The second part carries therefore the only new information in the sentence. In Winter's terms, the prepositional phrases in sentences 2 'by *ad*sorption and by *ab*sorption' are replacement by addition; the rest is disguised repetition.

The two paragraphs providing the Details are in a Matching relation, for the same reason as were the examples in **6.11** and **6.18**; they fulfil parallel functions in the larger organisation. Not all Preview–Detail relations intermesh with Matching relations, as we have already noted. The fact that some do, however, is one of the points that Preview–Detail relations and Generalisation–Example relations share in common, entitling us to regard them both as subtypes of the same relation. (Another point they share in common – the movement from a more general level of detail to a less general – is of crucial importance to our

Table 7.2

(It can be readily seen that)	the amount of gas retained	in such a manner [anaphoric reference to *at the surface of the metal by adsorption*]	is directly proportional to	the total surface area	of the metal exposed to the gas	
	The amount of a given gas retained	by a given metal by absorption	is function of	the mass	of the metal involved	(rather than the surface area exposed)
constant	repetition	by a physical method of gas retention by a metal	repetition (paraphrase)	physical quality	repetition (paraphrase [in this context])	
variable		which physical method		type of physical quality		

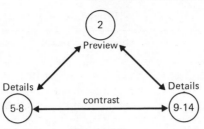

Figure 7.8

understanding of a particular discourse pattern called the Detail tree, and will be discussed when we discuss that type of organisation.)

If we place the sentences of each paragraph side by side according to the questions they answer, we can see that each paragraph answers largely the same questions in the same basic order. Once the overall sequence of the two paragraphs is revealed to be the same, it is possible to notice close links of the type found in **6.11**, **6.14** and **6.18** between the answers to the questions. For example, sentences 6 and 12, which both answer the narrow question 'How can one calculate the amount of gas retained?', can be set out as in Table 7.2. The phrase 'rather than the surface area exposed' reveals a clear Contrast between the two parts, picked up by the rest of the diagram.

Other pairs of sentences manifesting close links are 7 and 14*a*, which can be set out in a table form in the same way as 6 and 12, and 8 and 14*b* which are in a close complex paraphrase relation, each being the reverse of the other. Slightly less obviously linked are sentences 5 and 9, but even these are in near paraphrase for some of their length and show the closeness of their connection by having in common 'metal', 'gas' and 'in contact with' (paraphrased in this context as 'exposed to'). Difference is throughout emphasised rather than similarity. The reason for this is explained in the signalling sentence 3: 'These terms are often confused because of their similarity in spelling and pronunciation.' The Matching relation is therefore one of Contrast. We can represent the organisation of the passage as in Figure 7.8 (omitting sentences 1, 3 and 4).

3 Partly Matched Detail

While intermeshing between the Preview–Detail relation and Matching as illustrated in Section 3 is both common and interesting, it is, as we have already noted, by no means inevitable. An example of a Preview–Detail relation which does not intermesh with unambiguous Matching is **7.6** above, in which, as we have noted, sentence 1 carries the Preview and sentence 2 the Details. Sentence 2 is divided into three

Table 7.3

	shank	socket	mouth	barb
What is it made of?	✓	✗	✗	✗
What are its dimensions?	✓	✓	✗	✓
What is its shape?	✗	✓	✓	✓

parts, each of which picks up the Details of one of the parts mentioned in the Preview. Each part answers the broad question 'What are the details of x?' or 'Give me the details of x'. Since they answer the same question in the same context, why are the three parts not in a Matching relation? The answer lies in the Details they give. For in fact the request 'Give me the details of x' is very broad and can be met in a number of ways. Indeed a person so requested would in some circumstances be justified in replying 'What sort of details are you interested in?'.

If we examine **7.6** carefully from this point of view, we find that the three parts of sentence 2 do not all answer the same questions, though there is some overlapping. This can be demonstrated by putting sentence 2 into dialogue form, thus:

7.10 D: The harpoon consists of a 'socket', 'shank', and 'mouth'.
Q: What is the shank made of and what are its dimensions?
D: The shank, which is made of the most pliable iron, is about two feet long.
Q: What are the socket's dimensions and what is its shape?
D: The socket is about six inches long, and swells from the shank to nearly two inches in diameter.
Q: What is the mouth's shape?
D: The mouth is of a barbed shape.
Q: What are the barbs' dimensions and what is their shape?
D: Each barb or wither is eight inches long and six broad, with a smaller barb reversed in the inside.

Put in table form, the questions answered appear as in Table 7.3. Although two out of three of the questions are answered three times, no question is always answered. To the extent that they overlap, there is some degree of Matching; in so far as they differ, there is no Matching.

4 Types of Detail

Although the three parts of sentence 4 are shown in this way not to be in a full Matching relation, they are nevertheless closely linked. Quite apart from the overlapping shown in Table 7.3, we have the fact that the writer thought the parts near enough in content to warrant putting them all into one orthographic sentence. Moreover, it will perhaps have been noticed that the answers to the questions 'What are x's dimensions?' and 'What is x's shape?' are on several occasions in the original closely intermingled. The explanation for these signs of linkage lies in the fact that, though different, they are subtypes of the same type of Detail – the structure Detail. The structure Detail answers the question 'How would you describe x?' which is both broader than, say, 'What is x's shape?' and narrower than 'Can you give me the details of x?' The structure Detail is one of a number of types of Detail which answer questions narrower than 'Can you give me the details of x?'. Others are the function Detail which answers the question 'How does it function?' or 'What is its function?' and the composition Detail which answers the question 'What is it made of?'.

Instances of all three types of detail can be found in **7.11**:

7.11 *Rubber Dam Holds Water Inside and Out*
(1) In the Netherlands, there is a continuing need for economical ways of taking care of the situation that arises when a dyke fails. (2) What is required is something that can be brought into action very quickly to prevent flooding, but does not constitute a great expense or physical obstruction during the long years between emergencies. (3) The North-Holland Provincial Water Authority has developed an ingenious solution in the form of an inflatable dam made of steel sheets and rubber-nylon fabric.

(4) When out of use, this 'shell' dam lies almost flush with the bottom of the canal: a long, shallow steel box, set into a concrete base. (5) The top surface of the box, or shell, is a pair of steel lids, hinged to the sides of the shell at the outer edges. (6) The inner edges of the lids meet, and are joined to opposite edges of a sheet of the rubber-nylon fabric. (7) This sheet lies folded inside the shell.

(8) When a dyke breaks, releasing water from the canal, the correct emergency action consists of simply pumping the shell full of water. (9) The lids open, and the fabric sheet emerges to form a half-cylindrical roof. (10) The whole thing becomes a gigantic steel and rubber sausage.[5]

In this passage, sentences 1 and 2 provide a Problem and sentences 3–10 the Response. This can then be further divided into Preview ('an inflatable dam') and Detail (all that follows). The Detail is made up of composition Detail, structure Detail, and function Detail; as will become clear, these three types of Detail are linguistically distinctive. We will discuss each in turn.

(1)   Composition

In **7.11** composition Detail is embedded within sentence 3, as shown in **7.12**:

> **7.12**   The North-Holland Provincial Water Authority has developed an ingenious solution in the form of an inflatable dam *made of steel sheets and rubber-nylon fabric.*

The italicised part of **7.12** can be identified as providing composition Detail because (*a*) it answers the question 'What is it made of?'; (*b*) it contains the typical composition verb 'made of'; (*c*) it contains a prepositional group that fulfils the function of what we might term 'ablative of source'. This takes four typical forms:

> made *of* steel sheets,
> made *out of* steel sheets,
> made *from* steel sheets,
> made *with* steel sheets.

The last of these, as Leech and Svartvik (1975) have noted, need not involve the assumption that only steel sheets were used.

Another example of composition Detail, again embedded, can be found in sentence 2*a* of **7.6**, repeated here:

> **7.13**   The shank, *which is made of the most pliable iron*, is about two feet long.

(2)   Structure

Sentences 4–7 are identified as providing structure Detail. The criteria behind such an analysis are as follows:

(*a*)   Sentences 4–7 answer collectively the question 'How would you describe the dam?' (as opposed to 'How would you describe the way the dam works?').

(*b*)   The verbs are all typically used to describe states. They can be divided into three groups, namely, verbs of position (e.g., 'lie', 'stand', 'sit', 'rest'), verbs of contact (e.g. 'hinge', 'meet', 'touch', 'join') and verbs of equivalence (e.g. 'be', 'comprise', 'consist of'). It is also possible to meet verbs of shape.

(*c*)   The sentences all contain 'locative' phrases. Compare sentences 4–7 with sentences 8–10 in **7.14** below.

> **7.14**   (4) When out of use, this 'shell' dam lies almost *flush with the bottom of the canal*: a long, shallow steel box, *set into a concrete base.*

(5) The top surface of the box, or shell, is a pair of steel lids, hinged *to the sides of the shell at the outer edges.* (6) The inner edges of the lids meet, and are joined *to opposite edges of a sheet of the rubber-nylon fabric.* (7) This sheet lies folded *inside the shell.*

(8) When a dyke breaks, releasing water from the canal, the correct emergency action consists of simply pumping the shell full of water. (9) The lids open, and the fabric sheet emerges to form a half-cylindrical roof. (10) The whole thing becomes a gigantic steel and rubber sausage.

It will be seen that sentences 4–7 have all at least one locative phrase, but that there are none in sentences 8–10.

(*d*)   Sentences 4–7 are not organised on a time sequence nor can there be said to be a logical progression from point *a* to *b*. This does not mean that there is no order to the sentences; there is in fact a progression from General ('box') to Particulars ('top surface of the box') which are in turn further particularised ('outer edges', 'inner edges'). But it does mean that all the elements of the description are true at the same time.

(*e*)   The sentences employ items of dimension ('long', 'shallow'), position ('bottom', 'top') and shape ('surface', 'sides', 'edges'). These of course overlap with the prepositions of the locative phrases. Sentences 8–10 (the function Detail) employ these to a much smaller extent.

It will be observed that the Details of **7.6** meet all but one of these criteria. They answer the question(s) 'How would you describe the shank/socket/mouth/barb?', the verbs are either verbs of equivalence or shape, the clauses are not organised on a time sequence, and items of dimension ('long', 'diameter', 'broad'), position ('inside') and shape ('swells', 'barbed shape', 'reversed') are present. Only on the criterion of locative phrases do the Details in **7.6** fall down, there being only one such phrase. Overall, however, they are clearly structure Details.

(3) Function

Sentences 8–10 comprise function Detail. The features that make it recognisable as such are as follows:

(*a*)   it answers the question 'how does it function?'.
(*b*)   The verbs are all used to describe actions (pumping the shell full of water) or processes (the fabric sheet emerges). Verbs describing process appear in sentences which answer the question 'What happens/ed to Y?'. Verbs describing action on the other hand

appear in sentences which answer the question 'What does/did X do or what is done to Y?' or 'What does/did X do?' where X is human.

7.15   Q: What happens to the lids?
       D: The lids open.

but not

7.16   Q: What is done to the lids?
       D: The lids open.

(We would expect 'The lids are opened'.) Therefore 'open' is a 'process' verb in this context.

7.17   Q: What happens to the shell?
       D: It is pumped full of water.

but we find also

7.18   Q: What is done to the shell?
       D: It is pumped full of water.

Therefore 'pump' is an 'action' verb in this context.

The only verb in these sentences which does not describe an action or a process is the main verb of sentence 8. 'Consists' is a verb of equivalence, as noted above. The sentence of which it is the main verb nevertheless describes action because the right-hand side of the equivalence is a clause with an action verb and the left-hand side of the equivalence is the item 'action' itself:

7.19   the correct emergency *action* consists of simply *pumping the shell full of water.*

(c)   The sentences are linked in a time sequence. Between many of the clauses it would be possible to insert the words 'and then', because each sentence answers the question 'What happens next?'.

(d)   Sentence 8 contains a directional phrase ('from the canal'). It is usual to find at least one, since function is normally concerned with change of state.

Further examples of function and structure Details can be found in **4.10**, the discourse analysed in some detail in Chapter 4. There is in fact within its Response a Preview–Detail relation, where 'an air-cushion system' provides the Preview and the rest of the Response provides the Detail. This Detail can be analysed as in **7.20**.

7.20

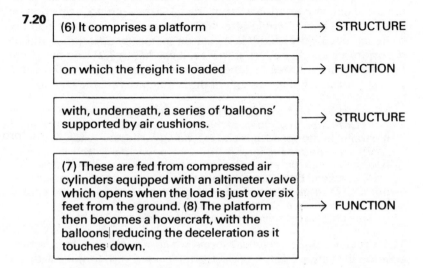

(6) It comprises a platform	⟶ STRUCTURE
on which the freight is loaded	⟶ FUNCTION
with, underneath, a series of 'balloons' supported by air cushions.	⟶ STRUCTURE
(7) These are fed from compressed air cylinders equipped with an altimeter valve which opens when the load is just over six feet from the ground. (8) The platform then becomes a hovercraft, with the balloons reducing the deceleration as it touches down.	⟶ FUNCTION

This looks more complex than it is. The reasons for the analysis are, we hope, fairly clear. 'It comprises a platform . . . with, underneath, a series of "balloons" supported by air cushions' answers the question 'How would you describe the air-cushion system?', has a verb of equivalence ('comprise') and a verb of contact ('support'), and employs an item of position ('underneath'). All these features demonstrate this sentence to be providing structure Detail. Sentences 7 and 8 ('These are fed', etc.) answer the questions 'How does the air-cushion system function?', have verbs of action and process, contain a directional phrase ('from compressed air cylinders'), and are in linked time sequence. Indeed 'then' is used as a conjunct to link the sentences. All these features show these two sentences to be providing function Detail. In addition, the relative clause 'on which the freight is loaded', contained within the 'structure' sentence 6, must also be regarded as providing function Detail. Although it does not by itself answer the question 'How does the air-cushion system work?', it does answer the question 'What function does the platform have?', it has a verb of action and a directional phrase ('on which', i.e., 'on to which') and it is the first stage of the series of actions described in sentences 7 and 8.

It should be noted before we leave this aspect of Preview–Detail relations that Detail need not fall into one of these three categories. To comprehend all types of Detail more categories will have to be set up; further work is needed before this will be a realistic possibility.

5　Unmatched Detail

In **7.8** the Preview contained an enumeration of the ways gases act on metals. That enumeration was not crucial to the sentence's function (in part) as Preview; it would after all have remained the same had the sentence been reworded 'Gases act on metals by *ad*sorption and by *ab*sorption'. In other cases, however, it can be. In **7.21** sentence 1 has the enumeration 'three technical terms which are needed'; this is the Preview for which the subsequent three sentences are the Detail:

> **7.21**　(1) We first explain three technical terms which are needed.
> (2) *Ordinate.* An *ordinate* of the graph is a line drawn from a point on it parallel to the speed axis and extending to the time axis.
> (3) *Area under the graph.* An *area under the graph* is an area bounded by the time axis, the graph itself, and by two ordinates.
> (4) *Gradient.* By the *gradient* of a line we mean the ratio between the number of units of speed parallel to the speed axis and the corresponding number of units of time parallel to the time axis.
> [This point is then expanded and illustrated.][6]

The Preview 'three technical terms which are needed' is in object position in sentence 1, the subject, adjunct, and verb forming with it a signalling sentence. Indeed one way in which signalling sentences might be incorporated into the organisation of the discourse might be via the Preview–Detail relation. If so, however, it will be a specialised use of the relation. In **7.21** the Preview is not simply part of a signalling sentence. To begin with, each of the Detail sentences is providing particulars of a 'technical term which [is] needed'. Moreover there is a symmetry of presentation typical of a Matching relation in sentences 2–4 (a symmetry which becomes still stronger if 4 is paraphrased as 'a *gradient* of a line is the ratio', etc.); this symmetry stems from the fact that all three sentences answer the same question, 'Give me the details of a technical term which is needed'. Were the signalling sentence to be removed, furthermore, the passage would collapse. This is not normally the case with signalling sentences. In **7.8**, for example, signalling sentence 4 can be removed without affecting the coherence of the text. Likewise, in **4.10** in Chapter 4 the signalling independent clause 'but this system has its problems' was removable. Sentences such as sentence 1 in **7.21** which are indispensable to the discourse we shall regard as Previews first and foremost and as signalling sentences only secondarily.

The important point to notice here is that despite superficial features in common with Matching relations elsewhere discussed, sentences 2–4 are not in a Matching relation because (1) they cannot be connected to each other by a question of the form 'Is what is true of x true of y?' or 'Compare x with y in respect of z,' and (2) paraphrase sentences of the denial or compatibility type cannot be inserted between the sentences.

The overall organisation of the passage can therefore be represented as in Figure 7.9, where 2, 3 and 4 form a coherent passage only because of their shared connection with 1.

Despite the different form taken by the Preview sentence in this example, the passage can still be projected into dialogue form employing the appropriate reader's request, without difficulty:

7.22 D: We had first better explain three technical terms which are needed.
  Q: Give me the details of one of them.
  D: Ordinate. An ordinate of the graph is a line drawn from a point on it parallel to the speed axis and extending to the time axis.
  Q: Give me the details of another of them;

and so on.

6 Larger Structures: Generalisation–Example Combined with Matching Compatibility

Discourses or longer passages are often organised by means of a combination of Generalisation–Example and Matching Compatibility. Discourses so organised tend to fall into two general classes. The first has a number of Examples all given approximately equal weight, whereas the second tends to concentrate attention on one of the Examples at the expense of the others. We shall begin by looking at an instance of the first class. In the discourse that follows, the Generalisation–Example relation does not organise the whole discourse but is embedded within a Problem–Solution pattern. Nevertheless it dominates the article and is a good example of how the relation can organise a large portion of a discourse:

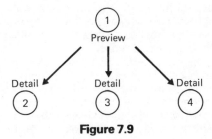

Figure 7.9

7.23   (1) In the hierarchy of criminals, forgers and safe-crackers have long enjoyed elite status because of their special skills. (2) Now they may be topped by the computer criminal. (3) According to Stanford Research Institute Computer Specialist Donn B. Parker, who recently completed a study of 100 crimes involving computers, the potential for illicit gain from the machines is so vast that dishonest employees and even ambitious outsiders will increasingly be tempted to put their knowledge to unlawful use. (4) A handful of key-punch crooks have already thought of ingenious ways to defraud the Brain, with varying results. (5) Some examples:

(6) ▶ Palo Alto Programmer Hugh Jeffrey Ward learned, from customers of a computer firm in Oakland, code numbers that enabled him to give orders to the firm's computer. (7) Ward claims that, on instructions from his superiors, he told the Oakland computer to print out a program for plotting complex aero-space data in graph form. (8) His company presumably planned to market the program which was valued at $12,000 or more, to the Oakland firm's own customers. (9) He was caught through a telephone company tracer and received a suspended sentence.

(10) ▶ Minneapolis Programmer Milo Arthur Bennett, whose firm handled computer work for the National City Bank of Minneapolis, programmed the computer in 1966 to ignore an overdraft in his own account at the bank. (11) He was caught and prosecuted in four months – but only because the computer broke down and the bank's accounts were checked manually.

(12) ▶ An employee of the New Jersey National Bank electronically siphoned $128,000 out of 33 of the bank's accounts and into the balances of two outside accomplices. (13) The trio were caught because the bank switched to new computers that did not give the 'inside man' time to erase the withdrawal data from the defrauded customers' bank statements, as had been planned.

(14) ▶ Jerry Schneider, a 21 year-old UCLA engineering graduate, studied Pacific Telephone and Telegraph's computer by posing first as a journalist and later as a customer. (15) He learned enough to place commercial orders for telephone equipment simply by punching the right beep tones on his own touch telephone. (16) He then picked up the equipment and sold it through a dummy firm. (17) Incredibly, the telephone company let his unpaid bills accumulate for three years. (18) The Los Angeles district attorney charged that Schneider stole $1,000,000 worth of goods in that manner, and the engineer drew a 40-day jail sentence. (19) Now on probation, he is setting up a firm to advise businesses on how to protect themselves against the kind of computer theft he used to practise.

(20) ▶ A Washington, DC, man takes the prize for elegant – and successful – simplicity; he pocketed all the deposit slips at the writing desks of the Riggs National Bank and replaced them with his own electronically coded forms. (21) For three days, every customer who came in without a personal slip and used one of the 'blank' forms was actually depositing money into the culprit's account. (22) The thief

reappeared, withdrew $100,000 and walked away; he has not yet been found.

(23) To cut down the rising incidence of automated rip-offs, companies that own computers are installing more and more gadgetry to improve security. (24) The Defence Department is working on guidelines designed to prevent unauthorised use of multi-access computers used by military contractors. (25) 'Computer audits', in which certain uses of the computer are carefully monitored, and computer ID cards are also growing in popularity. (26) Such measures make computer crime more difficult, but then smart crooks usually have a way of escalating their skills right along with the law. (27) For one thing, says Parker, they can enroll in one of the computer courses now offered as vocational rehabilitation in many US prisons.[7]

The Problem–Solution pattern within which the Generalisation–Example relation is used can be shown as follows:

7.24 A: What is the problem?
B: [Sentences 1–22]
A: What responses have been made?
   or (more naturally)
   What solutions have been tried?
B: [Response 1: sentence 23]
   [Response 2: sentence 24]
   [Response 3: sentence 25]
A: Do these responses (or solutions) work?
B: [Sentences 26–7]

We have therefore a Problem–Solution pattern in which over 80 per cent of the discourse comprises the Problem element. (Justification of the analysis outlined above is not given here; for details of how Problem–Solution patterns are justified, see Chapters 3–5). Of the 80

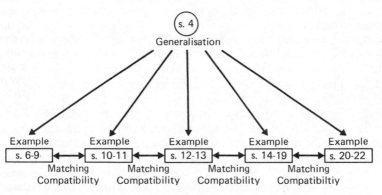

Figure 7.10

Table 7.4

	(s.6–9)	(s.10–11)	(s.12–13)	(s.14–19)	(s.20–2)
Who was a key-punch crook?	s.6	s.10	s.12	s.14	s.20
subdivided into					
Where did he come from?	s.6(*i*)	s.10(*i*)		s.14(*ii*)	s.20
What was his job?	s.6(*ii*)	s.10(*ii*)	} s.12	s.14(*iii*)	—
What was his name?	s.6(*iii*)	s.10(*iii*)	—	s.14(*i*)	—
What ingenious way did he defraud the Brain?	s.6–8	s.10	s.12	s.14–16	s.20–1
What was the result of his fraud?	s.9	s.11	s.13	s.18	s.22
subdivided into					
Was he caught?	s.9(*i*)	s.11(*i*)	s.13(*i*)	s.18 (implied)	s.22
How/Why?	s.9(*ii*)	s.11(*ii*)	s.13(*ii*)	—	—
What happened to him in consequence?	s.9(*iii*)	—	—	s.18(*ii*)	—

per cent devoted to Problem, all but three sentences comprise a Generalisation–Example relation. The internal organisation of that relation is shown in Figure 7.10.

The Generalisation–Examples relation is signalled quite clearly by the signalling phrase labelled in the discourse as sentence 5 (with an implicit *Here are . . .*). The Matching Compatibility relation binding the five Examples together is shown by the fact that not only do all five paragraphs answer the same overall questions with respect to the rest of the discourse (which would not by itself be sufficient evidence of matching) but they also all answer approximately the same (detailed, internal) questions in approximately the same order. This is shown in Table 7.4. Shortage of space prevents the full presentation of answers; the reader might wish to check how each question is answered by checking with the original. For this purpose sentence numbers are given in each column.

As can be seen, the degree of parallelism in the answering of the questions in the left-hand column is high. All five examples answer all three questions, and there are only minor differences in the answering of the question subdivisions. The Roman numerals indicate the order in which the question subdivisions are answered; even here there is a high degree of parallelism. Only one of the examples, the fourth, answers extra questions. Sentence 17 answers the question 'Why was he not caught earlier?', apparently taking as read the fact that he was caught, and sentence 19 answers the question 'What happened to him after his sentence?'. Example 5 supplies less information than the others only because the success of that criminal venture has presumably meant that less is known; it does, however, answer the additional

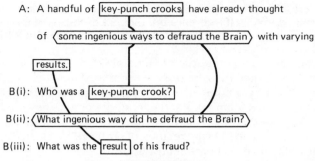

A: A handful of key-punch crooks have already thought

of some ingenious ways to defraud the Brain with varying

results.

B(i): Who was a key-punch crook?

B(ii): What ingenious way did he defraud the Brain?

B(iii): What was the result of his fraud?

Figure 7.11

question (in sentence 20), 'How do you evaluate this man as a criminal?'.

It should be noted that the three questions being answered are directly related to the original generalisation, as shown in Figure 7.11. In other words, there are the same close links between Examples and Generalisation as we found in our analysis of the short extracts.

It was mentioned above that discourses organised by means of combining Generalisation–Example and Matching Compatibility fall into two main classes. Discourse 7.23 was an example of the first class where a number of Matched Examples to a Generalisation were given equal weight. We must now look at an example of the other class of discourse organised by Generalisation and Matched Examples, where one of the Examples is allowed to dominate at the expense of the others. A good instance of this type of discourse is 'The Hampstead Murder' by Christopher Bush, which begins as follows:

7.25 (1) Life is a curious thing. (2) That has been said so many times and experienced so many more that it is trite enough to be boring. (3) But surely its divergencies and its strange juxtapositions are not in themselves boring. (4) Take from life its undoubted and verified coincidences, and where is the spirit of adventure? (5) Or again, trace to their first sources happenings that are momentous – at least to some people – and how trivial are the things that set them in motion. (6) A man in Inverness lights his pipe with a paper spill and a man in Brighton breaks his leg in consequence. (7) Because of a bankruptcy in Cornwall a Yarmouth fishing smack goes down at sea. (8) A man writes a letter to *The Times* and the result is the Hampstead Murder.

(9) 'A bit far-fetched, surely!' you say.

(10) I don't know. (11) Let's take a look at the last and then we may perhaps judge of the others.

(12) You may not recall the Hampstead Murder. (13) There is no special reason why you should. (14) It created no excitement what-

ever. (15) A woman – a lady if you like – was found strangled in a drawing room . . . [From here on, the rest of the story recounts the details of the murder and the circumstances that led up to it.][8]

Before we can discuss the role of Generalisation–Example in organising this passage and thus the story, we must first note that the passage is characterised by a number of references to the reader. Though of interest in the development of a theory of discourse, they are ignored here; they serve the dual role of relating the story to the reader and signalling (in sentence 11) the relation of sentence 15, etc. to sentences 1–8. They play no direct part in the pattern.

Apart from the first four sentences which are complexly organised, the over-all organisation of the passage is relatively straightforward. The complexity of the first four sentences is best demonstrated by projecting them into dialogue as in **7.26**.

7.26   D: Life is a curious thing.
  Q: Evaluate the originality of that claim.
  D: That has been said so many times that it is trite enough to to be boring.
  Q: Is that true of the curiousness of life (as opposed to the statement of its curiousness)?
  D: (Surely) its [i.e. life's] divergencies and its strange juxtapositions are not in themselves boring.
  Q(*i*): Give me an example ⟨of what you mean by its divergencies and its strange juxtapositions⟩.
  Q(*ii*): Can you justify that claim?
Q(*iii*): Give me an example ⟨of what you mean by life being curious⟩.
D: Take from life its undoubted and verified coincidences, and where is the spirit of adventure?

Two features distinguish **7.26** from most of the projections into dialogue that we have so far given. The first of these is that the dialogue consists of two strands, one directly connecting sentences 1 and 4, the other acting as a commentary on the original claim made in sentence 1. The second distinguishing feature is that sentence 4 simultaneously answers three questions (none of them near-paraphrases of each other), two of which arise out of the commentary strand while the third arises out of the main strand. From here on, however, the organisation of the dialogue becomes much simpler. Discourse **7.27** takes up where **7.26** left off.

7.27   B: Give me another example ⟨of what you mean by life being curious⟩.
  A: (Or again) trace to their first sources happenings that are

momentous – at least to some people – and how trivial are the things that set them in motion.

B: Give me an example ⟨of a momentous happening that had at its source a trivial thing that set it in motion⟩.

A: A man in Inverness lights his pipe with a paper spill and a man in Brighton breaks his leg in consequence.

B: Give me another example ⟨of a momentous happening that had at its source a trivial thing that set it in motion⟩.

A: Because of a bankruptcy in Cornwall a Yarmouth fishing smack goes down at sea.

B: Give me another example ⟨of a momentous happening, etc.⟩.

A: A man writes a letter to *The Times* and the result is the Hampstead Murder.

B: Specify ⟨how a man's writing to *The Times* led to the Hampstead Murder⟩.

At this point, A can tell the story which takes up the rest of the discourse. We never in fact return to the general claim nor is any further opportunity given to 'judge of the others' as implicitly promised in sentence 11.

If we simplify slightly the complexity of the relations of the first three sentences, and ignore the evaluative/conversational sentences 9–14, we find we have the reasonably straightforward pattern shown in Figure 7.12. The Matching Compatibility relation binding sentences 6–8 is more clearly signalled than that binding sentences 4–5, about which doubt might legitimately be expressed. Accordingly, the line connecting sentences 4 and 5 is dotted as an indication of tentativeness.

Sentences 6–8 can be shown to be in matching compatibility by setting them out as in Table 7.5. Although the writer varies the syntactic shape of his sentences on each occasion, he has retained the same timeless non-past tense for each verb phrase (which of course cannot be used in the question that elicits them); this is another indication of compatibility. Likewise, despite the syntactic variation, he has taken care to signal clearly that the relationship between the two parts of the sentence in each case is Cause–Consequence – in sentence 1, by the use of the conjunct 'in consequence', in sentence 2, by means of the subordinator 'because', and in sentence 3, by the use of the vocabulary 3 item 'the result'. These features, plus the fact that all three sentences answer the same questions, as shown in Table 7.5, all add up to a clear indication of a Matching Compatibility relation holding between them.

The case of sentences 4–5 is, however, more complex. Again, the writer has given some indication of Compatibility. Both sentences begin with an imperative clause functioning as Condition and they are connected by 'or again' which shows that they are at least intended as

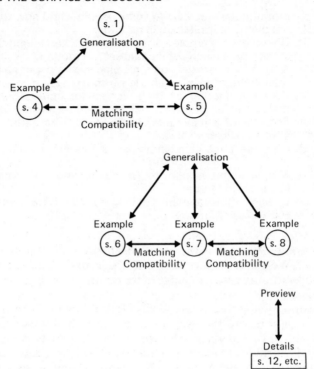

Figure 7.12

alike in being examples. Moreover, sentence 4 concludes with a rhetorical question and sentence 5 with an exclamation employing the item 'how'. Since the rhetorical question is a statement made in question form so as to be emphatic and the exclamation using 'how' is a statement made in exclamation form so as to be emphatic, a strong case can be made for regarding them as identical in function. All this suggests Compatibility. Nevertheless it is a fact that it is not possible to set up a table such as that given for sentences 6–8 in Table 7.5 without making the questions uninterestingly general. Likewise, whereas it is possible to set up trees showing how parts of sentences 6–8 relate to parts of the Generalisation in sentence 5, it is not possible to relate parts of sentences 4 and 5 to the Generalisation in sentence 3 with any certainty. Probably the most sensible solution is to regard 4 and 5 as weakly Matched; it is almost certainly the case that Matching runs on a cline from very strong to non-existent. The example we are examining would presumably come somewhere near the border-line that one arbitrarily would draw through the cline to distinguish Matching from non-Matching.

Table 7.5

	s. 6	s. 7	s. 8
What relatively trivial occurrence took place?	A man lights his pipe with a paper spill	a bankruptcy	a man writes a letter to *The Times*
Where?	in Inverness	in Cornwall	—
What relatively momentous occurrence took place as a result?	a man . . . breaks his leg in consequence	a fishing smack goes down at sea	the result is . . . [a] murder
Where?	in Brighton	Yarmouth	Hampstead

7 The Detail Tree

Some readers may have been surprised to see in Figure 7.12 that some sentences function both as Examples to other Generalisations and as Generalisations which are themselves exemplified. This is, however, quite normal. After all, we accept that a dog is an example of a mammal and that a mammal is an example of a vertebrate without worrying that a mammal is in the first case a general class and in the second an example. Of such duality of function, hyponymic trees are made.

What we have in **7.25** as set out in Figure 7.12 is a discourse pattern we call the Detail Tree. The Detail Tree exists wherever a discourse or passage is made of more than one level of detail, each level being connected to the one above by some form of General–Particular relation. In this case, the General–Particular relation predominantly used is the Generalisation–Example relation, though we also have one example of the Preview–Detail relation. The important factor, however, is that of different levels connected by General–Particular; which type of General–Particular is unimportant. Likewise, the presence of Matching relations is in no sense obligatory.

Sometimes Detail Tree patterns are more complex than the one we have just described. For one thing it is quite common for General and Particulars to be given in the same sentence. An example can be found of this in **7.8** where sentence 2 – 'Gases act on metal in two ways – by *ad*sorption and by *ab*sorption' – gave a Preview of what was to follow and in so doing set up a two-branched tree. In Figure 7.8 we drew a tree that was in fact a slight oversimplification; a more accurate representation of the tree is that given in Figure 7.13. In other words, 'Gases act on metals in two ways' provides the Preview and 'by *ad*sorption and by *ab*sorption' provide the Details of that Preview. They answer the question 'What are the two ways ⟨in which gases act on metals⟩?' or, more briefly, 'Specify the two ways'. 'By *ad*sorption' and 'by

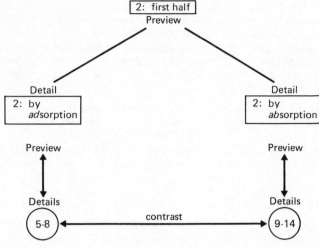

Figure 7.13

*ab*sorption' in turn act as Previews to two sets of Details, the first set being sentences 5–8, the second set sentences 9–14. In each case the sets of sentences answer the question 'What is *ad*sorption/ *ab*sorption?' or 'Specify what is meant by *ad*sorption/*ab*sorption'.

The change in presentation of course alters little in this case and would hardly be worth noting if it were not for the use of sentences such as 2 to set up and alter trees. This leads us to the second factor which affects the complexity of Detail Tree organisation. Writers (or speakers) can sometimes alter the tree pattern they are developing as they proceed. This makes identification of the organisation more difficult and can on occasion lead to what might be termed 'impossible objects' – discourses where two sets of signals lead to different and incompatible organisations.

An example of a Detail Tree pattern of the more complex sort just described is **7.28** below. (It will be noted that **6.11** was drawn from this passage.) We will first present the passage without comment and then analyse it in terms of Detail Tree patterning stage by stage so that the changes that occur in the writer's signalling of the organisation can be clearly seen as they happen.

7.28 (1) Two familiar examples of modern models are maps and architect's models of buildings. (2) These both fall into the category commonly known as iconic models. (3) Iconic models are models which are images of the real situation which they represent. (4) The word comes from the original Greek word *eikonikos* through late Latin into English. (5) Iconic models are images (or icons) of the real situation they represent. [Subtitle omitted at this point.]

(6) It is interesting to note that iconic models only represent certain features of that portion of the real world which they simulate. (7) For example, a map will only contain those features which are of interest to the person using the map. (8) Similarly, architects' models will be limited to include only those features which are of interest to the person considering employing the architect. (9) For example, interior furniture and plumbing are not normally included in architects' models. (10) The exclusion of irrelevant detail is an important point which is often misunderstood when thinking of models, be they simulation models or models of other types.

(11) The class of non-iconic models includes the more common types of mathematical model. (12) The mathematical model is an attempt to represent some part of the real world by mathematical relationships. (13) One of the most useful and frequently encountered classes of mathematical models is that of models which are designed for solution by a mathematical programming system. (14) In the simplest case these will be linear programming models, where a real situation is represented by a series of formal mathematical inequalities.[9]

Sentence 1 of this passage is organised on the same basis as the sentence from **7.8** that we reconsidered at the beginning of this section. It contains within itself both Generalisation ('modern models') and Examples ('maps' and 'architects' models of buildings'). At this stage our tree is straightforward (see Figure 7.14*a*). The very next sentence, however, redefines the relationship of the parts. We are told 'These both fall into the category commonly known as iconic models'. This tells us that 'maps' and 'architects' models' are examples not just of 'modern models' but of a subcategory of modern models 'commonly known as iconic models'. At this stage we have no evidence to suggest that the other categories of modern models will be given, so we have to assume 'iconic models' to be an Example of 'modern models' (see Figure 7.14*b*).

Sentences 3–6 give details of 'iconic models'. The relationship between 'iconic models' in sentence 2 and these sentences is one therefore

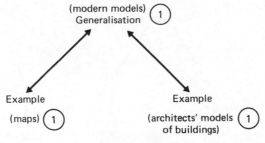

Figure 14a

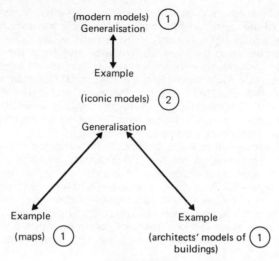

Figure 7.14b

of Preview–Detail. It is interesting to note that 'iconic models' in sentence 2 is now Example, Generalisation and Preview all at the same time. Our tree has therefore to be redrafted (see Figure 7.14c).

The next pair of sentences' relationship with sentence 6 has been discussed in some detail elsewhere.

All that needs to be added here is that maps and architects' models

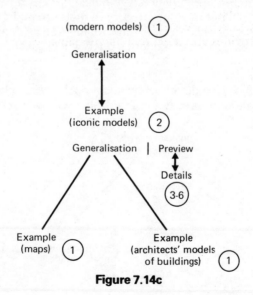

Figure 7.14c

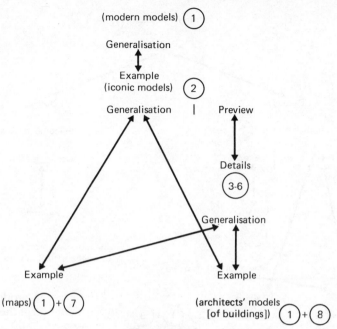

Figure 7.14d

are here examples of iconic models in respect of a specific feature – the limitation of detail to features of interest. Our tree must therefore be adapted accordingly (see Figure 7.14*d*).

The next two sentences do not affect our diagram substantially. Sentence 9 provides an Example to the previous sentence's General-

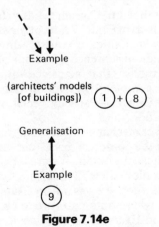

Figure 7.14e

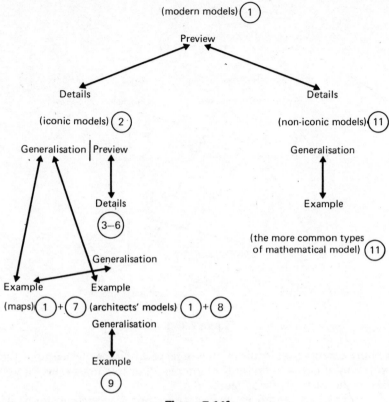

Figure 7.14f

isation, which means that our diagram needs to have an extension from the right-hand branch, as in Figure 7.14*e*; otherwise, though, no change is necessary. Strictly speaking, of course, sentence 9 is an Example only of the claim made in sentence 8 and not of architects' models as such. Our diagram disguises that fact; since however the diagram is not intended to be the complete description but simply to reflect the tree-like network of General–Particular relations, it will be sufficient to note the simplification.

Sentence 10 involves no change at all to our tree, being an Evaluation of the importance of the point just made, but sentence 11 on the other hand produces a radical alteration. We are introduced in this sentence to 'the class of non-iconic models'. This means that the earlier reference to 'iconic models' in sentence 2 was not an Example but one part of the Detail of a Preview, where both parts are to be given. Moreover, this sentence also gives an Example of 'non-iconic models' ('includes the

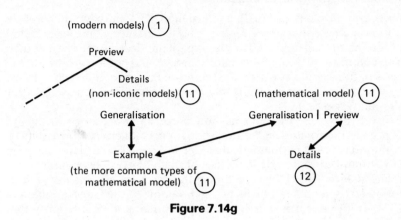

Figure 7.14g

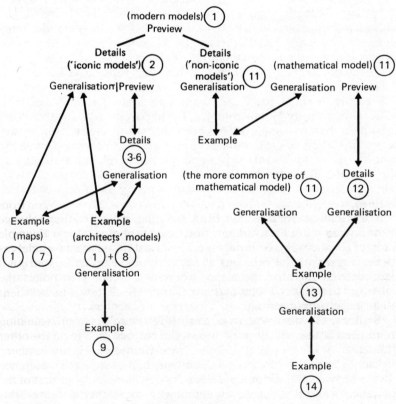

Figure 7.14h

more common types of mathematical model'). Our diagram therefore takes on a new shape (see Figure 7.14*f*). Sentence 12 provides Detail of 'mathematical model'. The class 'mathematical model' is wider than 'the common types of mathematical model' and not identical with 'the class of non-iconic models'. We therefore have two intersecting trees, as shown in Figure 7.14*g*. (Only the right-hand branch is given for simplicity's sake.)

From now on, the organisation becomes straightforward again. Sentence 13 provides an Example both of the Generalisation 'the more common types of mathematical model' in 11 and of the Generalisation 'an attempt to represent some part of the real world by mathematical relationships' in 12, thus combining the two trees still further. This is followed by sentence 14 which is an Example of the Generalisation in 13. In both cases, the signal of Example contains an Evaluation of that Example, i.e. 'one of the *most useful and frequently encountered* classes of mathematical model', and 'in the *simplest* case'. It is quite common for a reason to be given in this way for the selection of a particular Example. Our final tree now looks as in Figure 7.14*h*, though it should be said that the original in fact continues in much the same way for a good deal of its length. Moreover, what precedes our extract is also built on the Detail Tree structure. The final tree pattern is therefore far more complicated than that represented in Figure 7.14*h*.

Presented as in Figure 7.14*h*, there is no doubt that the Detail tree pattern seems forbiddingly complex. It is important to realise therefore that this apparent complexity has been almost entirely built out of two relations – the Generalisation–Example and the Preview–Detail relations – both subtypes of the General–Particular relation and both the simplest of building bricks. The Detail Tree only looks complex; it is in fact a pattern of organisation even simpler than the Problem–Solution Pattern.

In the analysis we have just been outlining, we were attempting to show how a Detail Tree can be retrospectively altered or developed by a writer (or speaker). Naturally therefore we drew no special attention to the signals of the relations as such. It would be quite wrong to deduce from this that the means whereby a Detail Tree pattern is conveyed to a reader/listener are any different from those discussed for other patterns of organisation. To begin with, sentences 1, 7 and 9 in **7.28** all use the word 'example' to signal their role. Other signalling items used in this passage are 'category' (sentence 2), 'type' (sentence 11), 'class' (sentences 11 and 13) and 'case' (sentence 14). Sentences 3, 5, and 12 are in the form of a definition, that is, *x* is *y*. Definitions always provide Detail for a previous Preview in nominal group form. Sentences 4 and 10 are in their different ways comments on the passage rather than part of the passage. Sentence 8 is signalled as Example by the use of the conjunct 'similarly' to relate it to the previous Example; sentence 6 is an extension of the definition of iconic models given in 3 and 5 but not couched in '*x* is *y*' form. In other words, throughout the passage signalling is clear and unambivalent. Similar signalling is used in speech.

8 Summary of Chapter 7

In the course of this chapter the following generalisations have been made:

(1) Context is crucial in deciding the nature of any relation.

(2) General–Particular relations can be either Generalisation–Example relations or Preview–Detail relations.

(3) Matching often occurs between Particulars in a General–Particular relation.

(4) Preview may show strong signals, weak signals, or no signals of the Detail to follow.

(5) Detail may be of several types which include Structure Detail, Function Detail and Composition Detail; there are precise criteria for establishing when such Detail has been provided.

(6) Matching Compatibility and Generalisation–Example may combine to create complex patterns of organisation for discourses and long passages, either with equal weighting between Examples or with extra weight on the last Example.

(7) Out of Matching and General–Particular relations may be built complex patterns that we have called Detail Trees.

(8) Detail Trees can only be definitively plotted out after a discourse/passage is complete, as it is always open to the writer/speaker to reinterpret the relationships between the parts as he progresses.

(9) Both members of a relation within such a tree may be held within the same sentence.

(10) Detail Trees may be weighted towards use of the Preview–Detail relation or the Generalisation–Example relation though rarely to the total exclusion of the other.

(11) The apparent complexity of Detail Trees disguises the essential simplicity of their construction.

Chapter 8

Some Theoretical Conclusions

1 Description and Theory

In the preceding chapters we have explored in some detail the ways in which discourse patterns of various kinds are constructed out of clause relations. We have further shown how these patterns are indicated to the reader by means of lexical signalling and repetition, and how they can be reconstructed by the analyst with the help of question and paraphrase tests. What we have not tried to do is place all this discussion of patterns into a theoretical framework. Description and theory must necessarily grow together, and just as the positing of a descriptive category presupposes a theoretical framework into which the category fits, so equally a theoretical framework presupposes some examination of data which require explanation. Too much passes as theoretical discussion that is closely related to the pastime of making paper planes. The models fly well and are elegant – but woe betide the man who expects them to fly far or to carry freight. The theoretical discussion that follows may not fly far but it has been designed to carry freight and if it does not work, the dismantled pieces may be of use to someone else later.

In this chapter we try to show the theoretical framework that appears to underpin the work discussed in previous chapters. No certainties are offered, only clues as to how the facts of discourse all fit together *vis-à-vis* spoken and written monologues.

2 Relation Networks

It was suggested in Chapter 2 that 'adjoining' in Winter's definition of the clause relation should be interpreted as meaning 'within the same discourse'. There are several reasons why such an interpretation would seem to be necessary. First, our analysis of many of the discourses we have analysed within this work has not assumed adjacency as a pre-requisite for the positing of a relation; furthermore, Winter's own practice and remarks suggest a liberal interpretation would be in keeping with his intention. Secondly, our ability to handle some problem cases is dependent on such an interpretation.

What are the implications of this modification? One of them is at first sight somewhat alarming, namely, that any sentence (or part of a sentence or group of sentences) may be in a relation with any other sentence (or part of a sentence or group of sentences) within the same discourse.

Let us consider further what this involves. It means that for a passage of four clauses' length, ABCD, we are positing a potential set of relations – AB, AC, AD, BC, BD and CD. Furthermore, for every clause, the subject, predicator, complement and object can, where present, relate with any clause or any component of any other clause; they may also of course quite naturally relate with each other within the same clause. Thus, assuming each clause has three components, a, b, and c, we are suggesting that our four-clause passage may now potentially contain the following set of relations – AB, ABa, ABb, ABc, AC, ACa, ACb, ACc, AD, ADa, ADb, ADc, AaB, AaBa, AaBb, AaBc, AbB, AbBb, AbBc, and so on, a total of ninety-six relations, excluding relations internal to the clause. It is not, however, being suggested that any passage ever does manifest all these possibilities; that way would madness lie. Rather, it is being suggested that this set of possibilities is always available and that though no one discourse ever realises anything like all the options, the totality of discourses will do so.

A useful analogy to this situation might be found in the family. In three generations, there could in theory be over seventy people in the form of brothers and sisters, parents, uncles and aunts, grandparents, great-uncles and great-aunts, cousins, nephews, nieces, second cousins, wives and husbands, brothers- and sisters-in-law, and so on. Thus in principle it might be possible for a person to have at least seventy relatives whom he knew personally. In practice, however, such a situation will seldom occur. In the first place, not every potential within the family will be realised. A brother may remain unmarried, thus removing a possible sister-in-law, a parent may have had no sisters, thus removing possible aunts, a cousin and his wife may have had no children, thus depriving one of possible second cousins, and so on. For each case, a potential, marked in the vocabulary of the language as such, is not fulfilled. In the second place, a person may have no direct contact with some of the relatives. Thus he may never have seen his nephews in Australia, one of his grandparents may have died before he was born, and he may not even know of the whereabouts of some of his great-aunts. These relatives, then, exist, but his knowledge of them is second-hand, derived from a relative acting as intermediary. Thus some relatives in any particular family are potentials not realised for that family and others are realised only in an unimportant way (from the point of view of one person within the family). In the same way, in any particular discourse, a clause may be unrelated to some of the other clauses, the potentials for relation not being realised for that discourse, and may be related to others only in an unimportant or tangential way. In the totality of discourses, however, all options will be fully realised. The tests whether two non-adjacent sentences are related are, as one would expect, the same as those for establishing the relation between adjacent sentences.

It will be noticed that, according to this view of the organisation of discourses, just as a sentence may be in a relation with any other sentence in the discourse, so also a group of sentences may be in a relation with any other group, single sentence, or part of a sentence. Such a formulation will account for the discourse organised on strictly hierarchical lines while also accounting for all the discourses that pose problems for a hierarchical model.

3   The Reader's Approach to a Discourse

One of the consequences of a network view of discourse is that it would not be possible to adopt an interactive model based on the use of the question test, since this would limit one to one 'interaction' at a time. If in principle a clause may be related to every other clause in a discourse, then in principle there are as many projections into dialogue as there are other clauses with which the clause may be related.

What status do the questions we have used then have? Are they merely convenient fictions for clarifying the relationship between sentences? In one sense they are just that, since no claim is made that the reader/listener internally asks the very questions provided or indeed any questions as such at all. In another sense, they are not, however; they are intended to reflect a crucial aspect of the interpretative process. While it is not suggested that precise questions are formulated, it is suggested that on the basis of (1) cultural and linguistic expectations about the type of discourse encountered and (2) what the writer/speaker has already said (including the title and the place of occurrence), a reader/listener hazards guesses as to the content to come and its relationship to what has preceded. In so far as they guess correctly, they have a smooth ride; in so far as they guess wrongly, their comprehension is slowed down to some extent. If they consistently guess wrongly, it can be doubted whether they properly comprehend at all, though the fault may lie with either encoder or decoder.

A simplified representation of what happens in written discourse is as follows. The writer initiates his discourse with a first sentence. The form and content of this first sentence are undoubtedly affected in only partly understood ways by a number of cultural expectations established for the medium in which the writing appears and aroused by the title. Nevertheless constraints are relatively absent for this first sentence and a reader's expectations of it are not particularly precise. The reader scans the first sentence and forms expectations as to the information that might follow. No harm is done by representing these expectations as questions. The writer then offers a further sentence which is scanned by the reader as a possible answer to one or more of his or her questions (or expectations). If something in the sentence signals that the question being answered is not one on the reader's short list, then the reader retrospectively has to re-create the question that it must be answering, and if this is in turn impossible, the reader assumes that the sentences are in fact unrelated and seeks a relation elsewhere in the discourse.

The three possible results of a reader's scanning of a sentence – recognition of the sentence as answering the reader's question, recognition of the sentence as answering another unanticipated question, and non-recognition of the sentence as answering any question anticipated or otherwise – are all the offspring of expectation and signalling. In the first place the reader interprets the sentence as an answer to one of his or her questions by using signals within the sentence as clues to how it relates to its predecessor. Thus subordinators, conjuncts, lexical signals and repetition all play a part in this process, as do verb tense and grammatical focusing. If there are no internal signals, then expectation is normally sufficient to carry the load. If an answer to question Q is expected and A will serve as an adequate answer to Q, then A will be read as the writer's answer to Q. If this is not to be circular, it must of course be assumed that question Q is in fact formulated prior to encountering answer A. An informal experiment performed by the author with twenty students can be interpreted as giving support to this assumption. The students were given a discourse sentence by sentence and asked to anticipate the questions that might be answered by the discourse after each sentence. With two exceptions, they always found no more than three questions that could be answered next and were always satisfied that the discourse answered at least one of them. The two exceptions were a sentence that strongly signalled information of a certain type to follow that was not forthcoming and the last two sentences of the discourse, at which point the students expected no further questions to be answered. Although it would be wrong to place much weight on such an experiment until it is replicated under more rigorous conditions, it suggests at least that the assumption that Q is formulated prior to A is not demonstrably absurd.

Where the question answered is not on the reader's shortlist, then internal signals are usually sufficient to rectify the reader's 'mistake'. It would of course be possible to argue that, given the speed at which most people read, all connections between sentences made by the reader are retrospective. If this assumption is made, then it will also be necessary to argue that when such retrospective connections are made, note is taken of earlier prospective signals at the same time. Since this requires that they are retained in the memory until needed, the difference between such a formulation and that offered here is slight.

If the question answered is neither on the reader's shortlist nor clearly signalled, then problems of interpretation are liable to arise, for example, where the relation of a sentence to its predecessor is vague or ambiguous (as opposed to being simply a multiple relation). It is interesting to note that a pair of sentences may be negatively signalled such that no reader could doubt that they are (initially) unconnected; accordingly problems of interpretation do not occur.

When readers have recognised a sentence as an answer to their question, retrospectively amended their question list in the light of

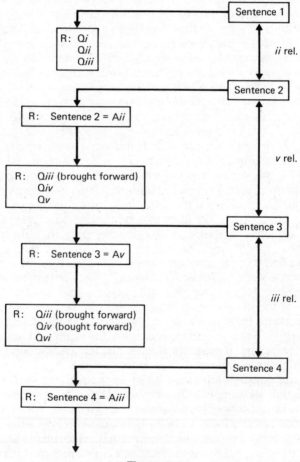

Figure 8.1

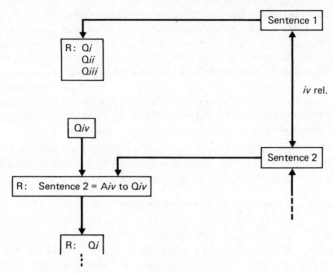

Figure 8.2

what they have found, or simply noted a sentence as unrelated to what has gone before, they then revise their list of questions to be answered which may or may not include some left unanswered from the previous time. This may be shown as in Figure 8.1.

Figure 8.1 does not show a reader's retrospective question-positing. This can be introduced as in Figure 8.2. It should be apparent that the paraphrase tests used throughout this book to establish relations are in some sense simulations of the process that a reader goes through in assessing how a current sentence relates to its predecessor(s). Consider, for example, a pair of sentences discussed briefly in Section 7, Chapter 2.

8.1   Peter went red. He knew he had been silly.[1]

If we attempt to connect these together using all possible subordinators and conjuncts, we find that not all the results are equally probable. For example, it is fairly difficult to find an interpretation of

8.2   Peter went red, but he knew he had been silly.

and nearly impossible to find one for

8.3   In order that he went red, Peter knew he had been silly.

Other possibilities are more likely such as

8.4   Peter went red because he knew he had been silly.

and

8.5   Because Peter went red, he knew he had been silly.

Of the two, **8.4** is clearly more likely but, out of context, the other cannot be dismissed. In the fuller context, however, there is no question of likelihood:

> **8.6**   'Peter, you're the silliest boy I ever knew to do a thing like that,' said William. 'You know we're not allowed in that pit. Now you've given us all a fright, and spoilt Bertie's new braces. I think you're just silly!'
> Peter went red. He knew he had been silly.

The trio of relations between the final sentence of William's speech and the two sentences of **8.1** puts paid to any consideration of **8.5** as an accurate paraphrase of **8.1**. 'Peter went red' cannot be the Cause of William's opinion which is in a Matching relation with Peter's own opinion.

It is suggested that such a sifting of potential paraphrases in the light of the context (linguistic and otherwise) takes place every time a reader encounters a new sentence which is not internally signalled as related to its predecessors in a particular way. It is certainly in principle testable whether readers regularly arrive at the same paraphrase for the same pair of sentences.

As presented in Figure 8.1 and as previously described, the account given above of how a reader encounters a discourse uses a number of temporary simplifications. First, as Winter has pointed out from the very beginning (for example, Winter, 1968), two clauses may be related in more than one way at the same time. Thus a sentence may answer more than one question that the reader has (or has not) anticipated. The diagram does not show this, though no great emendation is necessary to enable it to do so.

Secondly, a reader's question will, as we have seen, be particular to the discourse being read and therefore unique. The relation between two sentences will on the other hand be general and recurrent. It is assumed therefore that the relation and question link are in a General–Particular relation, an assumption implicit throughout this book. Another way of putting this is that a reader's question is likely to be a narrow question but that the question presupposed in a relation will always be broad. The relationship between broad and narrow questions was touched on in Chapter 2.

Thirdly, and very importantly in terms of the methods of analysis used in previous chapters, it is open to the discourse to highlight certain questions as ones that it will answer. Thus is may, and often does, anticipate what it is about to say. When this occurs in a discourse, the effect on the reader's interaction with the discourse can be represented as in Figure 8.3. In other words, a writer may enforce a question on a reader which he or she then, unsurprisingly, answers.

Fourthly, and related to the previous point, the presence of certain signals can be said to predict a relation. For example, a statement that reserves judgement on another's viewpoint, termed by Winter a hypothetical statement, predicts a statement of what the author believes to be true. Predictions can be overridden but will normally be fulfilled. They can be seen therefore not as pre-empting the questions that might arise in the reader's mind but rather as heavily weighting the options in favour of one of the possible questions. Labov (1972) found it necessary to attach to some of his grammatical rules probability estimates of their being met; it seems as if some such measure of probability must be attached to relation predictions, though since no work has yet been done on measuring their probabilities this is highly speculative.

In this context, it should be noted that some predictive statements appear to operate in a more comprehensive way than most. In Chapter 1 we remarked that the only coherent discourses produced by the 'Serious Consequences' game were the ones that began

8.7 Once upon a time there was a merchant; a man so rich that he could have paved the whole street and most of a small alley with silver.

Here the *Once upon a time* can be seen to have predicted a number of different features in the subsequent discourse. To begin with, as a strong signal of Situation, it set up an expectation of Problem to follow. This expectation met, Problem generated Response and thus the coherence of the discourses produced in the 'Serious Consequences' game was maintained. Secondly, though, it also set up an expectation of an entirely different kind; it set up an expectation that a fairy tale

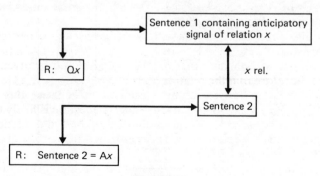

Figure 8.3

would follow that was so precise that both **1.4** and **1.5** included in their second sentence a reference to the merchant's 'beautiful daughter'. This type of prediction is very difficult to pin down in analysis but is nevertheless pervasive. No one encountering the first sentence of a scientific report would expect the second sentence to provide racy narrative. In short, part of a reader's expectations and therefore of the questions he or she will look to see answered are set up by the indications given as to the style/genre of the writing encountered.

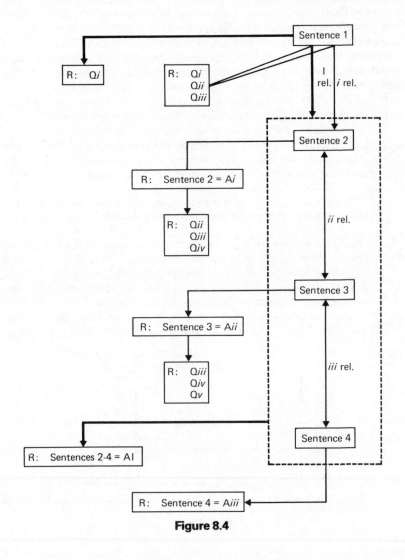

Figure 8.4

Fifthly, depending largely but not wholly on the generality of the questions being answered, the answers may vary in length from (part of) one sentence to a whole discourse. Thus our diagram must be further modified to allow for levels of questioning (see Figure 8.4; heavy lines indicate high-level questions, normal lines low-level questions). If this is correct, we have to account for the means whereby readers know their higher-level questions are being answered and how they recognise the point at which they have been answered. This we have only begun to do.

4 Signalling as Focusing and as Relation–Forming

What has been said in previous sections leaves certain matters unresolved. In particular, the two views of discourse organisation that we have so far considered appear to have little in common. On the one hand, we have a view of the discourse as a collection of multifariously related sentences, in which potentially any sentence, part of sentence, or group of sentences may be in a relation with any other, and on the other, we have a view of the discourse as interpreted as a dialogue in which the reader matches his or her expectations against the answers received. The latter view sees discourse as in part linearly organised; the former emphatically denies linearity of organisation for discourses. The two views reflect to some extent the perspectives of writer and reader. Writers are capable of revising what they write many times; each revision may introduce greater complexity of interrelatedness. They also may well write in a non-linear way, returning to earlier passages to insert extra material or indeed writing later passages before the earlier parts were even roughed out. This book was not written linearly. I wrote Chapter 3 first, then Chapter 4. I then drafted Chapters 6 and 7, moved back to Chapter 1, then forward to Chapter 5. Chapter 2 was then written, and then, as you might induce from this paragraph, Chapter 8 was completed, having however existed in a rough form since the drafting of Chapters 6 and 7.

It is moderately unlikely however that you read it that way (though not of course impossible). On the whole we read in a linear manner beginning at the beginning and ending (assuming we do not give up) at the end, though any footnotes, appendices or bibliography will not be so read. This point can of course be pushed too far; Roe (1977) has noted that scientific discourses are not necessarily read in this way; skipping may occur and reading may be governed not by page order but by cross-referencing in an index. Nevertheless most reading *is* linear (even if skipping occurs) and certainly will not reflect the order in which the work being read was written, except by accident.

If then we accept that discourses are built out of interconnecting parts, we must explain how a reader's linear approach to discourses permits a reasonable interpretation to occur. Part of the explanation for this need not be linguistic; no assumptions can be made by linguists about the storage of information once received. Part, however, is linguistic, and that is the role played by two features – signalling and custom.

Taking custom first, in Chapter 3 it was suggested that there are an infinite number of possible patterns of organisation for a discourse. This suggestion has been implicitly reinforced in this chapter. Yet as was remarked in Chapters 3 and 7, the Problem–Solution and Detail Tree patterns regularly re-occur; and in both cases specialised lexical signalling exists to indicate to the reader/listener when he or she is encountering such a pattern. If the claim is correct that there are an infinite number of discourse pattern possibilities, then the prevalence of any recurring patterns must be explained. This can be done if they are seen as culturally approved patterns which reflect (and perhaps to some degree influence) the Western world's concern with problem-solving and classification. Such culturally approved patterns greatly simplify the reader's task in seeking a linear path through a non-linear network.

The second feature to play a significant role in the relationship between network and dialogue is signalling. Throughout this book we have been concerned to show the ways in which discourse patterns may be signalled and the ways in which they may be elicited with the help of questions and paraphrases. Eliciting a relation is, however, not the same as recognising a relation that has been signalled. When a relation is signalled, a message is being communicated about the way in which the discourse should be interpreted: the writer/speaker is telling his or her reader/auditor to interpret the juxtaposition of the parts of his or her discourse in a particular way. When on the other hand a relation can be shown to exist by paraphrase or dialogue techniques but has not been signalled as related by any of the means discussed in this book, then a more muted message about the relation is being communicated to the reader/listener; the reader/listener is drawing conclusions based on the context and anticipated connections.

In the terms just outlined, signalled relations are relations given focus by the encoder and are therefore those most readily decoded by the reader/auditor. The connection then between the relation network and the reader's 'dialogue' becomes that between total set of relations and focused set. The connection is not neat. Obviously some non-linearly interpreted relations will be signalled. Nevertheless such a connection between the two views of discourse explains the significance of signalling for the anticipation of questions discussed in Section 3. Furthermore it offers one reason why a reader may find a discourse more difficult to read if signals of the type described in this book are not present. Apart from having to check each sentence more carefully against the possible questions, the reader of such a discourse is given fewer clues as to which relations are in focus and which not. Interpretation is consequently more difficult.

The theoretical framework sketched out in this chapter leads also to the tentative suggestion of one way in which we may come to value certain works of literature more highly than others. Whereas for most types of writing one reading has to be enough and therefore signalling has to be unambiguous and clear, for a literary work a number of readings may be both necessary, desirable and pleasurable. In such works a greater number of relational possibilities may be realised than in non-literary writing of the same length, and the focusing on certain relations may be less clear-cut. For such works extra readings would reveal extra unexpected connections and would lead to the detection of other focal relations than those noticed on the first reading. While it would be quite absurd to suggest that greater use of the network of possibilities is the only factor involved in separating successful literary writing from all other writing, the possibility that this plays some role should not be dismissed out of hand.

5 Rhetorical Ineptness

Sections 2–4 were arguing that there are three potential descriptions of any discourse – the description of the complete network, the description of the clearly signalled relations and patterns, and the description of the reader's interpretation of the discourse. These three possibilities are less discrete than they appear. Analysts attempting to describe the focused patterns of a discourse are functioning as careful readers and are therefore describing what they think significant in that discourse. Analysts attempting to describe the complete network of a discourse are responding to something in the language that makes them know a relation exists and are therefore describing only what has been signalled to them even if what is serving as the signal is still a mystery. A further complication is that as we learn more about signalling devices, our notion of which serve to focus a relation may have to be altered. Even if we allow for such fuzziness, the distinction between the types of description is worth maintaining as it enables us to talk about ways in which discourses may go wrong. Essentially we should want to say that all discourses must, willy-nilly, be describable in terms of the total set of relations that exist within them – such a network is the *discourse organisation*. Where a culturally approved pattern exists or where the relations or patterns are clearly signalled, discourses are also describable in terms of the set of focused (or formed) relations that exist within them – such a set is the *rhetorical organisation*. If writers or speakers fail to relate one or more of their sentences to any of the other sentences in their discourse, then they are not producing coherent discourses but fragments of a discourse. If on the other hand writers or speakers relate all the parts of their discourses but fail to show their readers a clear pathway through the parts, then their discourses are coherent but rhetorically inept.

Rhetorical ineptness may arise either from under-signalling so that no clear focus of attention is found or mis-signalling so that the reader is wrongly directed as to what to expect. (A third type of rhetorical ineptness is discussed in Section 6.) An example of the first type of ineptness is the following:

8.8　*An Eye on Drunken Drivers*
(1) A 'breathalyser' indicates the amount of alcohol in a person's body rather than his reaction to that alcohol. (2) Dr Donald E. Sussman has developed a device which measures the unsteadiness of a drinker's eyes – just one of the neurophysiological effects of drinking. (3) The device, developed at the Cornell Aeronautics Laboratory, Buffalo, makes a pictorial record of what happens to each of a driver's eyes when he looks at a target light in a black box.

(4) The box, which takes up very little space and could be fitted into any police station, had a head-rest, two target lights at a distance of three and four inches, and a third light visible in a mirror at a distance of 46 inches. (4) The lights are flicked on in sequence and a motion-picture camera photographs the subject's eyes. (6) Forty frames per second are recorded by the camera. (7) Light comes from a strobo-scope with 1·5 millisecond flashes.

(8) The films are processed and a score calculated for a four-second period while the subject is looking at each light. (9) Each iris movement greater than 0·1 inches is counted.

(10) A series of tests showed that the number of involuntary eye movements went up as the subjects drank more. (11) With no drink, the count was less than one, but the count was 1·8 after the first drink, rising to 6·8 after the fourth drink. (12) The blood alcohol level and the number of involuntary eye movements were not well correlated. (13) Further tests may allow an 'impairment scale', based on the subject's score, to be established.[2]

This discourse has been given to innumerable groups of students with the question 'Is Dr Sussman's device a (relative) success or is it a (relative) failure?'. Almost without exception the groups divide down the middle on the matter, some seeing the lack of correlation reported in sentence 12 as an indication that the device is doing what was intended of it, others seeing the lack of correlation as evidence of its failure to match the breathalyser in reliability. (Experienced statisticians inform me that the proper interpretation is that there is insufficient information on which to form an opinion one way or the other.)

Table 8.1

	a 'breathalyser'	indicates the amount of	alcohol in a person's body
	a device . . .	measures	the unsteadiness of a drinker's eyes
Constant	a device	measures	a drinker's body
Variable	nature of device		what is measured regarding it

Clearly any discourse open to such differing interpretations is not succeeding in communicating all that it might (unless one adopts the somewhat perverse stance of assuming that it is acceptable that readers should form unintended evaluations of the work described). The explanation for this appears to lie in under-signalling.

The function of sentence 1 is crucially vague with regards to the rest of the discourse. It is partly related to sentence 2 in a Matching relation as is shown in Table 8.1. The relation is one of Contrast, shown by 'rather than' in sentence 1 and the ability to paraphrase 'his reaction to that alcohol' as 'the effects on him of drinking alcohol' and 'the neurophysiological effects of drinking' as 'the neurophysiological effects on him of drinking alcohol'. The difficulty lies in deciding whether this is the only relation holding between sentences 1 and 2. We have a number of indications that sentence 2 may be the beginning of a Response section. In particular we note the full complement of Attribution signals – agent (Sussman), national origin (at the beginning of sentence 3) (Buffalo), 'have-ed' plus 'develop', and a general statement of the nature of a device described in greater detail immediately below; we are, however, unable to characterise this general statement as being one of a Response for lack of other signals. Given sentence 2 as a potential Response we are forced to re-examine sentence 1 as a possible statement of Problem, but it carries no explicit signal of Problem unless 'rather than' is allowed to bear more weight than it should. Similarly we are forced to search for an Evaluation of sentence 2's putative Response; the only Evaluation of the Results (sentence 12) leaves unclear whether the device is meant to improve upon the breathalyser but 'not well' would in other circumstances suggest an unsolved Problem. In short, if a Problem–Solution pattern is intended, it is under-signalled, and the relations of which it would have been made up have not been formed let alone focused. Two minor changes would have made all clear. If a Problem–Solution pattern was intended, sentence 1 could have been reworded 'The problem with the "breathalyser" is that it indicates . . .' and sentence 12 added to thus: 'As expected the blood alcohol level . . .'. If on the other hand this interpretation was to be avoided, the inclusion of an appropriate purpose clause (for example, 'To measure this also . . .') in sentence 2 to eliminate the reading of sentence 1 as Problem would have helped and the addition of the disjunct 'Unfortunately' to sentence 12 have made the Evaluation unambiguous.

Under-signalling may lead to failure to communicate a clear message; mis-signalling on the other hand may result in a different kind of frustration for the reader. An example of a discourse that is capable of worrying readers is the following:

8.9 *March 1976: The Night Sky. The Error that Proved Right*
(1) Pluto is often regarded as the most distant of the nine known major planets in our solar system. (2) Its discovery came as a result of a search instigated by Percival Lowell and carried out at Lowell's planetary observatory in Arizona. (3) Lowell had examined observations of the position of Uranus and deduced that, in addition to Neptune and the other known planets, some other sizeable body was exerting a gravitational pull on Uranus. (4) His calculations, published two years before his death in 1916, predicted the pressure and possible position of a massive planet six times larger than the earth which was oribiting the sun in a period of 282 years.

(5) Clyde Tombaugh found the new planet in 1930 close to Lowell's predicted position in Gemini, but it became apparent that Pluto (the assigned name incorporated Lowell's initials) was fainter and smaller than anticipated and would need to be unbelievably dense to account for the gravitational pull on Uranus diagnosed by Lowell. (6) Astronomers now believe that the early observations of Uranus used by Lowell to make his predictions were in error, and that his accurate prediction was a fortuitous accident.

(7) Observations of Pluto now show it to have a diameter of about 6,400 km and a mass, derived from its small gravitational influence on the position of Neptune, of only one-tenth that of the earth. (8) These parameters, which are similar to those of Mars, confirm that Pluto has little in common with the other outer planets (Jupiter, Saturn, Uranus and Neptune) which are all massive, with deep atmospheres. (9) A 20 per cent brightness fluctuation in a period of 6 days 9 hours is taken to indicate the length of Pluto's day, while a calculated temperature of −230 deg. centigrade implies that any Plutonian atmosphere probably lies frozen on its surface.

(10) Its slow rotation period, and the fact that Pluto's 248-year eccentric orbit of the sun actually takes it within the orbit of Neptune, have led some astronomers to speculate that Pluto was originally one of Neptune's moons which became detached as a result of a close approach to Triton, the largest of Neptune's present moons. (11) Possibly, this encounter could explain why Triton is the only major moon in the solar system which rotates round its planet in the opposite direction to the planet's axial rotation. (12) There is no chance of a collision between Pluto and Neptune since the tilts of their orbits are such that they do not intersect at any point.

(13) Pluto will move nearer the sun than Neptune in 1979 on its way to the perihelion, the closest point to the sun, in 1989. (14) At magnitude 13.8, it has been glimpsed with a telescope of 5 in. aperture, but a telescope with double this aperture would probably be required normally. (15) Opposition occurs this year on March 30, north-east of the star Epsilon Virginis.[3]

The problem with this discourse lies in its very first sentence. As has been shown in some detail by Winter and others, a statement of views that are left unendorsed by the author (a Hypothetical statement) strongly predicts a statement of the author's own views (the Real). The consequence of delaying fulfilment of such a prediction is that the reader requires it with ever greater urgency; this is used to great rhetorical effect by Shakespeare in Antony's speech at Caesar's funeral (see Hoey and Winter, 1982). In **8.9**, however, the effect is altogether different. The avowed topic of the article as presented in the title is not Pluto's position in the solar system *vis-à-vis* other planets but Pluto's discovery as a result of an incorrect calculation. As such, the delay of nine intervening sentences, and the fact that the Real, when finally given, is offered parenthetically in a nominal group of the kind you are reading at the moment, serves only to distract attention from what is being said elsewhere. When I first encountered this article I hardly noticed the 'error that proved right', so anxious was I to be disabused of my erroneous view of Pluto as the furthermost planet. In a class of twenty students ignorant of the relation Hypothetical–Real, all predicted, given the first sentence, that the next would tell what a correct view of Pluto's position would be, and all were surprised when they found that the next sentence did not offer this information.

Such a discourse is clearly not unclear. It is not under-signalled but mis-signalled. What problems it causes are problems of unrealised expectations not problems of interpretation. The writer has in effect told the reader to expect a particular question to be answered and then delayed supplying information that could serve as an acceptable answer to that question.

6 Relations as a Finite Set

Given an infinite number of possible patterns, it is necessary to presuppose a finite number of relations and a finite number of possible paraphrases, broad questions and signals for each relation. Although both presuppositions have at present to be taken on trust, as comprehensive testing of them has yet to be undertaken, informal checking on a large scale suggests that they are correct. Two points need, however, to be made in this connection. First, the relation between two parts of a discourse may be a 'weak relation' (Jordan, 1978); the connection need be no more than 'What happened next or at the same time?' or 'Tell me something (more) about *x*'. In other words, time sequence and maintenance or (allowed) change of topic are types of relation in the same way that Cause–Consequence and Matching Contrast are. This does not make everything possible, however; many combinations are excluded as before. Compare

> **8.10**   Father stops the car and I jump out with Ruff. We run into the garden and up to the door. My friends come out to get into the car.[4]

with

> **8.11**   My friends come out to get into the car. We run into the garden and up to the door. Father stops the car and I jump out with Ruff.

Although both the original and reversed versions are made up of descriptions of actions, only the original is interpretable, the three sentences being connected in a time sequence relation representable by the questions 'What did we do then?' and 'What happened then?' respectively. Likewise in **8.12** the sentences are connectible by the question 'Tell me something (else) about the river', whereas in **8.13** no such connecting question is possible.

> **8.12**   There is a river with caravans by it. On the river there are two boats.[5]
>
> **8.13**   On the river there are two boats. There is a river with caravans by it.

Of course, **8.13** is unacceptable in part because of its flouting of a basic rule of cohesion (**8.11** also breaks such a rule but less conspicuously); 'a' plus repeated noun-head will only have anaphoric (backward-looking) reference if it appears within a generalising statement. What this underlines is that the grammatical facts of cohesion are inextricably bound up with the clause relations holding between statements. Whereas Halliday and Hasan (1976) consider each cohesive relation in isolation, however, we are concerned to show what communicative function those relations have regarding the relation of the clauses, etc. as a whole. Thus it is not sufficient to observe the existence of a cohesive tie; its significance in communicating the relation holding between the statements in which its members appear must also be described before its value in providing 'texture' to the discourse can be estimated. If such a perspective on cohesion is adopted new insights into the nature of some of the devices in English are likely to be achieved (see, for example, Jordan, 1978, on *this* and *that*).

The second point that needs to be made about the finiteness of the number of relations and paraphrases/questions/signals pertaining to relations is that this finiteness would appear to be subject to a cline of generality from narrow to broad. So just as Smith and Wilson (1979) represent presuppositions as in Figure 8.5, so also we may represent questions as in Figure 8.6, with equivalent diagrams leading to 'what happened?' from 'What did John steal?' and from 'What number of horses did John steal?'. Likewise for relations themselves we noted in Chapter 3 that Stimulus–Response is a subclass of Cause–Consequence and in Chapter 5 that the latter relations and Condition–Consequence are in some circumstances indistinguishable and therefore by implication related in a more intimate way than, for example, Cause–Consequence and Matching Contrast. In other words, the categories with which we have been dealing are assumed to

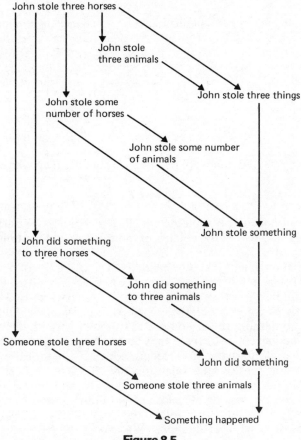

Figure 8.5

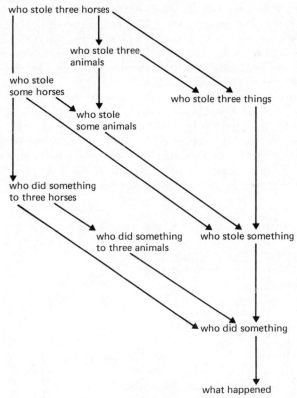

Figure 8.6

be finite but not sharply separated in all circumstances. We are talking about the finiteness of the colours of the rainbow not the finiteness of peas in a pod.

One final comment needs to be made. The examples of connection by the most general relations were taken from a children's reading book. Children's writing can be typically characterised as predominantly concerned with the questions 'What happened next?' and 'Tell me something (else) about x'. Although such children do not produce incoherent discourses; they do produce discourses that would be regarded, if they were produced for adults, as rhetorically inept.

The reasons for this are straightforward. It has been pointed out in several places that all signals are evaluative and all relations are evaluative of the joint significance of two or more parts of a discourse. Accordingly a passage organised on the simplest bases is devoid of all but the most basic of evaluations. We expect, however, a writer or speaker to comment on the significance of what he or she is saying in a more precise way. If he or she does not, and the discourse is accordingly unfocused, we usually reject what we are given as naive.

Secondly, if two statements are presented as related in a particular way, that relation is seen as a partial justification for the inclusion of the information. We are deemed to be interested in causes, purposes, similarities, exceptions and so on. On the other hand if the only connection between pieces of information is time sequence or maintenance of topic (for example), then some other justification, such as its likely interest value, is required. This type of justification may not be linguistically encoded; whether it is or not, it is unlikely that an extended stretch of discourse will be explicable in these terms. (As was noted in Chapter 7, many questions that come under the category 'Tell me something (else) about *x*' are describable in more precise ways.)

7 Summary of Chapter 8 and Final Observations

In this chapter we have suggested that
(1)   a strict hierarchical model of discourse should not be adopted for monologues;
(2)   a relation-network view of discourse should be adopted in its place;
(3)   questions are a reflection of the way a hearer/reader interprets a discourse in terms of expectations and retrospective relations;
(4)   signalling is used both to focus on particular relations as rhetorically important and to create relations where otherwise they could not have confidently been assumed to exist;
(5)   failure to give readers/hearers a clear path through a discourse is the consequence of rhetorical ineptness which may be caused by under-signalling and mis-signalling;
(6)   over-reliance on the most general relations also gives rise to rhetorical ineptness and is particularly characteristic of the writing of children;
(7)   the most general relations are time sequence and maintenance or (allowed) change of topic;
(8)   the finiteness of the set of relations is subject to a cline of generality from narrow to broad.

What we have not done is make any attempt to incorporate this monologue model into existing dialogue models. Clearly this must be done and done soon; a necessary preliminary for such work is further research into questions. Likewise some connection with speech act theory would be desirable but has not been attempted here. In both cases, the reason has been that it seemed best to present a truthful picture of what has so far been discovered about monologues without making claims as to completeness. We are acutely conscious of what a paltry beginning this book is, compared with the work that is still to be done. Our only consolation is that this book is a shanty-town built upon rock rather than a palace built upon sand. As such it awaits redevelopment with the confidence that what it offers is worth redeveloping.

Annotated Bibliography

Some readers will have brought to this book a considerable body of reading about discourse analysis and textlinguistics; others are likely to have brought relatively little. Likewise, some readers will want to pursue the study of discourse further; others, finding their palates sated or dulled by what they have been given, will be happy to leave further study to those with more enthusiasm or time. Inevitably therefore the needs of readers with regards to bibliographical data will vary enormously. Accordingly a decision has been taken throughout this book not to encumber the main body of the text with bibliographical detail which might simultaneously prove too little and too much but to supply instead an annotated bibliography as an appendix. The bibliography has been organised on a chapter-by-chapter basis and, where appropriate, on a section-by-section basis as well.

Chapter 1

Section 1

The term 'discourse analysis' was first introduced in a series of papers published in 1952 by Zellig Harris (Harris, 1952a, b, c) in which an attempt is made to modify the techniques of distributional analysis developed by the post-Bloomfieldians so that they can be used for the analysis of discourses. Transformations are introduced into the analysis as a way of discovering substitutable items. Harris (1952c) notes that one can make predictions about what will follow any particular sentence in a discourse and shows awareness of the cultural and stylistic importance of discourse work.

Kenneth Pike (1967 [1954–9]) shows a similar awareness and makes a number of challenging claims about the organisation of discourse in the course of his presentation of a model of language designed to account also for the organisation of human behaviour. Particularly relevant are chapters 1–5, 9–11 and 16, though the reader will find useful remarks elsewhere as well; he or she is however warned that the latter part of the work is particularly difficult. Pike's current position can be found in Pike and Pike (1977).

Section 2

There is a detailed discussion of the jumbled discourse (1.1) by Winter (1976) who analyses the 'right' result with a view to giving practical advice to report writers. He notes that the fundamentals of information structure form a consensus of agreement about the way we receive information.

Harper (1965) reports a similar, though smaller-scale, experiment; his results largely correlate with those given below but the conclusions he draws from them are to some extent different. Aaron *et al.* (1971) include a jumbled sentence 'game' in their Reading Systems Studybooks; the difference between the two exercises lies mainly in the fact that the children that form Aaron *et al.*'s readership have earlier had the same story in the normal order. Thus it becomes for them a test of memory as much as anything else.

Section 4

Among the linguists who have advocated treating the orthographic paragraph as a unit above the sentence are Christensen (1965), Becker (1965) and Young and Becker (1965, 1966). Those who have opposed this view have included Rodgers (1966) and Stern (1976), who both argue that work on discourse is hampered by belief in the existence of a unit coterminous with the orthographic paragraph. Longacre (1968, 1979 and elsewhere) uses the term 'paragraph' to describe a tagmemic level above the sentence but defines it on a non-orthographic basis.

The results of Koen, Becker and Young's paragraphing experiments were initially circulated in several mimeographed papers in the mid-1960s. Both the passages and the discussion in this section are derived from those papers, which have never, as far as I can ascertain, been published. A summarised account of their research was, however, published at the end of the decade (Koen *et al.*, 1969) in a largely statistically oriented paper; this confirms that a significant agreement is found between informants on the placing of paragraph breaks in a wide variety of texts in both normal and nonsense versions, noting however that the finding does not hold for children. There is some discussion of the paragraphing experiments in Young *et al.* (1970).

Section 6

Winter (forthcoming) provides a synthesis, with important modifications, of existing definitions of the sentence that takes into account his own work on the sentence in context. Sadly this was made available to the present author too late for it to affect this book.

Chapter 2

Section 1

The main places where Winter develops his concept of the clause relation are Winter (1968, 1969, 1971, 1974, 1976, 1977, 1979, forthcoming) and Hoey and Winter (1982). Of these Winter (1969) and (1976) exist in mimeographed form only, though the latter has had fairly wide circulation. His work is always characterised by a concentration on the task of describing real discourses, a concern with the means whereby a particular relation may be recognised, and a belief that the study of surface grammar and discourse analysis should go hand in hand.

Details of each of these references are given in the bibliographies attached to subsequent sections. Linguists who have worked with Winter's ideas include Dea (1977), Jordan (1978), Hoey (1979) and Edwards (1980).

Section 2

The first linguist to define clause relations was Quirk (1954). Quirk takes a single relation – the concessive relation – and shows the ways in which it is characterised in a particular language, namely, Old English. Both his use of the whole context and his use of paraphrase characterise the approach to discourse analysis adopted in this work. Thus, although Quirk concentrates on inter-clausal rather than intersentential relations, his approach is essentially that of a discourse analyst. His working definition of the concessive relation – 'the concessive relation may be said to exist between parts of an utterance when one part is surprising in view of the other' – forms the basis of the definition adopted by Winter (1971, 1974, 1977) as used in this book.

Section 3

Alternative names for the clause relation have been 'propositional relation' (Beekman, 1970a; Kathleen Callow, 1970) and 'interclausal relation' (Ballard *et al.*, 1971a, b); none of the terms suggested, however, fully reflects the complexity of the relations they label.

Although the notion of the clause relation was known to Poutsma (1914–29) and Jespersen (1914–49), their use of relations was almost exclusively in terms of connecting clauses within the sentence and not of connecting the sentence with its neighbours. Probably the first to use clause relations to clarify the organisation of discourse (though in these matters certainty is not easily achieved) was Beardsley (1950). Beardsley was concerned to integrate philosophical modes of thinking into the everyday world. It was therefore necessary for him to show the ways in which logical thinking could be reflected in language and, equally importantly, to show how language could be used intentionally or otherwise to disguise illogical thinking. To achieve these twin ends effectively, Beardsley had to undertake the first steps of discourse analysis. Because of the unexpected context in which his work appeared, however, his influence on linguists has been slight. That he is nevertheless still aware of the importance of discourse work is apparent in a paper given in the 1960s (Beardsley, 1965) in which he again discusses the various types of relations that hold between sentences, also commenting that 'faults of style must be faults of logic'.

In a series of papers in the 1960s Young and Becker (Young and Becker, 1965, 1966; Becker, 1965, 1966; Koen, Young and Becker, 1969; Young, 1968) explore ways of treating the paragraph, using a tagmemic model that incorporates a notion of clause relation. In Young, Becker and Pike (1970), there is less insistence on the paragraph and more on the discourse. Here they talk of 'generalised plots' which they define as 'made up of a sequence of semantic slots which may be filled with a variety of specific semantic elements provided that the choice of an element to fill one slot is appropriate to the choices made for the other slots'. These can be present at discourse or paragraph level. Examples of such 'plots' at paragraph level are 'B is an instance of A, B is a cause of A, B is a restatement of A, B is different from A, B is similar to A, A and B exist in temporal sequence, A and B exist in spatial array'. It will be seen that these plots are conceived entirely in relational terms.

Another tagmemicist who has utilised the notion of the clause relation is

Robert Longacre. In Longacre (1968), he is concerned to account for discourse, paragraph, and sentence structure in a number of Philippine languages. In his discussion of sentence structure the concept of the clause relation is clearly present in the form of sentence margins, the relation holding between the margin and the nuclear clause. The margins are divided into three main types – time, teleological and implicational margins. Time margins place the nuclear clause in a temporal relation with other events; they are important in establishing paragraph and discourse linkage. Teleological margins include cause margins, circumstantial margins (which serve to sketch the situations out of which actions have arisen), purpose margins, result margins and chance/anticipatory/hortatory margins (which offer a tentative and uncertain purpose or cause). Implicational margins include conditional margins, provisional margins (i.e. clauses beginning 'provided that . . .), possibility margins (i.e. clauses of the form 'should *x* happen, do *y*') and concessive margins. These relations, though handled at the sentence level, are recognised by Longacre to have implications at higher levels. In two papers (strictly speaking one divided into two) written jointly with Ballard and Conrad (Ballard *et al.*, 1971a, b) and in Longacre (1972) a distinction is made between interclausal relations and their typical 'surface' encoding. On the one hand we must have a formal statement of the relations, if possible in terms derived from logic, and on the other hand we must have a clear and comprehensive account of the ways in which each relation can be manifested in the language. This double description is necessary for two reasons: some relations can be manifested in more than one way, and some linguistic manifestations can signal more than one relation. (A similar observation by Winter, 1968, is discussed in Section 4 of Chapter 2.)

In Longacre (1979) paragraphs are argued to be grammatical units with a structure firmly built on the concept of the relation. Thus defined, the paragraph is seen to be describable in terms of three parameters:

(1)   binary versus n-ary constructions (in other words, a relation may be between two members only or may be between any number of members);

(2)   movement along a parameter with the following values: conjoining (e.g. contrast), temporal relations, logical relations, elaborative devices, reportative devices (e.g. 'evaluative observations by the composer of the discourse');

(3)   weighting considerations (i.e. whether the parts are of equal weight or whether one part is of greater importance).

Whether or not we accept the argument that these parameters describe the structure of a level that can usefully be called the paragraph – arguments were presented in Chapter 1 for the opposite view – there can be no doubt that the parameters provide an excellent basis for a proper classification of relations.

Much of Longacre's work on discourse has been fuelled by a missionary zeal in the strictest sense of those words. While in English there are innumerable translations of the Bible and most households have a (largely unread) copy on their shelves, there are still many languages in the world where the Bible has never been translated and very many more where it has been translated only in part and inadequately. As a devout Christian – Longacre (1976) culminates in a challenging statement of faith – Longacre has sought to make available to translators the fruits of his work on discourse, and many of his colleagues in the field have had an active missionary function. It should come as no surprise, therefore, that Bible translation has generated new ideas about and applications of the concept of the relation.

In a series of papers published in *Notes on Translation* (Beekman, 1970a, b, c; Blight, 1970; Kathleen Callow, 1970; J. Callow, 1970a, b; Jamieson, 1970) and in a subsequent book (Beekman and J. Callow, 1974) Beekman and his colleagues explore the use of what they term propositional relations as a way of representing the organisation of the content of a discourse.

The basic principle underlying the work of Beekman *et al.* is that concepts group into propositions, propositions into statements, statements into semantic paragraphs, semantic paragraphs into sections, and sections into larger units up to the total discourse. For Beekman *et al.* these 'levels' are arrived at pragmatically as the result of specific analyses of particular discourses; they have no validity as levels within a tagmemic description. Furthermore a single proposition may relate to any higher semantic unit.

This is the first important insight of Beekman *et al.*; relations do not occur neatly at one level at a time but occur between levels. Thus a nominal group may be in a relation with several (orthographic) paragraphs, or a single sentence in a relation with an entire discourse.

A second important insight that Beekman *et al.* develop is that propositional relations are both reflections of and developments from real-world relations. They divide these relations into two groups – perceptual relations, which are relations perceived in the world, such as sequence in time, alternatives, and differences, and conceptual relations, which are the writer or speaker's reworking of the perceptual relations. These include deductions, repetition for emphasis, explanation, and the giving of prominence to parts of the information. Both types of relation have their typical linguistic correlates, though these are not discussed in much detail, as it is Beekman *et al.*'s intention to explain what is shared between languages, not describe in detail the signalling system of any one language.

A third insight of Beekman *et al.* worthy of brief mention is that a proposition may be in relation with more than one other proposition, stated in a subdued form in Beekman (1970a) and more broadly in Beekman and Callow (1974).

Beekman *et al.* consider the organisation of very long discourses, for example, discussing in Beekman (1970a, b) and Beekman and Callow (1974) the organisation of the whole of the Acts of the Apostles. They also offer ways of getting at the 'central proposition' of a total discourse. Nevertheless all is for them subordinate to the needs of translation. Thus their use of propositions assumes a degree of abstraction from the language that may well be justifiable as a practical device for translators in preparation for their task but which is more arguable in the study of a language for its own sake. Similarly they show only a cursory interest in how relations are signalled as such to their readers, and their discussion of such signals, as they recognise, is sometimes naive. Some of the relations posited in their classification seem spuriously differentiated; they are in no position to prove otherwise because no signalling criteria are supplied nor are any other means offered of justifying a relation's existence in the classification. The presence or absence of a relation would, according to this, seem to be a matter of no more than intuition and practical value.

Section 4

In addition to Winter (1968), discussed briefly in the text, Winter has also written about subordinators and conjuncts in Winter (1971).

A number of other linguists have shared Winter's interest in the semantic functions of subordinators and conjuncts. Quirk (1954) was concerned to study them as the main means of signalling the concessive relation in Old English. Harris (1952b) lists, as in an equivalence or transformation relationship, pairs such as the following:

Co-operatives succeed by economising.

and

Co-operatives economise: thus they succeed.

Sledd (1956) argues that, subject to the restraints of context, we have a number of options available in English for clarifying the logical relation holding between two clauses; these include subordinators and conjuncts. Karlsen (1959) notes, in passing, that conjuncts (or half-conjunctions, as he terms them) indicate logical relations between clauses and briefly lists the logical relations they may indicate.

All these either refer to their signalling function in passing or, in the case of Quirk, concentrate on a relevant subset. More representative coverage of the possibilities is given by Young *et al.* (1970), though without discussion, and by Hutchins (1977b) who adapts Longacre (1970) so as to set up classes of conjuncts; he does this by converting Longacre's classes of sentence margin into classes of conjuncts, following a hint of Maryott's given in Longacre (1968) that conjuncts might be treated as a special type of sentence margin.

The two most detailed descriptions in recent years have been Quirk *et al.* (1972) and Halliday and Hasan (1976). Quirk *et al.* discuss the function of conjuncts both as signals of relations along with other syntactic devices used for the same purpose, and in terms of their syntactic characteristics and differences. Halliday and Hasan treat them within the broader category of conjunction, one of four types of cohesive relation. Both descriptions involve a detailed classification of conjuncts/types of relation. Space, however, forbids reiteration here, especially as conjuncts and subordinators will be found to be of relatively minor importance to the analytical system described in this work, except in so far as paraphrase is concerned. Accordingly the reader is referred to the works cited in this section for fuller accounts of conjuncts and subordinators.

Section 5

The importance Winter attaches to lexical signalling is apparent in Winter (1974) and is even hinted at in Winter (1968). It is in Winter (1977), however, that its significance is systematically worked out. In this monograph he offers evidence for recognising the existence of the special vocabulary of lexical signals, gives a full, though not comprehensive, list of such signals, and works out in detail the criteria for identifying them in the context of a theory of clause relations. A shorter form of the argument with a slightly different emphasis is to be found in Winter (1978). Hoey (1979) uses Winter's work to illuminate discourse organisation.

There are brief references to lexical signalling in the writings of other linguists. Jespersen (1933) notes that two or more expressions 'may have exactly or approximately the same meaning and yet, grammatically speaking, belong to totally different categories so that they should not be named by the same term', and gives among his examples:

He came to the tryst because he admired her

and

His admiration for her was the reason why he came to the tryst,

a pair which clearly foreshadows Winter's comparison of vocabularies 1 and 3.

Quirk *et al.* (1972) suggest the relationship between grammatical and lexical signals in the examples accompanying discussion of connectives in chapter 10 of that work, though the nature of the relationship is not explored. Gopnik (1972) notes that items like 'increased', 'changed', 'remained constant' are implicit comparatives. She also notes the existence of words which refer to the whole of the previous discourse (e.g. 'this evidence', 'these findings'); this, as is shown in Chapters 3–7, is an important function of lexical signalling.

Perhaps closest to Winter's position is Farnes (1973), who makes reference to 'signposts that tell the reader where he is going', 'signposts along the route', 'signposts that tell the reader where he has come from' and 'signposts or instructions on how to receive or comprehend a text'. Sadly, these categories are left undeveloped, rather less than four pages being devoted to them. Furthermore, his 'signposts' are somewhat confusingly divided into 'content' and 'structure' signals, a division that separates 'We have outlined the causes of the Industrial Revolution' from 'The main points of the area have been outlined'.

This distinction appears to derive in part from Francis (1958), who adopts a less developed but essentially similar position. Francis notes: 'The use of special grammatical devices in a situation-sentence (i.e. the sentence that begins a conversation) to forecast sequence-sentence (i.e. a sentence that continues the utterance of the same speaker) to come is really a special case of an aspect of grammar that has been very little studied: the whole question of the foreshadowing of grammatical structure.' He adds: 'The careful listener, . . . like the careful driver, is subconsciously alert to signals that forecast what the situation will be a few seconds later.' He cites as examples of this 'foreshadowing', 'in the first place' and 'on the one hand' but assigns to rhetoric, not grammar, examples such as 'let us consider the second point' which, he says, 'forecast something about the subject-matter, rather than the structure into which it is formed'.

Section 6

The two places where Winter develops most fully his conception of repetition as a signal are Winter (1974, 1979). In the former work, he shows repetition to be a key feature of his clause-relational approach to discourse; in the latter, he updates his original position in the light of work subsequent to (1974) and makes the earlier insights more accessible. Hoey and Winter (1981) show how the study of systematic repetition can be used for the purposes of literary stylistics.

Harris (1952a, b) uses repetition as the basis for setting up equivalence classes in discourse. His refusal to consider the semantic significance to the discourse of the repetition hinders him, however, from discovering anything from these classes once set up. Dixon (1965) also notes the existence of repetition in discourse and makes it an important aspect of his approach to linguistic description. Unfortunately his abandonment of all customary clause categories has made his suggestions in this area less accessible than they otherwise might have been.

More successful perhaps than either of these in demonstrating the importance of repetition in discourse studies is Harper (1965). Harper is less concerned than Winter with systematic repetition. He seeks rather to demonstrate the high frequency of lexical repetition in discourse. Examining the relationship of adjacent sentences in Russian and English, he concludes that there are repetitions of nouns and/or adjectives in 70 per cent of all sentence pairs, there are repetitions of root morphemes and technical symbols in a further 10 per cent, and repetition by pronominalisation or synonymy in another 8 per cent. Thus only 12 per cent of sentence pairs are not connected by some form of repetition device. As we show in Chapters 6 and 7, had he considered non-adjacent pairs, the ratio of unconnected sentences would have been still lower.

Leech (1965) observes repetition and grammatical parallelism as part of Dylan Thomas's technique in 'This Bread I Break'. He also notes (Leech, 1969) that if there are more than two stages in the pattern created by the parallelism, the last stage is liable to be seen as climactic. He observes that the relation between parallel elements 'is, broadly speaking, a connection either of similarity or of contrast'.

Longacre (1968) shows that in some Philippine languages the main clause of a sentence may be repeated in a subordinate clause in the next. This type of linkage is much more regular and systematic than anything apparent in English. Grimes (1972) describes this phenomenon as 'overlay' and claims that it distinguishes sharply the organisation of these and other languages from that of the Western European languages. In the light of Winter's and Harper's observations about repetition, one would want to argue that the difference should be seen as one of degree rather than kind.

Others who have also looked at the role of repetition in discourse are Gopnik (1972) who is, however, concerned with repetition between sentences that have already undergone transformational analysis or 'decomposition'; Van Dijk (1973), who notes that coherence is a function of the degree of repetition in a discourse, and Brazil (1975, 1978), who shows that a phenomenon similar to that of repetition and replacement as postulated by Winter can account for many features of the intonation patterns employed in English.

Rimmon-Kenan (1979) and Suleiman (1980) discuss the importance of repetition in accounting for literary text. Rimmon-Kenan states that 'repetition is present everywhere and nowhere', a paradoxical formulation of the idea that 'even when the whole sign is repeated, difference is introduced through the very fact of repetition, the accumulation of significance it entails, and the change effected by the different context in which it is placed'. She goes on to distinguish between repetitiousness, where repetition produces a sense of sameness, and repetitiveness, where repetition adds force and intensity. This is summed up in her second paradoxical formulation: 'Constructive repetition emphasises difference, destructive repetition emphasises sameness (i.e. to repeat successfully is not to repeat).'

Suleiman is similarly interested in the nature and function of repetition. She attempts to set up means of categorising discourses according to the different types of redundancy/repetition occurring in them. As an aid to doing this, she painstakingly subclassifies repetition into a variety of types, some identifiable with forms of repetition already discussed, others of a form as yet unanalysable in linguistic terms. Her work, though flawed by confusing literal repetition with repetition perceived but not provable, is nevertheless of value in highlighting the pervasiveness and variety of repetition in discourse.

Section 7

Paraphrase is used frequently in Winter (1974, 1977) in particular but is present to some degree in all his work as a test of relations. Harris (1952b) employs it to set up equivalence classes. Quirk (1954) uses it as a means of identifying instances of the concessive relation in Old English.

Gopnik (1972) examines the structures of scientific texts starting from the assumption that 'some sets of texts are semantically equivalent'. This is a broader view of paraphrase than that Winter adopts or than is used here. There is value, however, in her notion of 'included paraphrase'; where what one passage says is included in what the other says, e.g. 'A table was purchased' is included in 'David purchased a table'.

Van Dijk (1973) states as one of the properties of a text-grammar that it will be able to 'consider the relations between clauses in complex or compound sentences as special cases of the more general textual relations between sentences, or rather between their underlying "propositions" or "logical forms", be these described in syntactic or semantic terms'. This, as he suggests, 'implies that any complex sentence can be paraphrased by a set of simple sentences'. Such indeed is shown to be the case in Chapter 4 where paraphrase is employed systematically to educe the organisation of a minimum discourse.

Section 8

Winter first introduces questions as a means of clarifying clause relations in Winter (1969); considerable use is made of them in all his subsequent work, particularly Winter (1974, 1976). He divides questions into two kinds – starting questions and continuation questions. Starting questions are questions that start new stages in a discourse. Continuation questions are questions which are determined by their starting questions. It was the use of questions that enables Winter to identify the Problem–Solution pattern discussed in Chapters 3, 4 and 5.

Bakhtin (1973 [1929]) was perhaps the first to use dialogue to illuminate the relationships holding between the parts of a prose passage. He claims that Dostoevsky's prose rarely reflects the writer's voice alone; as evidence he demonstrates that passages of monologue can be converted into dialogue quite readily in such a way as to account for many of their linguistic features. Sadly, Bakhtin's work met the disapproval of the Stalinist regime in Russia and it therefore exercised little influence until it was republished in 1963.

Apart from Winter, the only modern linguists to have made the conversion of monologue into dialogue a matter of central consideration have been Gray and Widdowson. Gray (1977a, b) argues that modern linguistics has no answer to the ancient problem of 'how to teach the composition of sustained discourse more precisely than simply by holding up examples and labelling them as good or bad'. He notes that 'a written discourse, if properly composed, can tell you what it means and in much the same way that dialog . . . conveys meaning – by raising questions and giving answers to them'. He proceeds to demonstrate that an acceptable piece of writing can be accounted for in terms of the implied questions that arise out of earlier statements and that conversely an unacceptable piece of writing cannot be so satisfactorily accounted for.

Widdowson (1979) sees reading as 'interaction between writer and reader mediated through the text'. This can be represented in the form of a dialogue in which the reader acts as questioner and the text as answerer. This position is very similar to that developed in Chapter 8.

Chapter 3

Section 2

A more inflexible position regarding hierarchy in discourse is that taken by Graustein and Thiele (1980), who argue that all discourses can be accounted for using clause relations in hierarchical formation. Longacre (1979) makes a similar assumption regarding paragraph structure.

Section 3

The four-sentence example discussed in this and subsequent sections was first briefly discussed in Winter (1976) though it predates that work in his lecture notes by some years. It has also been discussed in Hoey (1979).

Section 12

The category of Situation is similar in some respects to that of setting in Gleason (1968) and Grimes (1975), though it differs from setting in being definable only in terms of the complete discourse pattern.

Section 17

The approach adopted here to the Problem–Solution pattern is derived from Winter's accounts of it (1969, 1976). Brief mention is also made of the pattern in Winter (1977). Hoey (1979) uses the Problem–Solution pattern as a vehicle for discussing the nature of signalling in discourse. Jordan (1980) looks at the variety of forms the pattern can take in factual reporting.

The structure we have identified as Problem–Solution appears to have been first noted by Beardsley (1950). Young and Becker (1965) rediscovered it, identifying it as one of two important paragraph structures, the other being Topic–Restriction–Illustration; most of their attention is however devoted to the latter structure.

Labov and Waletsky (1967) and Labov (1972) identify the pattern in oral narratives: abstract–orientation–complication–action–evaluation–result or resolution–coda. Likewise Longacre (1972) identifies the following structure for certain narratives: aperture–setting–inciting moment–developing conflict–climax–dénouement–final suspense–closure. These, though not identical to the Problem–Solution pattern, are clearly related.

Grimes (1975) notes of the Problem–Solution pattern that

> Both the plots of fairy tales and the writings of scientists are built on a response pattern. The first part gives a problem and the second its solution . . . the content of the second part is dependent upon the content of the first part to a great extent. How to express this interlocking seems to be beyond us . . . but that is the shape of the relation.

Van Dijk (1977) draws attention to the narrative structure setting–complication–resolution–evaluation–moral, and to the scientific discourse structure introduction–problem–solution–conclusion. He notes: 'The structure of an argument . . . should be assigned independently of whether it is about engineering, linguistics or child-care.'

A more central role is given to the Problem–Solution pattern by Hutchins (1977a, b), who discusses it as it applies to scientific discourses and to the needs of abstracting. Hutchins's main task is to relate the various descriptions of the linguists so far mentioned (as well as others not discussed); he suggests that the Problem–Solution pattern is perhaps best seen as one of a series of 'oppositions' built out of patterns of expectation and 'as determined by the particular communicational functions it has to serve'.

Section 20

Winter (1979, forthcoming) discusses the relation of Situation and Evaluation in considerable detail, the latter work relating it to the verbs 'think' and 'know'. Hoey (1979) and Hoey and Winter (1982) also refer to it, though in less detail.

Chapter 4

Section 7

The discourse 'Balloons and Air Cushion the Fall' was originally found by Winter and used in teaching. It is briefly discussed in Winter (1976) and in greater detail in Hoey (1979) where it is analysed with the help of comparative fragments from other discourses.

Chapter 5

Section 8

Jordan (forthcoming) has independently come to similar conclusions about participant-linking which he discusses under the heading of 'people problems'.

Chapter 6

Section 2

Repetition is discussed in great detail in Winter (1974). Cohesion in general is treated fully in Halliday and Hasan (1976) and in Quirk *et al.* (1972). Jordan (1978) looks at some aspects of cohesion from a clause relation standpoint. For repetition as a signal, see the bibliography for Section 6, Chapter 2 above.

Harris (1952a, b) developed a technique that made no use of meaning criteria identifying equivalences between parts of a discourse. He termed his paraphrases 'transformations' and it was this that Chomsky borrowed and adapted for a different end in his own work (Chomsky, 1957 *et seq.*).

Section 3

The Matching relations are first posited in Winter (1968). They are central to Winter's discussion of clause relations in Winter (1974),where the interlocking functions of repetition and replacement are first analysed. Winter (1981) continues his work on these important aspects of clause relation theory. The terms 'constant' and 'variable' derive from Fowler (1965 [1926]).

Christensen (1965) talks of 'co-ordination' relations between sentences in a paragraph which are identified by 'likeness'. Although likeness is not defined, it would appear from his examples that his 'co-ordination' relations broadly correspond to Winter's Matching relations, though the relationship is never treated by Christensen as having meaning and is seen as a consequence of topic development. He notes of one of his examples:

> The repetition of structure . . . is all that is necessary to join sentence to sentence at the same level. Any connectives other than the simple *and* for the last member would be an impertinence – *again, moreover, in the same vein, in addition* would be a hindrance rather than a help. But repetition of structure *is* necessary; like things in like ways is one of the imperatives of discursive writing. Any attempt to introduce variety in the sentence beginnings, by varying the pattern or by putting something before the subject, would be like trying to vary the columns of the Parthenon.

Section 8

For Winter's own account of the 'Icy Roads' experiment and his analysis of the text, upon which the analysis here offered is built, see Winter (1976).

Chapter 7

Section 2

Winter discusses the General–Particular relations in Winter (1974). They are at the heart of Young and Becker's work; for details see the annotated bibliography for Section 3 of Chapter 2 above.

Section 3

The special status of sentences containing enumeration is discussed in Winter (1977) and Tadros (1981). Johns (1980) discusses large-scale matching organisation under the heading of the matrix, drawing on a number of sources including Allen and Widdowson (1974).

Section 5

Todd (1980) makes use of similar subdivisions of Detail, though categorised in a different way and defined using different criteria. See also Davies *et al.* (1980) in which important insights are offered into subclassifications of Detail, seen too late to be incorporated into the main body of the text.

Section 8

Bligh (1972) suggests that a common form of lecture organisation is the classification hierarchy – this is in principle the Detail Tree under another name. Allen and Widdowson (1974) likewise treat classifications as an important information-structure.

Chapter 8

Section 3

The possibility of a discourse's highlighting certain questions as ones that it will answer is discussed in some detail in Winter (1977) and is further developed in Cooper (1980, forthcoming) and Tadros (1981), both of whom are in different ways concerned with exploring the extent to which all relations have an anticipatory element. Winter (1977) uses 'anticipate' to mean that the clause makes explicit in advance what the next clause relation will be. Tadros (1981) prefers to use the term 'predict' for this, a term Winter (1977) uses to describe those circumstances where certain types of information are likely rather than are certain to follow. We follow Winter's usage here.

Discussion of the hypothetical–real relation can be found in Winter (1974, 1979), and Hoey and Winter (1982).

For discussion of the expectations raised by the style/genre of writing encountered, see Crystal and Davy (1969), Grimes (1975), Van Dijk (1977) and Cooper (1980).

Notes

Chapter 1

1 The first sentence of this 'passage' is taken from 'Upon Epitaphs' by William Wordsworth in *Prose Works* (1876), reprinted in *A Century of English Essays* (London: Dent, 1913).
2 The first sentence of this and the subsequent passage is taken from 'The Flying Trunk' by Hans Andersen, translated by Reginald Spink, in *Fairy Tales and Stories* (London: Dent, 1960).
3 This and the subsequent passage are taken from Young and Becker (1966); the work they cite is *Lincoln and his Generals* by T. Harry Williams.
4 From a letter dated 12 November 1971 circulated to all members of the British Film Institute by the chairman, Denis Forman.

Chapter 2

1 From Stanley Phillips, *Stamp Collecting*, 7th edn (London: Stanley Gibbons, 1959), p. 66.
2 From Mary Gaskell [1848], *Mary Barton* (London: Dent, 1967), p. 12.
3 From Hammond Innes, *The Strange Land* (London: Collins/Fontana, 1954), p. 18.
4 From Gore Vidal, *Julian* (London: Heinemann, 1962), p. 202.
5 From P. D. Eastman, *Big Dog . . . Little Dog* (London: Collins Picture Lions, 1973).
6 From Margaret Drabble, *The Needle's Eye* (Harmondsworth: Penguin, 1973), p. 192.
7 ibid., pp. 193–4.
8 Cited in Winter (1974); from *The Times*, 7 January 1966, p. 11.
9 Cited in Winter (1977).
10 From Martin L. Keen, *The How and Why Wonder Book of Science Experiments* (London: Transworld Publishers, 1964), p. 14.
11 From 'Car body structure design for corrosion prevention', paper given by J. Fenton at the 'Nature and Prevention of Vehicle Corrosion' conference held at the Hatfield Polytechnic, September 1972 (mimeo.).
12 Quoted in Winter (1974); from the *Guardian*, 8 November 1966, p. 8.
13 From Enid Blyton, 'Bertie's Blue Braces', in *Stories for Bedtime* (London: Dean, 1966), p. 148.

Chapter 3

1 Strictly speaking, 'thereby' is probably not optional. The sequence would be unacceptable or at least odd without the addition of 'thereby' to the fourth clause. Since it will be discussed in Section 5, it has been omitted here from our discussion.
2 I am grateful to Adrian Stenton for this and the following example.

Chapter 4

1 From Arthur Billit, 'In your garden: fruit', *Amateur Gardening*, 1 March 1975, p. 23.
2 From 'Technology review', *New Scientist*, vol. 46 (1970), p. 230. I am grateful to Eugene Winter for this example.

Chapter 5

1   Advertisement for Inter-dens Gum Massage Sticks, current in 1978.
2   From A. W. Rudge and D. E. N. Davies, 'Electronically controllable primary feed for profile-error compensation of large parabolic reflectors', *Proceedings of the Institution of Electrical Engineers*, vol. 117, no. 2 (1970), p. 351. I am grateful to P. A. Witting of the School of Engineering, the Hatfield Polytechnic, for drawing my attention to this passage.
3   'The Princess and the Pea' by Hans Andersen, translated by Reginald Spink, in *Fairy Tales and Stories* (London: Dent, 1960).
4   Sample text from paper by Anthony Davey given at the 4th Systemic Workshop held at the Hatfield Polytechnic, July 1977.
5   From Roger Hargreaves. *Mr Noisy* (London: Thurman Publishing, 1976).
6   From 'Rubber dam holds water inside and out' ('Notes on the News'), *New Scientist*, vol. 35 (1967), p. 281. I am grateful to Eugene Winter for this example.
7   From advertisement for Trihextin G, current in 1978.
8   From advertisement for Vibrelax, current in 1978.
9   From advertisement for Boots developing and printing service, current in 1978.

Chapter 6

1   From W. J. Reichmann, *The Use and Abuse of Statistics* (Harmondsworth: Penguin, 1964), p. 185.
2   From D. H. Lawrence, *Women in Love* (Harmondsworth: Penguin, 1960), p. 240.
3   From F. Scott Fitzgerald, 'Mayday', in *The Stories of F. Scott Fitzgerald*, Vol. 1 (Harmondsworth: Penguin, 1962), p. 65.
4   From Ivor Montagu, *Film World* (Harmondsworth: Penguin, 1964), p. 122.
5   From personal tape recording.
6   Newspaper source lost.
7   From Michael P. Foster, introduction to *Masters of Political Thought*, Vol. 1 (London: Harrap, 1942), p. 16.
8   From P. D. Eastman, *Big Dog . . . Little Dog* (London: Collins Picture Lions, 1973).
9   From W. C. Guthrie, *The Greek Philosophers* (London: Methuen, 1950), pp. 68–9.
10 From Alan Jenkin, 'Simulation under focus', *Computer Management*, March 1971, p. 38.
11 From W. Littler, *Elementary Chemistry* (London: Bell, 1961), p. 347.
12 From Gilda Lund, *Red Riding Hood also Goldilocks and the Three Bears* (Loughborough: Ladybird Books/Wills & Hepworth, 1958).
13 From C. W. Kearsey and R. W. Trump, *Introductory Physics* (London: Longman, 1960).
14 William Blake, 'The Clod and the Pebble', in *Complete Writings* (London: OUP, 1966), p. 211.
15 William Blake, 'A Poison Tree', in op. cit., p. 218.
16 Letter from Michael Tippett to the *Guardian*.

Chapter 7

1   From Christopher Bush, 'The Hampstead Murder', in *A Century of Detective Stories* (introduction by G. K. Chesterton) (London: Hutchinson, 1935), p. 405.
2   From W. H. Kingston [1851]. *Peter the Whaler* (London: Cassell, 1919), p. 181.
3   From Letter II (1864), in W. H. Gardner (ed.), *Gerard Manley Hopkins: A selection of his Poems and Prose* (Harmondsworth: Penguin, 1953), pp. 156–7.

4   From Wesley Cable, *Vacuum Processes in Metalworking* (New York: Van Nostrand Reinhold, 1960).
5   From *New Scientist*, vol. 35 (1967), p. 281; I am grateful to Eugene Winter for this example.
6   From P. Gant, *Mechanics* (London: Bell, 1961), p. 6.
7   From 'Key-punch crooks', *Time*, 25 December 1972.
8   From Christopher Bush, 'The Hampstead Murder', op. cit., p. 405.
9   From Alan Jenkin, 'Simulation under focus', *Computer Management*, March 1971, p. 38.

Chapter 8

1   From Enid Blyton, 'Bertie's Blue Braces', in *Stories for Bedtime* (London: Dean, 1966), p. 148.
2   'An eye on drunken drivers', in 'Technology Review', *New Scientist*, March 1970, p. 559.
3   'The error that proved right' in 'March 1976: The night sky', *Guardian*, 1 March 1976.
4   From A. E. Tansley and R. H. Nicholls, *Racing to Read*, Book 7.
5   ibid.

References

Aaron, Ira E., *et al.* (1971), *Scott, Foresman Reading Systems Studybook Level 10* (Glenview, Ill.: Scott, Foresman).

Allen, J. P. B., and Widdowson, H. G. (1974), *English in Physical Science*, English in Focus series (London: OUP).

Bakhtin, Mikhail (1973), *Problems of Dostoevsky's Poetics* [1929], trans. R. W. Rotsel (Ann Arbor, Mich.: Ardis).

Ballard, D. Lee, Conrad, Robert J., and Longacre, Robert E. (1971a), 'The deep and surface grammar of interclausal relations', *Foundations of Language*, vol. 7, pp. 70–118; reprinted in Ruth M. Brend (ed.), *Advances in Tagmemics* (Amsterdam: North-Holland Publishing Co., 1974), pp. 307–55.

Ballard, D. Lee, Conrad, Robert J., and Longacre, Robert E. (1971b), 'More on the deep and surface grammar of interclausal relations', *Language Data*, Asian-Pacific series, No. 1 (Ukarumpa, Papua N-G: Summer Institute of Linguistics Publications).

Beardsley, Monroe C. (1950), *Practical Logic* (New York: Prentice-Hall).

Beardsley, Monroe C. (1965), 'Style and good style', address delivered at a National Defense Education Act Institute for Advanced Study in English in 1965: published in G. Tate (ed.), *Reflections on High School English: NDEA Institute Lectures 1965* (Tulsa, Okla: University of Tulsa, 1966); reprinted in M. Steinmann (ed.), *New Rhetorics* (New York: Scribner, 1967).

Becker, Alton L. (1965), 'A tagmemic approach to paragraph analysis', *College Composition and Communication*, vol. 16, no. 4, pp. 237–42.

Becker, Alton L. (1966), 'Symposium on the paragraph', *College Composition and Communication*, vol. 17, no. 1, pp. 67–72.

Beekman, John (1970a), 'Propositions and their relations within a discourse', *Notes on Translation*, vol. 37, pp. 6–23.

Beekman, John (1970b), 'A structural display of propositions in Jude', *Notes on Translation*, vol. 37, pp. 27–31.

Beekman, John (1970c), 'Structural notes on the Book of Jude (1)', *Notes on Translation*, vol. 37, pp. 36–8.

Beekman, John, and Callow, John (1974), *Translating the Word of God* (Grand Rapids, Mich.: Zondervan).

Bligh, Donald (1972), *What's the Use of Lectures?* (Harmondsworth: Penguin).

Blight, Richard C. (1970), 'An alternate display of Jude', *Notes on Translation*, vol. 37, pp. 32–6.

Brazil, David (1975), *Discourse Intonation*, Discourse Analysis Monographs 1 (Birmingham: English Language Research, Birmingham University).

Brazil, David (1978), *Discourse Intonation II*, Discourse Analysis Monographs 2 (Birmingham: English Language Research, Birmingham University).

Callow, John C. (1970a), 'Structural notes on the Book of Jude (2)', *Notes on Translation*, vol. 37, pp. 38–41.

Callow, John C. (1970b), 'An outline of Jude', *Notes on Translation*, vol. 37, p. 42.

Callow, Kathleen (1970), 'More on propositions and their relations within a discourse', *Notes on Translation*, vol. 37, pp. 23–7.

Chomsky, N. (1957), *Syntactic Structures* (The Hague: Mouton).

Christensen, Francis (1965), 'A generative rhetoric of the paragraph', *College Composition and Communication*, vol. 16, no. 3 (1965), pp. 144–56, revised 1966; reprinted in M. Steinmann (ed.), *New Rhetorics* (New York: Scribner, 1967).

Christensen, Francis (1966), 'Symposium on the paragraph', *College Composition and Communication*, vol. 17, no. 2, pp. 60–6.

Cooper, Malcolm (forthcoming, a), 'Linguistic aspects of text difficulty', in A. Urquhart and J. C. Alderson (eds), *Linguistic Competence of Practised and Unpractised Non-Native Readers of English* (London: Longman).

Cooper, Malcolm (forthcoming, b), 'An investigation of the structure of academic written text', PhD thesis, University of Birmingham.

Coulthard, R. M. (1977), *An Introduction to Discourse Analysis* (London: Longman).

Coulthard, R. M., and Brazil, D. (1979), *Exchange Structure*, Discourse Analysis Monographs 5 (Birmingham: English Language Research, Birmingham University).

Crystal, David, and Davy, Derek (1969), *Investigating English Style* (London: Longman).

Davey, Anthony (1978), *Discourse Production: A Computer Model of Some Aspects of a Speaker* (Edinburgh: Edinburgh University Press).

Davies, F., Greene, T., and Lunzer, E. (1980), 'Reading for learning in science: a discussion paper', Schools Council Project 'Reading for Learning in the Secondary School'.

Dea, W. H. (1977), 'The sentence and beyond: clause relations and analysis of the language of literature', M.Phil. dissertation, CNAA, Hatfield Polytechnic.

Dixon, R. M. W. (1965), *What Is Language? A New Approach to Linguistic Description* (London: Longman).

Edwards, N. (1980), '"Difficulty" in text as a function of syntactic complexity: a study of syntactic complexity within and between sentences', M.Phil. dissertation, CNAA, Hatfield Polytechnic.

Farnes, N. C. (1973), 'Comprehension and the use of context', Unit 4, Reading Development, Educational Studies: a Post-Experience Course and Second Level Course. PE.261 (revised 1975) (Milton Keynes: The Open University).

Fowler, H. W. (1965), *Fowler's Modern English Usage* [1926], 2nd edn, (London: OUP).

Francis, W. Nelson (1958), *The Structure of American English* (New York: Ronald Press).

Gleason, H. A., Jr. (1968), 'Contrastive analysis in discourse structure', in James E. Alatis (ed.), *Georgetown University 19th Annual Round Table Meeting on Linguistics and Language Studies: Contrastive Linguistics and its Pedagogical Implications*, Monograph Series on Language and Linguistics No. 21 (Washington, DC: Georgetown University Press).

Gopnik, Myrna (1972), *Linguistic Structures in Scientific Texts*, Janua Linguarum Series Minor, 129 (The Hague: Mouton).

Graustein, Gottfried, and Thiele, Wolfgang (1980), 'Zur Struktur der Bedeutung von englischen Texten', *Linguistische Arbeitsberichte*, vol. 26, pp. 12–28.

Gray, Bennison (1977a), 'From discourse to dialog', *Journal of Pragmatics*, vol. 1, no. 3, pp. 283–98.

Gray, Bennison (1977b), *The Grammatical Foundations of Rhetoric: Discourse Analysis*, Janua Linguarum Series Minor, 51 (The Hague: Mouton).

Grimes, Joseph E. (1972), 'Outlines and overlays', *Language*, vol. 48, no. 3, pp. 513–24.

Grimes, Joseph E. (1975), *The Thread of Discourse* (The Hague: Mouton).

Halliday, M. A. K., and Hasan, R. (1976), *Cohesion in English* (London: Longman).

Harper, Kenneth A. (1965), *Studies in Inter-Sentence Connection* (prepared for USAF Project Fund), Memorandum RM-4824-PR (Santa Monica, Calif: Rand).

Harris, Zellig S. (1952a), 'Discourse analysis', *Language*, vol. 28, no. 1, pp. 1–30.

Harris, Zellig S. (1952b), 'Discourse analysis: a sample text', *Language*, vol. 28, no. 4, pp. 474–94; reprinted in *Papers in Structural and Transformational Linguistics* (Dordrecht: Reidel, 1970).

Harris, Zellig S. (1952c), 'Culture and style in extended discourse', in S. Tax (ed.), *Indian Tribes of Aboriginal America*, proceedings of the 29th International Congress of Americanists (Chicago: Chicago University Press), pp. 210–15.

Hoey, M. P. (1979), *Signalling in Discourse*, Discourse Analysis Monographs No. 6 (Birmingham: English Language Research, Birmingham University).

Hoey, M. P., and Winter, E. O. (1982), 'Believe me for mine honour: a stylistic analysis of the speeches of Brutus and Mark Antony at Caesar's funeral in *Julius Caesar*, Act III, Scene 2, from the point of view of discourse construction', *Language and Style*, vol. 14, no. 4.

Hutchins, W. John (1977a), 'On the problem of "aboutness" in document analysis', *Journal of Informatics*, vol. 1, no. 1, pp. 17–33.

Hutchins, W. John (1977b), 'On the structure of scientific texts', *UEA Papers in Linguistics*, vol. 5, no. 3, pp. 18–39.

Jamieson, Carole (1970), 'The relationals of modern mathematical logic', *Notes on Translation*, vol. 37, pp. 3–5.

Jespersen, Otto (1914–49), *A Modern English Grammar on Historical Principles* (Vols II–IV, Heidelberg: Winter; Vols V–VII, London: Allen & Unwin).

Jespersen, Otto (1933), *Essentials of English Grammar* (London: Allen & Unwin).

Johns, Tim F. (1980), 'The text and its message: an approach to the teaching of reading strategies for students of development administration', in H. von Faber (ed.), *Pariser Werkstattgespräch 1978: Leseverstehen im Fremdsprachenunterricht* (Munich: Goethe Instituts/British Council Paris), pp. 147–70.

Jordan, M. P. (1978), 'The principal semantics of the nominals *this* and *that* in contemporary English writing: a study within an expanded framework of clause relations and other approaches to discourse analysis with wider implications to all forms of substitution and other forms of cohesion', PhD thesis, CNAA, Hatfield Polytechnic.

Jordan, M. P. (1980), 'Short texts to explain Problem–Solution structures – and vice versa', *Instructional Science*, no. 9, pp. 221–52.

Jordan, M. P. (forthcoming), *Fundamentals of Information Structure* (London: Allen & Unwin).

Karlsen, Rolf (1959), *Studies in the Connection of Clauses in Current English: Zero, Ellipsis and Explicit Form* (Bergen: J. W. Eides, Boktrykkeri AS).

Koen, F., Young, R., and Becker, A. (1969), 'The psychological reality of the paragraph', *Journal of Verbal Learning and Verbal Behaviour*, vol. 8, no. 1, pp. 49–53.

Labov, William (1972), *Language of the Inner City: Studies in the Black English Vernacular* (Philadelphia, Pa: University of Pennsylvania Press).

Labov, William (1975), *What Is a Linguistic Fact?*, Peter de Ridder Press Publications in Linguistic Theory 1 (Lisse: Peter de Ridder Press).

Labov, William, and Fanshel, David (1977), *Therapeutic Discourse: Psychotherapy as Conversation* (New York: Academic Press).

Labov, William, and Waletsky, Joshua (1967), 'Narrative analysis: oral versions of personal experience', in *Essay on the Verbal and Visual Arts* (Seattle, Wash.: University of Washington Press), pp. 12–44.

Leech, Geoffrey (1965), '"This bread I break" – language and interpretation', *A Review of English Literature*, vol. 6, pp. 66–75; reprinted in D. C. Freeman (ed.), *Linguistics and Literary Style* (New York: Holt, Rinehart & Winston, 1970).

Leech, Geoffrey N. (1969), *A Linguistic Guide to English Poetry*, English Language series (London: Longman).

Leech, G., and Svartvik, J. (1975), *A Communicative Grammar of English* (London: Longman).

Longacre, Robert E. (1964), *Grammar Discovery Procedures: A Field Manual* (The Hague: Mouton).

Longacre, Robert E. (1968), *Discourse, Paragraph and Sentence Structure in Selected Philippine Languages* (Dallas, Texas: Summer Institute of Linguistics Publications in Linguistics and Related Fields, No. 21, Vols 1 and 2).

Longacre, Robert E. (1970), 'Sentence structure as a statement calculus', *Language*, vol. 46, no. 4, pp. 783–815; reprinted in Ruth M. Brend (ed.) (1974), *Advances in Tagmemics* (Amsterdam: North-Holland Publishing Co., 1974), pp. 251–83.

Longacre, Robert E. (1972), *Hierarchy and Universality of Discourse Constituents in New Guinea Languages* (discussion and texts) (Washington, DC: Georgetown University Press).

Longacre, Robert E. (1976), *An Anatomy of Speech Notions* (Lisse: Peter de Ridder Press).

Longacre, Robert E. (1979), 'The paragraph as a grammatical unit', in Talmy Givon (ed.), *Syntax and Semantics, Vol. 12: Discourse and Syntax* (New York: Academic Press), pp. 115–34.

Pike, Kenneth L. (1967), *Language in Relation to a Unified Theory of the Structure of Human Behaviour* [1954–9], 2nd rev. edn (The Hague: Mouton).

Pike, K. L., and Pike, E. G. (1977), *Grammatical Analysis* (Dallas, Texas: SIL Publications in Linguistics and Related Fields No. 53/The University of Texas at Arlington).

Poutsma, H. (1914–29), *A Grammar of Late Modern English*, 2nd edn (Gröningen: Nordhoff).

Quirk, Randolph (1954), *The Concessive Relation in Old English Poetry* (New Haven, Conn.: Yale University Press).

Quirk, Randolph, Greenbaum, Sidney, Leech, Geoffrey, and Svartvik, Jan (1972), *A Grammar of Contemporary English* (London: Longman).

Rimmon-Kenan, Schlomith (1979), 'Les paradoxes sur la répétition' (in English), Department of English, The Hebrew University, Jerusalem (mimeo.).

Rodgers, Paul C., Jr (1966a), 'A discourse-centred rhetoric of the paragraph', *College Composition and Communication*, vol. 17, no. 1, pp. 2–11.

Rodgers, Paul C., Jr (1966b), 'Symposium on the paragraph', *College Composition and Communication*, vol. 17, no. 2, pp. 72–80.

Roe, Peter (1977), 'The notion of difficulty in scientific text', PhD thesis, University of Birmingham.

Sinclair, J. McH. (1981), 'Planes of discourse in literature', mimeo.

Sinclair, J. McH., and Coulthard, R. M. (1975), *Towards an Analysis of Discourse: The English used by Teachers and Pupils* (London: OUP).

Sledd, James (1956), 'Co-ordination (faulty) and subordination (upside-down)', address to annual meeting of the Conference on College Composition and Communication; published in H. Allen (ed.), *Readings in Applied English Linguistics* (New York: Appleton-Century-Crofts, 1958); reprinted in M. Steinmann (ed.), *New Rhetorics* (New York: Scribner, 1967).

Smith, N., and Wilson, D. (1979), *Modern Linguistics: The Results of Chomsky's Revolution* (Harmondsworth: Penguin).

Stern, Arthur (1976), 'When is a paragraph?', *College Composition and Communication*, vol. 27, no. 3, pp. 253–7.

Suleiman, Susan Rubin (1980), 'Redundancy and the readable text', *Poetics Today*, vol. 1, no. 3, pp. 119–42.

Tadros, Angela (1981), 'Linguistic prediction in economics', PhD thesis, University of Birmingham.

Todd, Mark (1980), untitled ms. (mimeo.).

Van Dijk, Teun A. (1973), 'Models for text grammars', *Linguistics*, no. 105, pp. 35–68.

Van Dijk, Teun A. (1977), *Text and Context: Explorations in the Semantics and Pragmatics of Discourse* (London: Longman).

Van Dijk, Teun, A., and Kintsch, Walter (1978), 'Cognitive psychology and discourse: recalling and summarizing stories', in Wolfgang U. Dressler (ed.), *Current Trends in Textlinguistics* (Berlin and New York: Walter de Gruyter).

Widdowson, H. G. (1978), *Teaching Language as Communication* (Oxford: OUP).

Widdowson, H. G. (1979), *Explorations in Applied Linguistics* (Oxford: OUP).

Winter, E. O. (1968), 'Some aspects of cohesion', in *Sentence and Clause in Scientific English, Report of the Research Project 'The Linguistic Properties of Scientific English'*, (London: University College London, Department of General Linguistics).

Winter, E. O. (1969), 'Grammatical question technique as a way of teaching science students to write progress reports: the use of the short text in teaching', University of Trondheim (mimeo.).

Winter, E. O. (1971), 'Connection in science material: a proposition about the semantics of clause relations', in *Centre for Information on Language Teaching Papers and Reports*, No. 7. (London: Centre for Information on Language Teaching and Research for British Association for Applied Linguistics), pp. 41–52.

Winter, E. O. (1974), 'Replacement as a function of repetition: a study of some of its principal features in the clause relations of contemporary English', PhD thesis, University of London.

Winter, E. O. (1976), 'Fundamentals of information structure: pilot manual for further development according to student need', mimeo., Hatfield Polytechnic.

Winter, E. O. (1977), 'A clause relational approach to English texts: a study of some predictive lexical items in written discourse', *Instructional Science*, vol. 6, no. 1, pp. 1–92.

Winter, E. O. (1978), 'A look at the role of certain words in information structure', in K. P. Jones and V. Horsnell (eds), *Informatics 3*, proceedings of a conference held by the Aslib Co-ordinate Indexing Group, 1975 (London: Aslib).

Winter, E. O. (1979), 'Replacement as a fundamental function of the sentence in context', *Forum Linguisticum*, vol. 4, no. 2.

Winter, E. O. (forthcoming), *Towards a Contextual Grammar of English: The Clause and its Place in the Definition of Sentence* (London: Allen & Unwin).

Young, Richard (1968), 'Discovery procedures in tagmemic rhetoric: an exercise in problem solving', mimeo.

Young, Richard E., and Becker, Alton L. (1965), 'Toward a modern theory of rhetoric: a tagmemic contribution', *Harvard Educational Review*, vol. 35, pp. 450–68; reprinted in M. Steinmann (ed.), *New Rhetorics* (New York: Scribner, 1967).

Young, R., and Becker, A. (1966), 'The role of lexical and grammatical cues in paragraph recognition', in *Studies in Language and Language Behaviour*, Progress Report No 2 (Ann Arbor, Mich.: Center for Research on Language, University of Michigan).

Young, R., Becker, A., and Pike, K. (1970), *Rhetoric: Discovery and Change* (New York: Harcourt, Brace & World).

Index

Index

Page numbers in **bold** refer to discourses and numbers in *italics* refer to figures.